Painting and Wallpapering For Dummies®

Cheat Sheet

Choosing a Paint Roller

Nap Length	Job
¹/₄-inch	Very smooth surfaces like flush doors, plastered walls, and wide trim
³/₈- or ¹/₂-inch	Slightly irregular surfaces like drywall and exterior siding
³/₄ inch or longer	Semi-rough surfaces like wood shingles
1- or 1¹/₄-inch	Rough surfaces like concrete block and stucco

Wall Paint Calculator

To determine how much paint to buy, find the square footage of the area that you plan to paint, and divide by the number of square feet covered by a gallon of paint.

Total Wall Area:
[Total Length of All Walls] × [Wall Height] = Total Wall Area

Unpainted Areas:
[Window Height] × [Window Width] × [Number of Windows] = Window Area

[Door Height] × [Door Width] × [Number of Doors] = Door Area

Paintable Wall Area:
[Total Wall Area] – [Window Area] – [Door Area] = Paintable Area

Paint to Order:
[Paintable Area] ÷ 350 = Number of Gallons Needed for Smooth Walls

[Paintable Area] ÷ 300 = Number of Gallons Needed for Rough, Textured Walls or Unpainted Wallboard

Painting Tips

- Examine paint color chips in daylight and under the artificial lighting conditions in the room to be painted.
- Read the label and follow its directions.
- Don't skimp on the paint.
- Don't buy cheap paint or applicators.
- Don't paint in direct sunlight.
- Don't assume that paint hides imperfections or seals cracks.
- Seal stained areas with stain-blocking primers before you paint them.
- Describe your project to a paint dealer and ask questions before you buy your paint and applicators.
- Paint only clean, well-prepared surfaces.
- Kill mold and mildew with a bleach solution.
- Paint to a wet edge.
- Remove masking tape as soon as paint is tacky.
- Protect areas that you don't want to paint with drop cloths.

Painting and Wallpapering For Dummies®

Cheat Sheet

Lead Paint Information

To obtain the following free EPA pamphlets about lead-based paint, call 1-800-424-LEAD.

- *Protect Your Family From Lead in Your Home:* This pamphlet tells you how to identify when lead-based paint is likely to be a hazard and how to get your home checked.

- *Reducing Lead Hazards When Remodeling Your Home:* This publication describes simple procedures to follow when you're remodeling.

Choosing Exterior Paint Colors

- Light, one-color schemes make a house look larger.

- Dark colors and contrast between the body and the trim make it look smaller.

- Use single-color schemes to unify a house with a hodgepodge of different textures.

- Two or three colors or distinct tones can highlight trim details or special features on a proportioned home.

- Choose colors that complement the colors of unchanging house components, such as the roofing and brick or stone.

Wallpaper Calculator

Determine how much wallpaper to purchase by calculating the area that you plan to paper and dividing that number by the usable yield per roll of paper.

Wall Area:
[Total Length of All Walls] × [Wall Height] = Wall Area

Unpapered Areas:
[Window Height] × [Window Width] × [Number of Windows] = Window Area

[Door Height] × [Door Width] × [Number of Doors] = Door Area

Wallpapering Area:
[Wall Area] − [Unpapered Areas] = Wallpapering Area

Wallpaper to Order:
[Wallpapering Area] ÷ [Usable Yield] = Number of Single Rolls Needed

Usable Yield Charts:

Pattern Repeat (Drop)	Usable Yield (American Rolls)	Usable Yield (European Rolls)
0 to 6 in.	32 sq. ft.	25 sq. ft.
7 to 12 in.	30 sq. ft.	22 sq. ft.
13 to 18 in.	27 sq. ft.	20 sq. ft.
19 to 23 in.	25 sq. ft.	18 sq. ft.

The IDG Books Worldwide logo is a registered trademark under exclusive license to IDG Books Worldwide, Inc., from International Data Group, Inc. The ...For Dummies logo is a trademark, and For Dummies and ...For Dummies are registered trademarks of IDG Books Worldwide, Inc. All other trademarks are the property of their respective owners.

...For Dummies®: Bestselling Book Series for Beginners

Praise for *Painting and Wallpapering For Dummies*

"The Hamiltons do everything but roll on the paint or paste the paper for you. Here is specific, detailed, accurate information, including problem-solving and trouble shooting. Even a first-timer will feel confident about picking up a brush and transforming a room."

> — Judy Stark, Home Editor, *St. Petersburg Times* and
> President, National Association of Real Estate Editors

"The thickness of a coat (only about 2/1000ths of an inch) is all that stands between your most costly investment and the environment. Before you expose your house to the next season, get seasoned advice. Brush up with *Painting and Wallpapering For Dummies*. It's a smart way to start your next project!"

> — Thomas A. Kraeutler, Home Improvement Columnist and
> Radio/TV Host

"Gene and Katie have done it again. Their new book has everything. All you need now are the brushes."

> — Glenn Haege, America's Master Handyman and
> Host of Westwood One's *Ask the Handyman* radio show

Praise for Gene and Katie Hamilton

"The most comprehensive guide available for those of us who are 'home improvement challenged' . . . If you're thinking of starting a home improvement project, don't start until you've read Katie and Gene Hamilton's *Home Improvement For Dummies*."

> — Susan Powell, Host of Discovery Channel's *Home Matters*

"Whether you're looking for tips on rejuvenating wood floors or culling creative ideas for holiday decorating, pay a visit to Katie and Gene Hamilton."

> — *USA Today*

"Think of HouseNet as your home improvement toolbox, and caretakers Gene and Katie Hamilton as your helpful neighbors. Within these (online) pages you'll find remodeling tips, home repair tutorials, money-saving ideas, and a do-it-yourself message board."

> — *Chicago Tribune*

"For home renovators looking for tips, building specs, or simply someone to commiserate with at any time of the day or night, HouseNet is the place to go."

> — *Newsweek*

"Voted the best place on the Web for fixing up your home."

> — Editors of Kiplinger's *Personal Finance* magazine

"The latest in home improvement information and services is just a few mouse clicks away with the relaunch of HouseNet on the World Wide Web."

> — *Chicago Sun-Times*

"Before you embark on a home improvement project, check our HouseNet's cost guides to determine whether it's really worth doing yourself. The how-to section is particularly rich in detail and covers a broad range of topics, from how to install an air conditioner to instructions for the first-time wallpaper hanger."

> — Yahoo! *Internet Life,* New York

"HouseNet, with its magazine-style look, is a very inviting and easy-to-use home-related site. It will guide your repairs down to the smallest detail, including a calculator to help accurately figure measurements."

> — *Today's Homeowner*

 ™

References for the Rest of Us!™

BESTSELLING BOOK SERIES

Do you find that traditional reference books are overloaded with technical details and advice you'll never use? Do you postpone important life decisions because you just don't want to deal with them? Then our *...For Dummies*® business and general reference book series is for you.

...For Dummies business and general reference books are written for those frustrated and hard-working souls who know they aren't dumb, but find that the myriad of personal and business issues and the accompanying horror stories make them feel helpless. *...For Dummies* books use a lighthearted approach, a down-to-earth style, and even cartoons and humorous icons to dispel fears and build confidence. Lighthearted but not lightweight, these books are perfect survival guides to solve your everyday personal and business problems.

> *"More than a publishing phenomenon, 'Dummies' is a sign of the times."*
>
> — The New York Times

> *"A world of detailed and authoritative information is packed into them..."*
>
> — U.S. News and World Report

> *"...you won't go wrong buying them."*
>
> — Walter Mossberg, Wall Street Journal, on IDG Books' ...For Dummies books

Already, millions of satisfied readers agree. They have made *...For Dummies* the #1 introductory level computer book series and a best-selling business book series. They have written asking for more. So, if you're looking for the best and easiest way to learn about business and other general reference topics, look to *...For Dummies* to give you a helping hand.

1/99

PAINTING AND WALLPAPERING FOR DUMMIES®

PAINTING AND WALLPAPERING FOR DUMMIES®

by Gene Hamilton, Katie Hamilton, & Roy Barnhart

IDG Books Worldwide, Inc.
An International Data Group Company

Foster City, CA ◆ Chicago, IL ◆ Indianapolis, IN ◆ New York, NY

Painting and Wallpapering For Dummies®

Published by
IDG Books Worldwide, Inc.
An International Data Group Company
919 E. Hillsdale Blvd.
Suite 400
Foster City, CA 94404
www.idgbooks.com (IDG Books Worldwide Web site)
www.dummies.com (Dummies Press Web site)

Library of Congress Catalog Card No.: 99-62841

ISBN: 0-7645-5150-7

Printed in the United States of America

10 9 8 7 6 5 4 3 2 1

1B/RT/QV/ZZ/IN

Distributed in the United States by IDG Books Worldwide, Inc.

Distributed by CDG Books Canada Inc. for Canada; by Transworld Publishers Limited in the United Kingdom; by IDG Norge Books for Norway; by IDG Sweden Books for Sweden; by IDG Books Australia Publishing Corporation Pty. Ltd. for Australia and New Zealand; by TransQuest Publishers Pte Ltd. for Singapore, Malaysia, Thailand, Indonesia, and Hong Kong; by Gotop Information Inc. for Taiwan; by ICG Muse, Inc. for Japan; by Norma Comunicaciones S.A. for Colombia; by Intersoft for South Africa; by Le Monde en Tique for France; by International Thomson Publishing for Germany, Austria and Switzerland; by Distribuidora Cuspide for Argentina; by Livraria Cultura for Brazil; by Ediciones ZETA S.C.R. Ltda. for Peru; by WS Computer Publishing Corporation, Inc., for the Philippines; by Contemporanea de Ediciones for Venezuela; by Express Computer Distributors for the Caribbean and West Indies; by Micronesia Media Distributor, Inc. for Micronesia; by Grupo Editorial Norma S.A. for Guatemala; by Chips Computadoras S.A. de C.V. for Mexico; by Editorial Norma de Panama S.A. for Panama; by American Bookshops for Finland. Authorized Sales Agent: Anthony Rudkin Associates for the Middle East and North Africa.

For general information on IDG Books Worldwide's books in the U.S., please call our Consumer Customer Service department at 800-762-2974. For reseller information, including discounts and premium sales, please call our Reseller Customer Service department at 800-434-3422.

For information on where to purchase IDG Books Worldwide's books outside the U.S., please contact our International Sales department at 317-596-5530 or fax 317-596-5692.

For consumer information on foreign language translations, please contact our Customer Service department at 1-800-434-3422, fax 317-596-5692, or e-mail rights@idgbooks.com.

For information on licensing foreign or domestic rights, please phone +1-650-655-3109.

For sales inquiries and special prices for bulk quantities, please contact our Sales department at 650-655-3200 or write to the address above.

For information on using IDG Books Worldwide's books in the classroom or for ordering examination copies, please contact our Educational Sales department at 800-434-2086 or fax 317-596-5499.

For press review copies, author interviews, or other publicity information, please contact our Public Relations department at 650-655-3000 or fax 650-655-3299.

For authorization to photocopy items for corporate, personal, or educational use, please contact Copyright Clearance Center, 222 Rosewood Drive, Danvers, MA 01923, or fax 978-750-4470.

is a registered trademark or trademark under exclusive license to IDG Books Worldwide, Inc. from International Data Group, Inc. in the United States and/or other countries.

About the Authors

Gene and Katie Hamilton are the husband-and-wife author team of the popular and witty syndicated newspaper column "Do It Yourself . . . or Not?", *Home Improvement For Dummies,* and over a dozen bestselling books on home improvement. They're also the founders of www.housenet.com, the largest home and garden Web site for homeowners and do-it-yourselfers on the Internet. The Hamiltons have been featured in numerous publications and television shows, including: HGTV, CNN, *Today,* and *Dateline.* In their 20 years as home-repair experts, they've successfully remodeled 14 homes (and they're still married!).

Roy Barnhart is a lifelong do-it-yourselfer and former professional building and remodeling contractor. He enjoyed eight years as Senior Building and Remodeling Editor for two national home improvement magazines. For the last nine years, he has worked as a freelance writer, editor, and consultant. Roy has contributed articles to over a dozen home improvement magazines, including *American Homestyle, American How-To, Family Handyman, House Beautiful, Remodeling, Today's Homeowner* and *Woman's Day.* He has also contributed to three books including *The New Reader's Digest Complete Fix-It-Yourself Manual, The Stanley Book of Home Improvement* and *The Reader's Digest Book of Skills and Tools.* He is currently the author of a weekly column on HouseNet (Gene and Katie's favorite Web site!).

ABOUT IDG BOOKS WORLDWIDE

Welcome to the world of IDG Books Worldwide.

IDG Books Worldwide, Inc., is a subsidiary of International Data Group, the world's largest publisher of computer-related information and the leading global provider of information services on information technology. IDG was founded more than 30 years ago by Patrick J. McGovern and now employs more than 9,000 people worldwide. IDG publishes more than 290 computer publications in over 75 countries. More than 90 million people read one or more IDG publications each month.

Launched in 1990, IDG Books Worldwide is today the #1 publisher of best-selling computer books in the United States. We are proud to have received eight awards from the Computer Press Association in recognition of editorial excellence and three from Computer Currents' First Annual Readers' Choice Awards. Our best-selling *...For Dummies*® series has more than 50 million copies in print with translations in 31 languages. IDG Books Worldwide, through a joint venture with IDG's Hi-Tech Beijing, became the first U.S. publisher to publish a computer book in the People's Republic of China. In record time, IDG Books Worldwide has become the first choice for millions of readers around the world who want to learn how to better manage their businesses.

Our mission is simple: Every one of our books is designed to bring extra value and skill-building instructions to the reader. Our books are written by experts who understand and care about our readers. The knowledge base of our editorial staff comes from years of experience in publishing, education, and journalism — experience we use to produce books to carry us into the new millennium. In short, we care about books, so we attract the best people. We devote special attention to details such as audience, interior design, use of icons, and illustrations. And because we use an efficient process of authoring, editing, and desktop publishing our books electronically, we can spend more time ensuring superior content and less time on the technicalities of making books.

You can count on our commitment to deliver high-quality books at competitive prices on topics you want to read about. At IDG Books Worldwide, we continue in the IDG tradition of delivering quality for more than 30 years. You'll find no better book on a subject than one from IDG Books Worldwide.

IDG BOOKS WORLDWIDE

John Kilcullen
John Kilcullen
Chairman and CEO
IDG Books Worldwide, Inc.

Steven Berkowitz
Steven Berkowitz
President and Publisher
IDG Books Worldwide, Inc.

VIII WINNER
Eighth Annual
Computer Press
Awards ≥1992

IX WINNER
Ninth Annual
Computer Press
Awards ≥1993

Computer Currents Readers Choice 1995

X WINNER
Tenth Annual
Computer Press
Awards ≥1994

XI WINNER
Eleventh Annual
Computer Press
Awards ≥1995

IDG is the world's leading IT media, research and exposition company. Founded in 1964, IDG had 1997 revenues of $2.05 billion and has more than 9,000 employees worldwide. IDG offers the widest range of media options that reach IT buyers in 75 countries representing 95% of worldwide IT spending. IDG's diverse product and services portfolio spans six key areas including print publishing, online publishing, expositions and conferences, market research, education and training, and global marketing services. More than 90 million people read one or more of IDG's 290 magazines and newspapers, including IDG's leading global brands — Computerworld, PC World, Network World, Macworld and the Channel World family of publications. IDG Books Worldwide is one of the fastest-growing computer book publishers in the world, with more than 700 titles in 36 languages. The "...For Dummies®" series alone has more than 50 million copies in print. IDG offers online users the largest network of technology-specific Web sites around the world through IDG.net (http://www.idg.net), which comprises more than 225 targeted Web sites in 55 countries worldwide. International Data Corporation (IDC) is the world's largest provider of information technology data, analysis and consulting, with research centers in over 41 countries and more than 400 research analysts worldwide. IDG World Expo is a leading producer of more than 168 globally branded conferences and expositions in 35 countries including E3 (Electronic Entertainment Expo), Macworld Expo, ComNet, Windows World Expo, ICE (Internet Commerce Expo), Agenda, DEMO, and Spotlight. IDG's training subsidiary, ExecuTrain, is the world's largest computer training company, with more than 230 locations worldwide and 785 training courses. IDG Marketing Services helps industry-leading IT companies build international brand recognition by developing global integrated marketing programs via IDG's print, online and exposition products worldwide. Further information about the company can be found at www.idg.com.
1/24/99

Dedication

We dedicate this book to Joseph Provey, a longtime mutual friend and former editor of several home improvement magazines. It was Joe, then editor-in-chief of *The Family Handyman,* who supported and encouraged our early efforts as authors and it was through Joe that we authors met, worked together, and became friends. Joe encouraged Roy to put his years of building and remodeling experience to paper — initially as a writer and later as building and remodeling editor for two national home improvement publications. Our thanks to Joe for all the years of sharing, learning, working, and exploring together.

Authors' Acknowledgments

When our own personal experience fails us in one way or the other, we turn to experts to make sure that we present the best information that we can. Our thanks to all the chemists and other experts at Pittsburgh Paints, Benjamin Moore Paints, Wm. Zinsser & Co., Paint Quality Institute, and EPA National Lead Information Clearinghouse for their patient explanations and valuable information. We are very grateful, too, for the careful and most helpful technical review of Tom Philbin, a veteran painting contractor and himself an author of three books on painting.

We have also learned a great deal of information from paint store managers, other do-it-yourselfers, trade shows, and a host of resources too numerous to mention. In particular, Roy would like to thank the many painting and wallpapering experts that have assisted him over the last 15 years. These experts helped him respond to the thousands of readers' questions contained in the Q&A columns that he's edited and authored. He would also like to offer a special thanks to John Gaynor, who set high standards in his effort to communicate good advice.

We've enjoyed working with our friends at IDG Books — everyone from Holly McGuire, the acquisitions editor to Jennifer Ehrlich, editorial manager, and project editor Andrea Boucher, who has maintained a steady head and steadfast hand at making sure this book is as good as it can be.

We're pleased with the fine work of the illustrators at Precision Graphics, who have gone the distance to translate our words to clear and concise drawings that make this a user-friendly and informative "show and tell" book.

As always we are indebted to our agent Jane Jordan Browne, who continues as our guiding light and good friend.

And last, but surely not least, we thank our good friend Joe Truini, whose wit and wisdom make this book enjoyable as well as enlightening. His quirky sense of humor makes even the most perplexing painting and wallpapering projects laughable.

Publisher's Acknowledgments

We're proud of this book; please register your comments through our IDG Books Worldwide Online Registration Form located at `http://my2cents.dummies.com`.

Some of the people who helped bring this book to market include the following:

Acquisitions, Editorial, and Media Development

Project Editors: Andrea C. Boucher, Brian Kramer, Stacey Mickelbart

Acquisitions Editor: Holly McGuire

Copy Editor: Tina Sims

Technical Editor: Tom Philbin

Editorial Managers: Kelly Ewing, Rev Mengle, Jennifer Ehrlich

Editorial Assistants: Paul E. Kuzmic, Alison Walthall

Production

Project Coordinator: E. Shawn Aylsworth

Layout and Graphics: Linda M. Boyer, Laura Carpenter, Angela F. Hunckler, Brent Savage, Kathie Schutte, Janet Seib, Michael A. Sullivan

Proofreaders: Christine Berman, Jennifer Mahern, Nancy Price, Marianne Santy, Ethel M. Winslow, Janet M. Withers

Indexer: Liz Cunningham

Special Help

Christine Meloy Beck, Jerelind Charles, Nicole Haims, Darren Meiss, Pamela Mourouzis, Jade Williams

---

General and Administrative

IDG Books Worldwide, Inc: John Kilcullen, CEO; Steven Berkowitz, President and Publisher

IDG Books Technology Publishing: Brenda McLaughlin, Senior Vice President and Group Publisher

Dummies Technology Press and Dummies Editorial: Diane Graves Steele, Vice President and Associate Publisher; Mary Bednarek, Director of Acquisitions and Product Development; Kristin A. Cocks, Editorial Director

Dummies Trade Press: Kathleen A. Welton, Vice President and Publisher; Kevin Thornton, Acquisitions Manager

IDG Books Production for Dummies Press: Michael R. Britton, Vice President of Production and Creative Services; Cindy L. Phipps, Manager of Project Coordination, Production Proofreading, and Indexing; Shelley Lea, Supervisor of Graphics and Design; Debbie J. Gates, Production Systems Specialist; Robert Springer, Supervisor of Proofreading; Debbie Stailey, Production Control Manager; Tony Augsburger, Supervisor of Reprints and Bluelines

Dummies Packaging and Book Design: Patty Page, Manager, Promotions Marketing

◆

The publisher would like to give special thanks to Patrick J. McGovern, without whom this book would not have been possible.

◆

Contents at a Glance

Cartoons at a Glance

By Rich Tennant

"You did an excellent job, Dave. But two months seems a long time to paint the bathroom."

page 27

page 5

"I would try using less varnish remover."

page 77

"Honey– can you toss me the bug spray, quickly? I think I disturbed something in the gutter."

page 119

"Frank and I decided to go for a sort of speckled finish."

page 217

page 173

Fax: 978-546-7747 • **E-mail:** the5wave@tiac.net

Table of Contents

Part IV: Painting and Finishing, Inside and Out...........119

Chapter 11: On the Outside Looking In: Painting the Exterior of Your Home 121

Introduction

• •

Welcome to *Painting and Wallpapering For Dummies,* a manual for people who are about to roll up their sleeves and get involved in the number one do-it-yourself home improvement activity — no, not raiding the fridge — painting. Following the *...For Dummies* tradition, our goal is to present a lighthearted, but not lightweight, book that gives would-be do-it-yourselfers the know-how and encouragement to get started so that they can reap the rewards of these activities. We know from our own renovation experience and our involvement with HouseNet Inc., a home improvement resource on America Online and the World Wide Web, that there's always room for improvement and always more to learn, so we also want to provide a valuable resource for seasoned do-it-yourselfers.

The result is a book that contains more than you need to know to get started and all that you need to know to achieve great results on most painting, finishing, and wallpapering tasks. With a solid foundation, you'll also find that you have the good sense to know when to ask questions, which expert to ask, and how to judge whether the expert really knows what he's talking about. Hint: Don't trust anyone who thinks that spackle is a Swedish breakfast treat or that an orbital sander is Colonel Sanders's great-grandson.

How to Use This Book

You can use this book in three ways:

- ✔ If you want information about a specific topic, such as what may be causing your paint to peel or when to use water-based varnish, you can flip to the index and be directed to the relevant page or pages.

- ✔ If you want general information about a topic or project, such as choosing the right paint applicator or wallpapering a room, just flip to that part or chapter. The chapter headings and the tip icons in the margins get you to the information you want. Occasionally, we refer you to related information in other chapters.

- ✔ If you want to cover all the bases, read the whole book. You'll discover options that you never knew you had. Although you probably won't keep all this stuff in your head, you'll be surprised at the information you do retain.

The book is organized in six parts, and the chapters within each part cover specific topics in detail. The content generally follows the flow of the work — planning, gathering tools and materials, becoming familiar with techniques, preparing the work surface, applying the finish or wallpaper, and cleaning up. Although wallpapering is presented separately, design decisions, preparation, and other wallpapering tasks often involve procedures or issues discussed in the introductory and painting parts of the book.

Part I: Before You Get Started

Sure, painting can be a simple matter of opening a can and brushing on the paint, and if wallpapering weren't an anyone-can-do-it task, it wouldn't be one of the hottest-selling do-it-yourself projects. More often than not, however, there's more to it than meets the eye, so be sure to look before you leap. A little planning will keep you from getting in over your head or from making costly mistakes. These first four chapters give you an overview of the work so that you can know what you can handle yourself and how to hire a pro for the rest.

Part II: Finishes, Applicators, Techniques, and Cleanup

With all your good intentions and great design ideas, you won't get the results you want unless you use the right materials, tools, and techniques. Hundreds of paints and other coatings are available. Many may be *okay* for your project, but with the information contained in this part, you'll be able to quickly narrow your options and choose the one that's *best*. Here's the place to find out about scrapers, ladders, brushes, rollers, and other "old reliables," as well as dozens of newer tools, including power painting and spraying equipment, that save you time and give you better results. Finally, to keep those tools in good working order, check out the chapter on cleanup. It's loaded with ideas that make this, the final step, an easy task.

Part III: Preparing Your Surfaces for Paint

If painting and wallpapering consisted only of applying the paint or wallpaper, we'd all have a lot more free time, but preparation is 90 percent of the work. Unfortunately, it's also the single most important factor in determining the success of a project, so you don't want to skimp on this process.

This part describes how to prepare existing surfaces for paint, wallpaper, or other finishes. You find out what you don't need to do (that's a good start, right?) and discover the easiest ways to handle the stuff that you do need to do. Many of the procedures will save you time in the long run, which is an important point to remember. Painting may be fun, but I'm sure we can all come up with an activity that we'd rather be doing.

Part IV: Painting and Finishing, Inside and Out

Now for the fun part — applying the finish. Here's when you start to reap the rewards of all that planning and preparation. The first two chapters in this part deal with exterior painting projects — everything from painting and staining your siding to special outdoor projects.

Moving indoors, the next few chapters cover painting rooms and refinishing natural woodwork. Want something special? Check out the chapter on decorative finishes. You'll astound your friends (and yourself) with the beautiful creative finishes that you can do yourself.

Part V: The Wonderful World of Wallpaper

Looking for a long-lasting interior wall finish that adds a designer's touch to any room in your home? Try wallpaper. In this part, you find out how wallpaper can help you achieve a variety of design goals. You also discover how to choose a paper that is suitable both for those objectives and for your skill level.

Finally, you get the step-by-step installation instructions that will make your very first installation or repair project a success. If you're more interested in removing existing wallpaper than putting it on, we've got you covered (or should we say, uncovered?) here, too.

Part VI: The Part of Tens

No ...*For Dummies* book would be complete without the Part of Tens. And we think that you'll find the chapters in this part especially useful — and the information valuable. One chapter highlights, the ten best decorative painting tips. You also get a chapter that leads you to ten great painting and wallpapering Web sites.

Those Funny Little Icons

We use the familiar ...*For Dummies* icons to help guide you through the material in this book:

Get on target with these great time-saving, money-saving, or sanity-saving inspirations from people who have "been there, done that."

Always remember these key tidbits of information that come into play in many aspects of your painting, finishing, and wallpapering improvements.

We don't want to scare you off, but some of the projects described here involve poisonous chemicals and tools that can be dangerous, even deadly, if not approached properly. This icon alerts you to potential hazards and signals information about how to steer clear of them.

Some painting, finishing, and wallpapering mistakes are so common that you can see them coming from a mile away. Let this icon serve as a warning that you're treading in trouble-prone waters. Why learn from your own mistakes when you can learn from other people's?

Some products on the market do such a darn good job that we can't resist sharing them with you. This icon points you to them and to the related techniques that we recommend to help you do a job better or faster.

Some people are into home improvement for the artistic rewards. Some people hope that the projects help them by improving the resale value of their homes. But others take up these home improvement jobs just for the tools. If you have an obsession for gadgets and gizmos that can make your task easier, keep an eye out for this icon.

This book doesn't bombard you with a bunch of technical trivia, but we think that some of these tidbits are too good to pass up. Some are helpful, and others are just interesting (at least to some of us). But like so much data in this Information Age, you can probably live without it.

At one time, we relied on storytellers for all our information. We still learn a lot, or at least get a good laugh, from the stories that we hear. This icon marks the better stories that we'd like to share with you.

Part I
Before You Get Started

In this part . . .

Hopefully you're reading this because you know that starting out well informed is always best, and not because you've gotten yourself into a mess and need a hand. (Yes, we know — most people operate the messy way. It's human nature.) Regardless, welcome!

In this part, you find out how to evaluate the job and your abilities and how to plan accordingly, which is the key to making a job go smoothly. And while painting and wallpapering projects are among the safest home improvement tasks, some very real dangers do exist that you need to know about. What's the sense, after all, of a beautifully wallpapered bedroom if your only view is an institution-green wall in a hospital room?

On a lighter note, we know that there's a little bit of artist in all of us. Take a look at the chapter on color (and the color insert) to help you choose and use your palette for maximum effect.

Chapter 1

Planning Your Project

- -

In This Chapter

▶ Painting — a bargain by any standard

▶ Tips that make any painting, finishing, or wallpapering task run smoothly

▶ Planning a major interior or exterior painting task

▶ Hiring professionals

- -

You probably don't need a market survey to tell you that "I'd rather be painting (or wallpapering) my house" bumper stickers aren't breaking any sales records — except perhaps for the fewest ever sold. Yet more people probably tackle painting, finishing, and wallpapering than any other type of home improvement project. If you think about it, it's no real mystery why people paint and wallpaper their houses. Applying a fresh coat of paint or hanging wallpaper is the easiest and most economical way to transform a room or a home's exterior and to make it uniquely your own.

Painting and wallpapering tools and materials are relatively inexpensive. If you're a first-time painter or wallpaper hanger, you'll also be happy to know that you can acquire the necessary skills on the job. Just start small to gain experience.

 With good preparation and planning, any job — big or small — will go smoothly, and you'll reap the rewards of an attractive, long-lasting finish. Take advantage of the wealth of great design tips in books (such as *Home Decorating For Dummies,* by Patricia Hart McMillan and Katharine Kaye McMillan, published by IDG Books Worldwide, Inc.) and magazines. Good results depend on being well informed about products, tools, and techniques.

Analyzing Paint Failures

Quite often, the reason for painting is associated with some paint failure. If your paint job fails prematurely and you're faced with repeating the job sooner than you expected, find out the cause and the solution. By doing so, you can avoid making a similar mistake or having the problem recur because you failed to follow the proper procedure. The color insert in this book describes some of the most common paint failures and how to deal with them. If you don't see your problem identified, be sure to consult a paint professional. Don't risk having your hard work peel off before your very eyes.

Preliminary Work

Anyone who has painting, refinishing, and wallpapering experience knows that preparation is the time-consuming part of the task. Skip this vital step, and your work is doomed to failure. Make a list of every preparation task that you can think of and allow for some surprises, especially on exterior house painting projects. See Part III for guidance on traditional prepping tasks, such as scraping, sanding, cleaning, and removing paint, varnish, and other finishes. If your preparation work involves removing wallpaper, refer to Chapter 15.

For siding repair, drywall and plaster repair, and a host of other related repair work, check out *Home Improvement For Dummies,* by Gene and Katie Hamilton (IDG Books Worldwide, Inc.).

Figuring the bill

First up, figure the cost of materials. Cost is one factor that you can usually establish with reasonable certainty. Plop yourself down at the kitchen table with a pad and paper. Then, as silly as it may feel, close your eyes and imagine your project. (You may as well make it a sunny day.) In your mind, walk through every little detail, opening your eyes only long enough to jot down notes or to keep from falling asleep.

In order to get a good estimate of the cost of the paint or wallpaper, take the measurements of the room or area where you'll be working. Make a few simple calculations (see the Wallpaper Calculator and Wall Paint Calculator on the Cheat Sheet in the front of this book for help), and you have a reasonable estimate of the paint or wallpaper required.

Don't forget to figure up the cost of tools, both ones that you may need to buy and those that you prefer to rent. For people who love any excuse to buy a nifty new tool, that's like telling a teenager, "Don't forget to eat."

Figuring the time

How much time can you really devote to your painting project? If you are planning a small project that steals you away from the boobtube for only a few hours, don't even worry about it. For the biggies, such as painting and refurbishing 29 windows, calculating the time that each task takes is very important.

While taking your kitchen-table tour of the project, imagine time for trips to the store, time to move furniture or set up ladders, and even time to fix the kids' lunch. Jot down the time as well as the materials associated with each task.

Also, you can get a professional estimate of time and cost. On a large project, it's wise to get at least one estimate that you can stack against all that you know would be involved if you tackled the job on your own.

Scheduling the work

The bigger the job, the more planning is required. Although we discourage a neophyte do-it-yourselfer from starting with a major project, a big painting job can usually be broken down into manageable stages. Unlike a kitchen or bath remodel, which is best done all at once and preferably as quickly as possible, painting is a task that lends itself to a piecemeal approach.

Whatever the size of the project, from refinishing a table or painting a room to painting the entire exterior of your home, take the time to assess exactly what amount of time is required and how you will fit it into your schedule.

Sizing up your abilities

There's no sense in beating around the bush: Some people are handy, and some are not. But it's also true — more often than not, we think — that those who may not think of themselves as handy are pleasantly surprised at just how much they can do when they just get started.

You also need know-how. You may be able to handle a power sander, but if you don't know that sanding across the grain scratches the wood or that veneer is typically less than $\frac{1}{16}$-inch thick, you can ruin a piece of furniture. Reading this book is a good start.

Required skills and know-how vary not only by the complexity of the project but also by the material being used. Some wallpaper, for example, is notoriously difficult to work with and, at the same time, very expensive. Some paints, such as two-part epoxies, require advanced skills and extra-careful handling if they are to be used effectively and safely.

If you don't know, then ask questions, read the label (now there's a novel thought), hop on the Internet, or visit the library. The right information is as important as the right tools and skills. Learning by mistakes is effective (and perhaps inevitable), but it's the hard way to go about painting and wallpapering.

Large painting projects include both skilled and unskilled tasks. Even if you're not a do-it-yourselfer and you have no desire to become one, you can participate in projects and save money by doing the grunt work and leaving the skilled work to your spouse (or a professional). Incidentally, the reverse also can be true: You may have the ability and desire to handle the skilled work but want to save time by hiring a helper for the more basic tasks.

Weighing the worth of a warranty

Paint manufacturers guarantee their products, but failures due to product defect are extremely rare. Even if a manufacturer does replace the paint, you're left with the sometimes-monumental task of removing the failed product and reapplying new. Defects in wallcoverings are not rare, but if you inspect the roll before you install it, you can often work around a local defect. If not, the maker will certainly replace any defective roll. But again, you are responsible for the removal and replacement of defective rolls that you install.

Professionals may offer additional warranties that cover the application. By electing to do it yourself, you assume that risk. Under normal circumstances, and if you exercise appropriate care in the preparation and application of the finish or wallpaper, you may not be concerned about accepting that risk. If you have had repeated paint failures, for example, make sure that you have sound professional advice before you tackle the job yourself. It may make sense to hire a professional who is willing to guarantee his or her work.

The comfort factor

When evaluating your project, make sure that you feel comfortable doing the work. If you are apprehensive about a job, trust your feelings. For example, if you don't feel comfortable using a power washer to blast dirt off before you paint on your nice wood shingles, then hire a professional for that part of the job, and do only the portion of the task that you feel comfortable doing.

This comfort factor is most important when it involves your concerns for safety. If you feel anxious about getting up on a high ladder or are concerned about doing even minor work involving lead paint, by all means hire a pro. (For more information on the dangers of lead paint, see Chapter 2.)

Chapter 2

Personal and Environmental Safety

*P*ainting, refinishing, and wallpapering are among the safest home improvement activities you are likely to undertake. Because people today are much more aware of environmental and health risks, taking appropriate precautions has never been easier. But what people don't know or don't think about causes most injuries, illnesses, accidents, and damage to the environment. Keep these special safety tips in mind:

✔ Don't inhale or ingest dust, fumes, or any of the harmful ingredients in paint and related products.

✔ Watch out for electrical hazards, including (but not limited to) the dangers of uncovered outlet boxes.

✔ Reduce the risk of injuries due to tripping or falls by being extra careful when using ladders and scaffolding.

✔ To prevent fires or explosions, follow label instructions when using solvents or products containing flammable ingredients.

✔ Listen carefully when your spouse says, "Please finish painting our bedroom." For some reason, spouses often interpret that request as "Take the weekend off to play golf."

Personal health is completely and absolutely intertwined with the health of the planet. Increased environmental awareness, safer handling and disposal of toxic materials, and improved, less polluting paints and finishes are replacing ignorance and disregard for environmental concerns. Many federal, state, and local envirnomental agencies have enacted laws protecting the environ-ment and have literature or experts available to answer any questions you may have. So if you're not sure, please ask!

Using Caution When Handling Paint Products

Paints, stains, and related products may produce attractive results on your walls and furniture, but if you use them incorrectly, the effects on your body aren't as pleasant. Read the warnings on product labels and remember these safety precautions:

- Keep paints, stains, and related products, such as solvents, mildew-cides, and cleaners, away from children so that they aren't tempted to drink these poisonous materials.

- If you can use an acceptable less toxic or more environmentally friendly alternative, do it. For example, use non-toxic paint remover instead of one that contains methylene chloride (which is banned in many states), use phosphate-free cleaners rather than TSP (trisodium phosphate), and use water-based finishes instead of solvent-based ones.

- If a label says to use the product with adequate ventilation, work with this substance only outdoors or in cross-ventilated rooms. Most of these products are too toxic or flammable to be used in a basement area.

- Wear an approved respirator (*not* a disposable dust mask) when spray-ing paints or stains or when working in areas that are difficult to ventilate.

- Nesting instincts often trigger painting frenzies in the months before a new baby arrives. However good the intentions, the health conse-quences for the developing fetus can be severe. Chemical fumes inhaled enter the bloodstream quickly and so have a direct pipeline to a fetus. Treat the mother-to-be to a hotel weekend during such work.

- Protect your eyes from dust, flying debris, and chemicals. Wear goggles when working with most tools and when scraping, washing, scrubbing, spraying, sanding, nailing, drilling, and . . . well, the list goes on and on. When you're not wearing the goggles, keep them around your neck. If your goggles are out in the garage when you're on a ladder, you're not likely to climb down to get them.

- Keep the lids on paints and solvents when they're not in use and put them well out of the reach of young children. Set up paint-mixing or brush-cleaning areas outdoors, if possible, and also out of children's reach.

✔ Reduce the risk of danger by eliminating the source of the problem. Dispose of leftovers rather than store them if you probably won't use them. Store solvents, cleaning chemicals, and leftover paint in a locked metal cabinet.

✔ Remember what your mom or dad told you when you were a kid: Wear clean underwear in case a bus hits you. No, that's not it. Oh yeah, wash your hands before you eat. If you eat, smoke, or drink without first washing your hands thoroughly after working with dust, cleaning products, and other chemicals, you inadvertently ingest contaminants.

✔ Take extraordinary precautions when you run into lead paint. (See the section "Lead, the environment, and you" in this chapter for more on working with lead paint.)

VOCs and the air we breathe

Volatile organic compounds (VOCs) contribute to ozone pollution. Essentially all paint solvents are VOCs. Paint companies, with a little push from a big uncle (Sam) and pollution-conscious states such as California, have made great progress in developing alternative products that contain few or none of these harmful by-products and yet meet high performance expectations. Unfortunately, many applications still call for oil-based paints. Set up a procedure in which you recycle solvents and dispose of waste properly, which you can find out about in Chapter 7.

Lead, the environment, and you

Lead, an extremely toxic substance, was found in most interior and exterior paints produced before the late 1970s, when its use was banned. An estimated 75 percent of homes built before 1978 contain lead-based paint. If your home has lead-based paint, exercise caution whenever repairs are made around the home.

Understanding the risks

Lead that enters the body affects children's developing nervous systems and causes learning disabilities or reduced intelligence. Adult nervous systems are also affected, leading to memory and concentration problems. Lead poisoning can also cause high blood pressure, digestive problems, kidney damage, and many other health problems.

Lead enters the body in the form of dust or fumes that are either inhaled or ingested. The creation of lead dust is not limited to sanding or other procedures used to remove paint. Everyday actions, such as simply opening and closing windows and doors, generate lead-contaminated dust.

We urge anyone who lives in a home or apartment that was built before 1978 to contact the National Lead Information Center (NLIC) to obtain valuable literature concerning this serious environmental and health hazard. The literature and the call are free. Of the many helpful and informative documents available, two EPA booklets are particularly good: *Protect Your Family in Your Home* and *Reducing Lead Hazards When Remodeling Your Home*. Call 1-800-424-LEAD to have the material mailed, or download materials directly from the NLIC Internet site, www.nsc.org/ehc/lead.htm./

Testing for lead and assessing the risk

Do-it-yourself lead-paint test kits are less reliable than professional testing methods. If the kit test indicates that lead is present, you can be confident that you do indeed have lead. The problem arises when you get a negative result from a home test kit. You cannot wholly rely on a test that indicates that the paint is lead-free. In that case, have professional testing done. Use a professional tester especially if you are planning any remodeling or redecorating project that would disturb the surface, if the paint is visibly chipped or peeling, or if you have very young children.

Testing, however, is only the first step. Lead-based paint poses little risk if it is in good condition and properly maintained. A trained professional can assess the risks and make appropriate recommendations for interim controls, which temporarily reduce the hazards, or for abatement, which permanently removes, seals, or encapsulates lead-based paint with special materials, not just ordinary paint. Only certified or licensed abatement professionals should do this work. Check the Yellow Pages under "Lead Inspection and Control," or contact your state or local agency for a referral.

Dealing with lead paint

If you are planning to paint, refinish, or wallpaper and any of the repair or preparation work will remove or disturb lead paint or create dust, the best advice is: Don't do it yourself. Don't allow any uncertified professional painting contractor to do the work, either. In addition to posing certain safety risks, hiring uncertified contractors may be illegal. Many states and localities have adopted laws that require only licensed or certified professionals to do such work.

We have no doubt that the preceding advice is sound for most people, and a virtual no-brainer for large projects such as stripping all the paint off your exterior siding or interior trim. On the other hand, we recognize — as does the U.S. Environmental Protection Agency — that it is neither practical nor realistic to expect that many homeowners won't work on certain smaller projects just because they involve lead paint.

If you undertake any painting or wallpapering project that may disturb lead paint, we recommend that you do the following:

✔ Become familiar with the risks involved in working on a project that involves lead paint, and with any local regulations that may apply, before you make any decisions about whether to do the work, who will do it, and how it will be done.

✔ If the work you plan is permitted and you decide to do it yourself, make sure that you know the proper procedures and precautions to take.

When you do prep work involving lead finishes, never dry sand or dry scrape (that is, without wetting the surface as you sand or scrape), and never use propane torches or heat guns to remove lead-based paint. There are many limitations and precautions when working with lead paint that are beyond the scope of this book.

Eliminating Fire Hazards

Firefighters are terrific people, but you probably don't want them coming over to your home unexpectedly — if you know what we mean. Therefore, take the necessary precautions to eliminate fire hazards. Be sure to read the label on any product that you use, looking for the word *flammable* or *inflammable*. Remember, the vapors of flammable liquids travel far from the source, and they are more dangerous than the liquid itself because of their explosive nature.

A remodeler friend of ours told us a terribly sad story about a job that he did restoring a fire-damaged house. Vapors from chemicals that the owner had been working with in the kitchen spread throughout the house. Somewhere, a spark ignited the fumes. The fire didn't just spread quickly; it simultaneously ignited all over the house, destroying it.

If you know that you are using a flammable chemical, remember the following:

✔ Never spray flammable products near an open fire or standing pilot light.

✔ Don't smoke while spraying or otherwise handling paint or paint products.

✔ Don't underestimate how far fumes can travel from the source.

✔ Do not use these products near flame or fire, or near electrical equipment that could spark.

✔ Use extreme caution when softening paint with a heat gun or propane torch. Small cracks in the surface may admit flame or enough heat to ignite the usually very dry material behind the surface. Such fires can spread without being noticed and are difficult to access and extinguish.

✔ Keep a fire extinguisher handy when working around flammable materials with heat guns and propane torches.

✔ Turn off all gas appliances, such as water heaters, that may light unexpectedly. Follow manufacturers' instructions to shut off any standing pilot lights, too. Do not light the pilot until the fumes have cleared.

✔ Handle paint-soaked or solvent-laden rags, drop cloths, and newspapers properly. If they are tossed in a garbage can or stored in an unventilated area, they may ignite spontaneously. Wash them and air-dry them outdoors. Then they are safe to store or throw in the trash.

Contrary to popular belief, it is not safe to simply store solvent rags in a closed metal container. The container must be half-filled with water, too.

Avoiding Accidents and Injuries

Tripping is a very real hazard in a work site that is covered with drop cloths, open paint trays, and buckets. To complicate matters, your hands are full, and your attention is usually focused up on a wall or ceiling. Utility knives, paint scrapers, heat guns, and other tools also present some risk when used improperly or carelessly. In addition, decorating projects often involve the risks associated with minor electrical work, such as temporarily removing outlet covers or light fixtures. However, the primary cause of injuries, especially serious ones, is the improper use of ladders and scaffolds.

When you are pressed for time or nearing the end of a job, it's hard to stop. But don't overwork. Risks are the greatest when you are overtired.

Using ladders and scaffolds

Choose a ladder that is more than adequate to support your weight and allow for heavy loads. Ladders are rated for heavy duty (Type I, up to 300 pounds), medium duty (Type II, up to 250 pounds), and light duty (Type III, up to 200 pounds).

A stepladder should feel solid and not wobble when you move on it. To raise a tall ladder, brace the end against something solid and walk it up to a vertical position. Then pull the base away from the wall a distance equal to one-fourth of its working length.

Tool rental outlets rent ladders and scaffolding by the day, week, or month and also offer a range of accessories. Ladder jacks allow you to extend a platform between two extension ladders. Stabilizers allow you to safely reach a wider area. Some rental outlets do not rent pump jacks or pipe scaffolding to non-professionals. Can you guess why? Here's a hint: lawsuit. Ask for instructions on proper and safe use of any equipment that you rent.

If you're painting the upper portion of a one-story home or working high on interior walls or ceilings, you can stretch a wide plank between two ladders or between a pair of sawhorses for scaffolding. We suggest something much better — a sturdy 2-foot-wide rolling scaffold. It is more stable, has a nice wide platform, and rolls around easily.

To be safe when using ladders or low scaffolding, follow these tips:

- Use ladders only for the purpose for which they were designed.
- Inspect ladders for structural defects, such as broken or missing rungs and broken or split rails or cross-braces.
- Set ladders only on stable and level surfaces unless you tie or brace them in order to prevent accidental shifting.
- Position extension ladders at the proper angle. The horizontal distance from the house to the foot of the ladder should be about one-quarter of the working length of the ladder (the extended length of the ladder).
- Platforms for scaffolds supported on sawhorses, ladder jacks, or pump jacks should be at least 12 inches wide, and preferably wider.
- If you place a platform on sawhorses, ladder jacks, or pump jacks, extend the platform at least 6 inches, but not more than 12 inches, over the supports.
- When ascending or descending a ladder, face the ladder and keep at least one hand free to grasp the ladder.
- Don't carry heavy or awkward objects that may cause you to fall, and make sure that tools are secured in a tool belt or proper holder.
- Don't climb or stand on the cross bracing on the rear of stepladders unless the ladder is specifically designed for access from both sides.
- Never stand on either the top of a stepladder or its top step.
- Don't stretch. Keep the trunk of your body within the ladder rails.
- Don't ever attempt to move, shift, or extend a ladder while you are on it.
- Never stand below an occupied ladder, unless you like the ringing sound that follows a hammer bouncing off your head.
- When you get off a ladder, don't leave any tools on it that may fall on someone's head. Keep the area around the bottom of a ladder clear, too. And just in case someone is lurking where you don't expect, don't move a ladder without looking up.

Handling hand and portable power tools

Use tools only as the manufacturers intended. Don't put sharp or pointed tools in your pocket — one deep knee bend and you'll hit a high note only dogs can hear. Use a tool belt or tool apron. Protect your eyes whenever using hand or portable power tools.

Here are some safety tips for specific types of tools:

- **Heat guns and torches:** Heat guns and propane touches can cause third-degree burns if they are not handled carefully. Don't underestimate the heat output of a gun just because there's no flame; remember that the flame on a torch extends well beyond the visible portion, especially in the bright sunlight. Don't inadvertently touch the hot metal tip.

- **Scrapers:** To avoid skinned knuckles, wear gloves and be careful working in tight places. Clamp a scraper in a vise or to a work surface to sharpen it, and keep both hands on the file.

- **Power tools:** Lock-on switches on power tools are handy but can be inadvertently locked when the tool is being carried. Keep the working end of a plugged-in tool away from your legs or other body parts, and always make sure that the switch is off before you plug in a power tool.

An electrifying experience you don't need

Removing and replacing all electrical outlet covers for painting takes far less time than painting around them or cleaning off the paint you may get on them. Always turn the power off at the circuit breaker or fuse box to eliminate any possibility of an electrical shock while you're working around the open outlets with metal tools and wet brushes. Electrical shock, though rarely fatal, can cause you to fall or have an accident.

So your first step should be to plug an extension cord into a receptacle that is on a different circuit from the room you are working in and extend the cord to the work area so that you can plug in work lights. Then head to your electric service panel. Locate and shut off the circuit for the work area according to the legend on the inside door panel.

If a negligent electrician did not identify the circuits, you'll have to use the following trial-and-error process: Switch off the breakers (or unscrew the fuses) one by one until you locate the right one. To help you find the right circuit breaker, plug in a radio and turn the volume way up; when it goes off, you'll know that you've switched the right breaker. Or you can have a helper alert you when a lamp goes off.

As a reminder to leave the breakers off until the work is done, put tape over the breaker switch until the covers and fixtures have been reinstalled.

To avoid damaging sensitive electronic equipment, especially computers, turn off such devices before you start messing with breakers.

After you switch off the circuit breakers, it's safe to remove the fixtures, right? Wrong! Use an electrical tester to verify that the power is off at receptacles and light fixtures, as shown in Figures 2-1 and 2-2. Ceiling lights and receptacles are most often on separate circuits. Sometimes more than one circuit can be present in an outlet box, and sometimes not all receptacles in a room are on the same circuit. Cap wires with wire connectors or electrical tape.

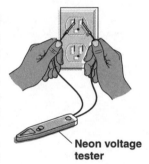

Figure 2-1: Insert probes into each receptacle to verify that the power is off.

Neon voltage tester

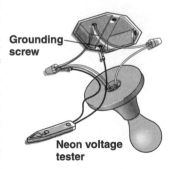

Figure 2-2: If necessary, carefully twist off wire connectors to probe the two wires connected to a light fixture.

Grounding screw

Neon voltage tester

Chapter 3

Brushing Up on Color

• •

In This Chapter

▶ Understanding the power and importance of color

▶ Developing a color scheme

▶ Letting the light in

▶ Choosing interior and exterior colors

• •

Choosing color is at the heart of nearly every decorating and exterior-finishing project. Color is a powerful medium. It can stimulate or calm or bring joy or create discomfort. The right color can visually raise or lower ceilings or make a house appear larger or smaller. Perceptions are what decorating is all about. Color schemes can also highlight features that deserve attention and camouflage those that don't.

Aside from its emotional and aesthetic impact, color has many practical implications. Under certain lighting conditions, the right color can reduce eye fatigue, while the wrong choice can make working nearly impossible.

Nevertheless, the primary consideration for choosing a color is personal preference. That's why decorating experts often advise people to choose the colors of their favorite clothes for their walls. The colors that you wear are probably also the colors that you'll like in a decorating scheme. (Paisleys and plaids don't count.)

For some people, choosing colors can be a daunting, even paralyzing, prospect. They may take five years to finally decide what color to paint a house, and even then — yeah, you guessed it — they pick white. Bolder folks choose off-white. But this reluctance to experiment with color seems less true today than in the past. Today, more people are excited about color and are more willing to experiment.

Whether you are timid or brave, try to become familiar with some basic color theory and design guidelines. And remember to use the information to expand, not limit, your possibilities.

Mark the page where the color insert begins, because you'll want to refer to it several times throughout this chapter.

Color Theory 101

Isaac Newton — the apple-on-the-head scientist — developed the color wheel when he was observing the effects on sunlight as it passed through a prism. (To see a color wheel in all of its colorful glory, flip over to the color insert in this book.) The wheel contains the 12 basic colors from which all identifiable gradations of color (called *hues*) are derived:

- **Primary colors:** The three *primary colors* (red, yellow, and blue) are the most brilliant and are spaced an equal distance from each other on the color wheel. Although all the other basic colors are derived from some mix of these three, the primary colors cannot be achieved by mixing any of the other colors.

- **Secondary colors:** When any two primary colors are mixed together in equal proportions, the resulting color is called a *secondary color*. Each of these three secondary colors (orange, green, and violet) is centered between the two primary colors that are mixed to create it.

- **Tertiary colors:** *Tertiary colors* result when a primary color is mixed with an adjacent secondary color. The six tertiary colors (red-orange, yellow-orange, yellow-green, blue-green, blue-violet, and red-violet) are positioned between the two colors mixed to create them.

But where do black, white, and gray fit in? Black, white, and gray — which is mixed only from black and white — are *non-colors*. But black and white, though non-colors, can add a lot to color. For example, if two different colors have an equal amount of white and black added to them, they have the same intensity of color, called *tone*. But adding more white increases the intensity of the color, creating a *tint*. Adding more black decreases intensity, creating a *shade*.

It's All a Big (Color) Scheme

The combination of colors used in a room or on the exterior of a house is called a *color scheme*. Use the color wheel (see the preceding section "Color Theory 101" and the color insert) as an initial step in choosing colors that *harmonize,* or go well together. Most color schemes fall into three categories: monochromatic, analogous, and complementary.

✔ **Monochromatic** schemes use one hue. This harmonious approach is perhaps the safest one — after all, you're using only one color — but it can be boring if you don't vary the *value* (tone) from light to dark. You can vary the tone with the color shades or tints that you choose or with different texture. A color looks quite different on a smooth surface than it does on a rough one.

✔ **Analogous** schemes use two or more hues that are adjacent to one another on the wheel and, therefore, are very closely related. Typically, one hue is dominant and is used, for example, on the body of a house exterior or the walls of a room, and the other hue is an accent. Using analogous colors allows you to highlight yet unify and harmonize.

✔ **Complementary** schemes employ hues that fall opposite each other on the color wheel. (See the color insert.) The combination of these colors produces the greatest degree of contrast. For two-color schemes, choose two colors that lie directly across from each other, called *direct complements*. For three-color schemes, you can use either *split complements* or *triad complements*. Instead of choosing a direct complement, split the complement by choosing the next lighter and darker colors — the colors adjacent to the direct complement. Choose a triad of complementary colors by placing an *equilateral triangle* (the sides are all the same length) anywhere on the wheel with colors at the points.

When using related or complementary color schemes, one hue must be the dominant one. If you don't have a dominant color and you try to balance the colors equally, the more zebra-like your room or house exterior will appear. We're not knocking these beautiful creatures, but a little zebra goes a very long way.

If you want to see how a certain color scheme looks, try painting some large samples, such as poster board. Apply the paints in approximately the same proportion that they will actually be used on the house — a large sample for the body paint and proportionately smaller samples for trim and accent colors.

Natural and Artificial Lighting

There would be no color without light, and the quality of that light affects your perception of color. The difference lighting makes can be subtle and beautiful or dramatic and attention-grabbing. Natural light changes color and intensity according to the season, the weather, the time of day, and whether the light is direct or reflected.

Light reflected from surrounding surfaces or natural environments alters color. A house that's nestled in evergreens under the gray, overcast skies of the Pacific Northwest appears quite different from an identically painted home in a sandy Southwest desert under clear, bright skies. Indoors, artificial lighting and the colors of rugs, walls, and furniture reflect light onto each other.

Artificial light may be needed during the day, and obviously, it is the only source of light at night. Keep in mind that colors are their truest, in bright white light, such as the light given off by halogen lamps. Colors become warmer under incandescent light. "Cool-white" fluorescent lamps approximate sunlight and so work best for supplemental day lighting. Use "warm-white" fluorescent lamps for areas usually lighted only at night.

Interior Inspirations and Tips

The interior of your home, especially the private areas, is your personal domain. Here is where you have the greatest opportunity for self-expression. In the process of making your house your own, here are some color tips to keep in mind:

- Furnishings are a major component in an interior color scheme. It's cheaper to match paint to furniture rather than the other way around.

- If you like changing wall colors, stick to neutral-color furnishings — they go well with a wide variety of colors.

- If furniture, Oriental rugs, or wall art are the focus, the colors in those furnishings will be the truest and stand out the most against a white background.

- Limit the use of vivid wall colors to rooms that you use only occasionally.

- Pastels tend to calm and produce a relaxed atmosphere.

- Two- and three-color schemes allow you to highlight features. Maintain the same tone for more harmony.

- *Cool* tones (those toward the blue end of the spectrum), monochromatic color schemes, and gloss sheens tend to add light and space and may make a room look less cluttered.

- *Warm* colors (those toward the red spectrum) can help a room that has harsh day lighting.

- Dark colors and paint with a visually flat sheen lower a ceiling. The effect can be increased by staining or painting the floor a dark color (or by using dark carpeting).

- Lower a ceiling or widen a narrow space by emphasizing horizontal elements, such as stencil borders or chair rails.

- Emphasizing vertical elements by painting them a different color or tone makes a room seem taller.

- If a room is poorly proportioned, you can camouflage the problem with a monochromatic and monotone color scheme. Or just close the door.

Exterior Color Considerations

Some important differences exist between exterior and interior painting. Exterior work is typically done all at once and requires more preparation work and more-expensive paint that can stand up to weathering and heights. You have fewer color decisions in exterior painting because typically you're selecting basically only one or two colors, not colors for nine different rooms. Finally, the exterior is the face that you present to the public. All things considered, you have less room for experimentation when choosing exterior colors, and you may need to consider the opinions of others. Plainly put, yes, your neighbors will care if you paint your house bright purple.

Typically, people want their homes to harmonize with others in the area. Your neighborhood may even have zoning restrictions that specify historic colors or other conformities. The closer neighboring homes are, the more important it is to consider how the colors relate. Walk through your neighborhood and check out the finishes and color combinations on houses that appeal to you.

You also need to consider three different areas when painting a house exterior: the body, trim, and accents.

- **The body, or siding,** of the house is the largest area and is the dominant color.

- **The trim** is the second component, which you can emphasize by using contrasting colors or different tones or *de-emphasize* by coloring the trim the same as the body.

- **Accents** — such as shutters and entry doors — make up the third area. You can emphasize accent areas by using a contrasting color when they're attractive or downplay them by using the same color as the body when you don't want to call attention to them. Gutters and downspouts that are painted should be camouflaged by matching or blending with the color behind them.

If you are painting vinyl siding, choose a color or shade no darker than the existing one. Dark colors absorb heat, which can expand the siding enough to make it buckle. Similarly, avoid painting south-facing steel entry doors in dark colors. They can get too hot to handle.

Exterior Color Design Tips

Many of the same design considerations for choosing an interior color apply outdoors, too. (See "Interior Inspirations and Tips" earlier in the chapter for more information on interior design tips.) In choosing colors for the exterior of your house, keep in mind the following guidelines:

- ✔ Light and monochromatic color schemes make a house look larger. Dark colors and contrast between the body and the trim make it look smaller.

- ✔ Use monochromatic color schemes to unify a house with many different textures. Use different colors to emphasize different textures.

- ✔ Emphasizing the horizontal lines by painting them a different color makes a house appear longer and lower to the ground; emphasizing the vertical features makes it appear taller.

- ✔ Emphasize or de-emphasize the effects of a shadow caused by roof overhangs, porches, and so on by painting the shadow area dark or light, respectively.

- ✔ Use two or three colors or distinct tones on a beautifully proportioned home or to highlight trim details or special features.

- ✔ Choose colors that complement the fixed colors of house components, such as the roofing and brick or stone.

- ✔ The more natural the environment, the more important your color decision. For example, a home that is painted pale colors in the desert not only reflects heat but also picks up the color of beautiful sunsets. And pink may not be the best choice for a house in a national forest!

- ✔ Don't trust a salesman in a red plaid jacket with bright yellow slacks to pick out your paint colors.

Some paint dealers feature computer-assisted color selection. Some systems include a variety of standard house designs that you can "paint" on-screen, choosing colors from the company's exterior palette. On other systems, you can scan a photo of your own home and "paint" it on-screen. We're not talking virtual reality here, so we wouldn't base a decision on this process alone, but any input helps.

Part II
Finishes, Applicators, Techniques, and Cleanup

The 5th Wave   By Rich Tennant

"You did an excellent job, Dave. But two months seems a long time to paint the bathroom."

In this part . . .

Half the battle with a painting or finishing project is choosing the right finish and applicator for the specific task you undertake. The other half is getting your hands on tools and related supplies that make your task easier. And then there's the half of knowing what you're doing, including how to clean up. (I know, the math may not be right, but it always seems like there's more than just one task when painting.) Whether you've never picked up a paintbrush or you're a seasoned paint-it-yourselfer looking for information that will make your job easier and the results better, this part is for you.

Chapter 4

Choosing the Right Finish

- -

In This Chapter

▶ Covering the basics

▶ Understanding the different types of finishes

▶ Choosing the right exterior and interior finish for the job

▶ Figuring out the labels on paint cans

▶ Estimating how much paint you need

- -

*T*he greatest painting and finishing hurdle you're likely to face isn't on your walls or ceilings; it's in the aisles of your home center. Faced with mile-long shelves loaded to the ceiling with mountains of paints, stains, and other finishing products, you stand there musing, "How the heck do I know what kind to buy?" Fear of the unknown is natural, so take heart. You may not be genetically gifted with knowledge of paints and finishes, but you can become more informed rather easily.

Beyond the ornamental purposes that paint, varnish, and other finishes provide, they bond with wood or other materials to protect the surfaces from heat, moisture, sunlight, chemicals, dirt, stains, and even fire. Depending on the formulation and the application, a finish prevents (or slows) degradation caused by weathering and sunlight, wood rot, mildew growth, and rust. It also limits excessive expansion and contraction due to changing moisture content and temperatures. It keeps things cleaner and, once they get dirty, makes them easier to clean. And you thought paint only added color.

A Primer on Primers and Finishes

The coatings that you apply to various surfaces to protect and beautify them fall into three categories:

✓ **Opaque:** This category includes paints, enamels, solid-color stains, tinted shellacs, and other primers and sealers.

✓ **Semitransparent:** Examples include pigmented stains, dye stains, and tinted varnishes.

- ✔ **Transparent:** Varnishes, clear shellacs, some sealers, polyurethanes, and various oils are considered transparent.

Paints, stains, clear finishes, and other coatings have three primary ingredients:

- ✔ **Pigment** provides color and hiding power. Paint has a lot of pigment, so it is an opaque finish. Semitransparent stains have less pigment or use dyes, and clear (transparent) finishes have no pigment.

- ✔ **Binder** is the material that keeps the pigments in suspension, binds them, and provides the backbone for the dried paint film. Modern paints use mostly plastic resins or synthetic rubber as binders. In water-based paints, binders are usually latex, vinyl, acrylics, or modified alkyds; in modern alkyd paints, the binders are synthetic resins called *alkyds.* In traditional oil-based paints, the binders are linseed, tung, soya, or other natural oils.

- ✔ **Solvent** is the liquid that makes an otherwise gooey mess a coating that is easy to apply. Along with *driers,* it also determines how fast the coating dries. It is what you use to thin the paint or clean up spills and tools. As the solvent evaporates, the paint film hardens. With some of the newer water-borne paints, drying and curing additionally rely on a chemical process (*cross-linking* of molecules, for the budding chemists among us). Water is the solvent for traditional latex paint and the newer *water-borne coatings*. Petroleum distillates (mineral spirits, lacquer thinner, and so on) are the solvents for alkyd paints, and natural oils derived from plants such as linseed oil are the solvents in traditional oil-based paints.

Because pigment and binders are all that's left after the coating dries, these *solids* are why you'll hear, "The heavier the can, the better the paint inside."

The balance between pigment and binders determines the sheen or gloss. The higher the pigment relative to binder, the more *matte* or flat (dull) the finish and the better the hiding power. The more binders there are (and the better their quality), the more shiny, durable, and washable the surface will be.

Additives shape a finish's properties. An additive may determine how a paint contacts or wets the surface, control the drying time, prevent a ceiling paint from spattering, or prevent separation in the can. Other additives may control growth of mildew, improve leveling qualities (so that brush marks won't show), make the paint go on with less effort, reflect ultraviolet (UV) radiation, make the finish penetrate or adhere better to certain surfaces, or make the paint dripless.

Water-based or oil-based?

Paints, stains, varnishes, and other clear coatings, both interior and exterior, are available in oil-based and water-based versions.

In the last 20 years, paint manufacturers have virtually eliminated lead in paint and have eliminated or greatly reduced the amount of ozone-producing chemicals called *volatile organic compounds* (VOCs). Until the mid-1980s, the development of water-based finishes, such as latex paints, was largely a game of catch-up with oil-based products, which offered superior penetration and bonding, leveling, shine, protection, and washability. But in the last ten years, a wave of entirely new types of water-reducible (water-borne) finishes that are based on new synthetic polymers has hit the market.

Thanks to much-improved performance qualities, such as scratch and stain resistance, do-it-yourselfers can tackle most home painting and finishing projects as effectively or even better with water-based coatings than with oil-based ones. However, there are still a few applications for which oil-based finishes are preferred or even required.

So why all these efforts on the part of manufacturers? In general, water-based products are not as harmful to your health or the environment. Water-based coatings always dry quicker and have fewer odors. Consumers also like the easy cleanup of water-based products.

What most people call *latex* or *water-based* paints actually are latex, acrylic-latex, vinyl-latex, or modified alkyd paints. The names are derived from the types of *resins* that form the paint film. Latex, which is natural rubber, and acrylic vinyl-latex and modified-alkyd are synthetic alternatives. There are, however, important differences in the quality of the resins, and therefore the paints. Of the three, acrylic-latex is the best quality.

First things first

Base coats include *primers* and *sealers,* or combination *primer-sealers,* which serve the purposes of both. Base coats are applied under a *topcoat* to provide better adhesion and/or to seal the surface for a more even finish application, or in some cases to prevent stains from bleeding through the topcoat.

Primers are formulated to adhere well to bare surfaces and provide the best possible base for other paint to stick to. Latex- and oil-based primers are available for virtually all interior and exterior surfaces. All new unpainted surfaces, patched areas, and spots that you make bare in the preparation stages needs *priming* before you paint.

If you're painting with a color that's significantly darker or lighter than that of the existing finish, use a tinted primer and a topcoat instead of the three or more topcoats that might otherwise be required. Ask your paint supplier to tint an interior primer to the approximate color of the planned topcoat.

Most primers (also called *undercoaters*) contain very little pigment and none of the ingredients that give topcoats shine, durability, and washability. Apply topcoats as soon as possible after the primer dries. (Primers generally dry fast.) Some primers can be topcoated in as little as an hour.

Sealers, or more commonly *primer-sealers,* should be used if you're painting a material that varies in porosity, such as newly installed drywall or woods such as fir. The seal prevents a topcoat from being absorbed unevenly, which would give the finish a blotchy appearance or uneven texture. Sealers also block stains. If you have kids, for example, you may have marker or crayon stains on walls. To prevent bleedthrough, apply a *stain blocker, stain-killing sealer,* or *white-pigmented shellac*. These primer/sealers are available in spray cans for small spots and in quart and gallon containers for large stained areas. You should also use them to prevent resin from wood knots from bleeding through topcoats. Having had mixed results with the stain-sealing effectiveness with these products, especially when it comes to knots, we always apply two or three coats.

Some finishes, notably floor-and-deck enamels and varnishes, are thinned for the base coat rather than using a separate primer or sealer. Certain topcoats do not require a primer on certain surfaces. For example, you don't need to prime when you're recoating well-adhered paint with an identical paint (latex semi-gloss over latex semi-gloss, for example) and are not making a significant color change.

Fortunately, you don't need to remember these rules — just read the label on the can of topcoat paint. It will specify primer requirements, if any, for various surfaces.

Categorizing finishes

A *topcoat* is the finish that protects and sometimes colors the surface. Sorting through the myriad of choices — one manufacturer's catalog that we looked at listed hundreds of finishes in 90 categories — is not as difficult as it first seems. You'll see, for example, that most fall into one of the following categories:

- ✔ **Exterior paints** are formulated to withstand the effects of weather, damaging ultraviolet radiation, air pollution, extremes in heat and cold, expansion, and contraction. They include house paints (intended for the body of the house, but may also be used for trim), trim paints, and a variety of specialty paints, such as those for metal roofs, barns, aluminum or vinyl siding, and masonry surfaces.

You can use some exterior finishes indoors (read the label), but they are not designed to hold up to scrubbing as well as some interior paints; never use an interior finish outdoors.

✔ **Interior paints** include flat white ceiling paints, wall and ceiling paints in various sheen ranges from flat to gloss, trim paints, and enamels in higher gloss ranges. Consider using special interior paints that contain mildewcides (or fungicides) for high-humidity areas such as kitchens, bathrooms, and laundry rooms. Interior textured paints, intended for use on ceilings and walls, contain sand or other texturing materials. Use vapor-retarding paint on interior walls in homes that have had thermal insulation blown into wall cavities without the required vapor retarder.

✔ **Interior/exterior paints,** as the name suggests, can be used indoors or outdoors. Some alkyd, urethane, and water-based floor, deck, and patio enamels fall into this category.

✔ **Interior and exterior stains and transparent finishes** are formulated for interior, exterior, or interior/exterior use. Although people associate stains primarily with wood, stains are also available for concrete. Stains intended for interior applications offer little or no protection and must be top-coated with a protective, film-forming sealer finish such as varnish, or with a separate sealer and a wax or polish finish. Exterior stains have water-repellent and UV-reflecting qualities.

Transparent finishes are just that: *transparent,* not colorless. Alkyd and polyurethane varnish are amber colored and will grow more yellow with time. Polyurethane varnish has largely replaced alkyd varnish because it is more moisture- and stain-resistant.

Water-based clear finishes dry three to six times faster than alkyds. Milky, water-borne polyurethane varnish and water-borne acrylic finish dry clear and remain clear, so they're also excellent choices to use over pickled, pastel-stained, or painted surfaces. On the downside, they lie on the surface rather than penetrate, so they don't enhance or bring out the beauty of the natural wood as well as do penetrating finishes. Nor do they offer the stain- and water-resistance of oil-based finishes.

Recently introduced one-step stain-varnish combos stain, seal, and protect in one coat. They don't penetrate wood as well and are harder to maintain, so we recommend that you stick with the two-step approach whenever possible.

A varnish offers more protection than that of other sealer/finish approaches, such as shellacs, oils, and polishes. However, varnish does mask the beauty of the wood more than these alternatives, so it is not always used on fine furniture. Furniture oils, such as tung oil, boiled linseed oil, and Danish oil, are penetrating, wipe-on finishes with an amber color and satin luster. Oils offer very little moisture or stain resistance, but on the plus side scratches are easily concealed by recoating. This makes oils a good choice for wood that takes a beating — but only if stains and water are not big concerns.

Specialty finishes, including some primers, sealers, and topcoats, are formulated for very specific and usually demanding applications. Whenever your project seems to go beyond the basics, look for specialty products. Special primers are made for galvanized metal and mill-finish aluminum. Masonry sealers prevent dusting or leaching of alkalis. Two-part epoxy and two-part urethane paints are used when a particularly strong bond is required or when a finish must stand up to extreme abuse, such as on countertops or garage floors.

Altering Qualities with Additives

In addition to the additives that paint companies use in the manufacturing process, there are four notable paint additives available to consumers: driers, paint conditioners, mildewcides, and textures. Here are some of the ways you can use them to change the qualities of a finish to suit you specific needs:

✓ You can add a drier to oil-based paints to speed drying time. This feature may be important to prevent runs or, for example, to let you close a freshly painted exterior door by the end of a day. Use a drier sparingly, as it can adversely affect other properties or cause paint to dry too fast.

✓ Paint conditioners give paint better flow and leveling qualities (no brush marks), better penetration, better bond, and better coverage. Acrylic-latex trim paint can be quite sticky in warm weather, and flow conditioners make it easier to apply. Latex conditioners also can be used to slow drying time, making it easier to keep a wet edge.

✓ Surface or bonding conditioners help finishes bond better with problem surfaces, such as hardboard, plastic laminate, masonry, or old paint. Make sure that the bonding conditioner you choose will work on the type of paint you have.

Don't use a bonding conditioner in a final coat because it may affect sheen unevenly. Bonding conditioners require special brush-cleaning procedures.

✓ You can add mildewcide (also called *fungicide*) to exterior paint or paint for bathrooms to reduce the chances of mildew growth. However, keep in mind that they are generally effective for a limited time. Although most exterior paints already contain mildewcide in sufficient quantities for normal conditions, you may need to add more in certain warm, humid climates or problem areas. Some specialized bathroom paints with mildewcide, such a Perma-White, come with warranties against mildew growth.

Mildewcide is extremely toxic and may cause blindness if it gets in your eyes. Read the manufacturer's instructions and handle them with extraordinary care; or better yet, ask your paint dealer to do the mixing.

> ✔ Texture additives may have aesthetic and practical purposes. A special sand, for example, can be added to interior wall and ceiling paint for appearance or to mask a less-than-perfect drywall taping job. A fine abrasive, intended for floor and deck enamels, makes painted stairs and walks slip-resistant.

Choosing an Exterior Finish

Unless you're building a new home or residing in an existing one, your choices for what finish to use are dictated to a degree by your siding and the type and condition of any existing finish. For example, some finishes work better on smooth, painted wood, while others work better on rough, stained wood. So the first step is to narrow the options to finishes that are appropriate. Next, choose the ones that offer you the right combination of qualities. Finally, choose a color.

Paint versus stain

If you have new siding or siding that has been treated with only a semitransparent stain, your options are wide open. However, you can't stain over previously painted surfaces.

As a general rule, paint is the preferred finish for smooth siding, trim, and metal siding like steel or aluminum. It offers maximum protection from UV radiation and moisture. Stains are commonly used on natural wood siding, especially rough-sawn boards, or on other exterior wood surfaces, such as decks and fences.

Although paint lasts longer than stain, paint finish builds up and may peel or otherwise fail. If it does, you're in for a lot of work. Stains, on the other hand, may not last as long, but thanks to the penetration, they just weather away. Over the long haul, less cost and work may be involved if you choose stain. It is easier to apply, and preparation is usually limited to simple power washing.

Exterior latex paint

Latex is the hands-down favorite of homeowners and professional painters for most painted exterior surfaces. It is popular because it is easier to use and more environmentally friendly. Latex paint is more elastic and remains flexible, so it won't crack as the materials it is applied to expand and contract. Oil-based paint, on the other hand, becomes brittle with age. Latex paint has superior color retention over most oil-based paint, meaning that it doesn't fade as much. The paint film also permits interior moisture vapor to pass through, so latex paint is less likely to peel due to moisture problems. You can apply latex topcoats over either latex or oil-based primers.

Exterior alkyd paint

Alkyd paint may be a better choice than latex on a few surfaces. For example, if a house has numerous coats of alkyd or oil-based paint, it is generally best to stick with alkyd. Believing that alkyd-painted surfaces are generally easier to clean and have more sheen than latex paints, some professionals use latex on the body of the house but prefer to use an alkyd finish on trim or other high-contact areas, such as doors. We think that the advantages of latex outweigh these purported advantages of alkyd-based paint in the vast majority of applications. We are inclined to agree, however, with the professionals (including some paint company chemists) who say that alkyd paints, especially alkyd primers, are better products to use on problem areas.

Don't use alkyd paint over a latex topcoat. It's likely to peel off even a well-prepared latex finish because the latex expands and contracts too much for the relatively rigid film.

Exterior stain and clear coatings

Stains and clear coatings are the most natural-looking protective finishes for wood. Exterior stains and varnishes have mildewcides, offer greater ultraviolet (UV) protection than interior versions, and may have more water-repellent qualities, too. Stains are available in both oil- and water-based versions and are colored with dye and pigment. A semitransparent stain uses more dye for deep penetration but allows the wood grain to show. A solid-color stain uses more pigment to cover all existing color and grain but retains some textures and always contains a sealer, such as urethane or varnish. A solid-color stain offers better UV protection and hiding characteristics than semitransparent stain or transparent finishes, such as varnish. Solid-color stain penetrates more than paint and produces a thinner film, so it is not as likely to peel.

Stains can be applied only over new or previously stained surfaces, not painted ones. Oil-based semitransparent stains are a good choice for new wood siding, decks, and fences. These stains have a linseed-oil base, which offers good penetration of new wood (especially rough-sawn surfaces), while revealing the wood grain and texture. For best protection, use two coats of semitransparent stain on new wood surfaces.

If your goal is to conceal discoloration, solid-color stains have more pigment than semi-transparent stains and tend to hide the wood grain. This characteristic makes solid-color stain a better choice to finish pressure-treated wood that has a pronounced green or brown tint, which semitransparent stains may not cover.

Typically, the only treatment used for redwood is clear water repellent. Semitransparent stains won't cover the red. Tannin bleed is a problem with redwood, so if you want to change its color, you can use an oil-based solid stain, but only on rough-sawn redwood. For smooth redwood, you should prime and paint. When working with redwood, use a stain-blocking latex primer on air-dried siding and an alkyd primer on kiln-dried, regardless of the type of topcoat.

Choosing the Right Interior Paint

When you reach the paint department, you'll be faced with a choice between the two major types of paint: *alkyd* (oil-based) and *latex* (water-based). Alkyd paint may produce more durable and washable surfaces, but because cleaning up afterwards involves using paint thinner, also known as *mineral spirits,* it's not as user-friendly.

Latex paint is the more popular choice because it's much easier to work with and cleans up with soap and water. For first-time home painters, latex is the better choice because you'll get a professional looking job with a durable finish. Plus, latex paints dry quickly. Some professional painters insist on using alkyd paint, claiming it's more durable in particularly demanding situations.

One approach is to use alkyd paint on woodwork and trim, where a hard, durable finish can be washed frequently, and latex paint on the walls.

Interior paints come in different gloss ranges, or *sheens*. In the past, there were only three standard gloss ranges: flat, semi-gloss, and gloss. Today, you may be able to choose from up to seven gloss ranges, depending on the manufacturer and the type of paint. Keep in mind that these are *ranges* and so may vary from one product to another. Some manufacturers get a bit more creative in naming some of the sheens, but the most common ones are

- **Flat** paint is at the low (dull) end of the sheen spectrum. It's often used on walls or ceilings because it's easy on the eye. It reflects a minimum of light off the surface, reducing glare and helping to hide small surface imperfections but is generally not considered to be washable.

- **Eggshell, lo-luster,** and **satin** paints have increasing amounts of sheen, making them a little more dirt-resistant than flat paints, and washable. The slight sheen is generally noticeable only when the surface is side-lighted. It is a good choice for walls in hallways, children's bedrooms, playrooms, and other high-traffic areas.

- **Semi-gloss** paint has still more sheen that makes it even more washable than eggshell, lo-luster, and satin paints. Kitchen, bathroom, mudroom, and young children's room walls are likely candidates for paints with this sheen level. Semi-gloss is, perhaps, the most widely used latex trim paint.

✔ **Gloss** and **high-gloss** paints dry to a very durable and shiny surface. Glossy paints are the most dirt-resistant and scrubbable choice for interior trim and most woodwork. Gloss enamels are particularly hard and are an excellent choice for doors, furniture, and cabinets because the surface can withstand heavy cleaning. Some gloss enamels, called deck or floor enamels, are specifically designed for wearing surfaces, such as floors. High-gloss paint has an almost mirrorlike sheen.

Instead of two coats of an expensive topcoat, use a primer-sealer for the first coat over new drywall or other hard-to-cover surfaces. If there is a radical change in color or shade from the previous color, have your dealer tint the primer to the approximate pastel or mid-tone color of the topcoat. Primers cover fairly well but, more important, they seal the surface so that the topcoat will cover well. Primers are less expensive because as undercoats they don't need any of the expensive ingredients that make topcoats washable.

Finding the Perfect Interior Stain

If you think that variety is the spice of life, you're going to love shopping for wood stains. Stains are available in a wide variety of wood tones, as well as pastels. Your paint dealer probably has samples so that you can see how the various stains look on real wood. Let your decor and tastes determine which is the best for you. For nicely grained wood such as oak, a good choice is to use a penetrating stain that enhances the grain pattern. For furniture, cabinets, or moldings made of less attractive wood or mismatched pieces of wood, consider a using a *pigmented* stain (a colored "wiping" stain) or pastel stains because they conceal more.

Can't find that perfect color? Play chemist and mix together different stains from the same manufacturer to make your own unique stain or one that matches an unknown stain on existing wood. If you decide to experiment, be sure to mix enough stain to do the entire job. Measure and record the proportions carefully, because if you run out of stain in the middle of a project or if you need to mix up a batch for a future repair, matching the color or tone without a formula is difficult.

You can also make your own pigmented stain by thinning alkyd paint with mineral spirits. For example, for a deep black stain, thin flat black alkyd paint with mineral spirits. Start with a 50-50 mix and add mineral spirits, testing often on a scrap of wood, until you get just the result you want.

Estimating How Much Paint to Buy

To estimate the amount of paint that you'll need for a project, the first factor to consider is how much *surface area* you are trying to cover. You have to dust off a math formula that you first learned in the fourth grade: length (in feet) x width (in feet) = area (in square feet). When figuring estimates for smaller projects, remembering that there are 4 quarts in a gallon and 2 pints in a quart also comes in handy.

The second factor in determining paint needs is *coverage*. Paints and other coatings virtually all describe coverage in terms of the number of square feet (area) that 1 gallon of the finish covers. The coverage varies by product and is printed on the label.

The third factor to consider is the *condition of the surface*. A rough, porous, unpainted surface absorbs much more paint than a primed or already top-coated surface. A complex, six-panel, raised-panel door requires more paint than a flat, smooth door.

Estimating is not an exact science. Keep in mind that you can usually return standard colors, but not custom ones, so it's more important to be accurate when using custom colors. Although you don't want to waste paint, a reasonable amount of leftover paint is handy for touch-ups. If you're like most people who fail to record custom paint colors in a safe place, keeping some extra paint is also the only way you know what color you used before when you need to repaint! Follow this process:

1. **Find the total area.**

   The easiest surfaces to figure are interior walls and ceilings and exterior walls. In a room, just add together the length of all the walls and multiply the result by the height of the room, measured from floor to a level ceiling. The number you get equals the total square footage. If the room has a cathedral (sloped) ceiling, there are some triangular wall sections (usually two identical ones on opposite walls). Dust off one more math formula: area (of a triangle) = ½ base x height. Measure from the top of the wall (usually 8 feet above the floor) to the peak of the triangle. Multiply that number (the height) by ½ the width of the wall (the base) to get the square foot area of the triangle. If there are two identical triangles, either double that number or just multiply the height by the entire width in the first place.

   Ceilings usually require a fairly straightforward measurement — just multiply the room width by the room length for the total ceiling area. Add this to the square footage of the walls or leave it separate, depending on whether or not you're planning to use different-colored paints for the ceiling and the walls.

   The exterior of a home may be more complex than four rectangular walls and a couple of gables, but the procedure is basically the same. Just break up the surface into rectangles, multiply lengths by widths for each rectangular area, and total them up.

Don't bother to climb a ladder to measure the height of a triangular gable wall section; count the rows, called *courses,* of siding from the ground. Measure the *exposure* (the distance from the bottom of one course of siding to the bottom of the next course) on siding that you can reach easily, and multiply that number by the number of courses to come up with the height measurement.

2. **Account for windows and doors.**

   First, you need to deduct for the openings — windows and doors — to figure how much of that total wall area is going to be paintable area. Unless you have unusually large or small windows or doors, you can just allow 20 square feet for each door and 15 square feet for each window. Add up the areas of the openings and subtract that total from the total area. On the exterior, however, don't make any deductions unless an opening is over 100 square feet. Experience has taught the pros that this general rule helps to account for some of the typical exterior conditions described in Step 4.

   Similarly, calculate the total area of the trim. This measurement is a little trickier because widths are usually measured in inches while lengths are measured in feet. In many cases, you add up a number of widths and can round off the total to feet. For example, take door trim. The 3-inch inside casing + 6-inch jamb + 3-inch outside casing = 12 inches (1 foot) total width. The two sides and the head add up to roughly 17 feet in length. So, 1 foot x 17 feet = 17 square feet.

   If you plan to paint the windows and doors, use the following rules. Allow 20 square feet for each door (just the door, not the trim) and double that if you're finishing both sides. Although you subtract 15 square feet for each window to calculate paintable wall area, figure about 8 square feet to paint the sash and trim. The rest is glass.

3. **Make a preliminary calculation of gallons required.**

   Knowing the areas to be covered, divide the total square footage of paintable area by the coverage per gallon, which is stated on the label. Divide the paintable wall area by 350 (the square-foot coverage in each gallon can) to find the number of gallons of paint that you'll need for the walls. If a remainder is less than .5, order a couple of quarts to go with the gallons; if a remainder is more than .5 gallon, order an extra gallon.

4. **Factor in surface conditions.**

   Out go the formulas for this final step. It's time for *guesstimating*. The coverage stated on the paint-can label applies under typical, if not ideal, circumstances. A quality latex topcoat applied over a primed or painted, smooth surface, for example, covers about 350 square feet. Just like get-rich-quick schemes or lose-weight-fast diets, "Results will vary," and you rarely get as much coverage claimed on the label.

Wood shingles and rough-sawn cedar siding require more than the stated coverage, in part because the surface is rough and loaded with joints and cracks. There's also more area than first meets the eye. On lap or bevel siding (where horizontal boards overlap each other), you must factor in the underside. On a house with board-and-batten siding, you have many edges to paint in addition to the rough faces of the boards. That's why you don't deduct for doors and windows on exterior wall calculations.

Similarly, you'll use more paint if you're painting interior walls or ceilings that are unfinished, heavily patched, or dark in color. Plan on applying a primer and a topcoat or two topcoats. Oddly enough, you may get better coverage with a cheap paint, but the finish will not be as durable or washable, so pass over bargain paint.

You must make still further allowances for the following adverse conditions: surfaces that are weathered or dry; porous material; unprimed, unsealed, or unfinished surfaces; rough surfaces; molding with a complex or detailed profile; cornices or other trims that are assembled using numerous pieces of lumber or molding; raised-panel doors; overlapping surfaces; and high contrast between base color and topcoat. Even the type of applicator and your skills can affect the amount of paint you use. A paint sprayer, for example, can waste 10 to 25 percent on surfaces other than the one you're trying to paint (like the neighbor's car), depending on the type of sprayer and the wind conditions.

In most cases, especially small projects such as painting a room, you can allow from 25 to 50 percent extra if you are painting problem sufaces. On large projects, like painting or staining an entire house, seek the advice of experienced paint store personnel. If you are using custom colors, which usually can't be returned, be conservative and plan a second trip if you need more. If you think that you have particularly adverse surface conditions and you want to allow 50 percent more paint, multiply your total painted area by 1.5. If conditions are moderately adverse and you want to allow 25 percent more paint, multiply the painted area by 1.25.

Consumer Advice

The cost of the paint (or other finish) typically makes up 10 to 15 percent of the total cost of a professional paint job. Although a dollar-to-dollar comparison is not possible with a do-it-yourself job, you'll probably have a similarly high investment in labor compared to the cost of paint. So buy the very best paint that you can afford. Any difference in cost is usually not worth the reduced quality.

To ensure that you're using quality paint, stick with well-known name brands. While professional painters don't always agree on the best brand, the reputable ones do choose top-quality paint because they must stand behind their work.

Good paint companies all offer varying quality paint under their brand names. From company to company, the products are comparable in quality and offer similar warranties. The price difference can be substantial, sometimes as much as $10 to $15 per gallon, especially when you compare a regularly priced, high-end brand name with a chain store's top-of-the line house label on sale. However, the more expensive paints tend to offer better color retention, better elasticity, more reliable warranties, and a longer life.

Pay attention to paint sales. You'll find that they follow the seasons, with the best sale prices in the spring. We've also noticed that the quality paint brands seem to be offered on sale in the middle of the summer after the Fourth of July.

Reading (and understanding) labels

Paint manufacturers formulate coatings to meet the demands of particular projects and often identify them according to their intended use — ceiling paint, floor enamel, house paint, galvanized metal primer, aluminum siding paint, and so on.

If a coating is not identified with a particular project or you are considering a use other than the name implies, read the label to determine whether the product meets your needs. Although you may not need to read the entire label to do that, you may save yourself a trip back to the store, especially if you read the preparation and priming requirements. For unusual or demanding applications, ask for a product specification sheet to be sure that you understand *all* the requirements. Most manufacturers also have toll-free access to their technical departments if you have any doubts about the appropriateness of a product or how to use it.

To ensure compatibility between a primer and a topcoat or between a painted surface and a new coating, the safest bet is to use the same brand and follow that manufacturer's specific recommendations.

Chapter 5

Selecting and Using Applicators

- -

- -

*W*henever we know that a project is labor intensive, meaning that labor is a more significant factor than the cost of materials, that's our clue to look for top-quality tools that speed the process or make the work easier. The payback is always worthwhile. Painting is just such a job.

Buy the best applicators that you can afford, not counting Bob, the painter. The right applicators feel better in your hand, hold paint better, spread the paint on better, and do not leave loose brush bristles or roller-cover fuzz all over your new finish. They last longer, and so do you because, incidentally — you don't have to work as hard. If you're looking for info about using sprayers to apply paint, check out Chapter 6.

This chapter shows you how to pick an appropriate applicator, one that is designed for use with the type of finish that you're using — oil- or water-based paint or varnish or enamel — as well as the condition, size, and shape of the surface that you are painting. You'll also figure out the best way to use brushes, rollers, and pads to get a truly professional finish. And you can find out which (if any) specialty applicators and accessories may save you money, time, and effort.

The Team Workhorses of Painting

Indoors or out, most painting tasks call for one or more of the big three applicators — brush, roller, or pad. (Actually there are four workhorses, but the fourth, the paint sprayer, is out in its own pasture. See Chapter 6.) You can use all three applicators with oil- or water-based finishes, so the surface you plan on painting is the primary determining factor. The applicators sometimes produce slightly different textures, so that can also be a reason for choosing one type over another.

Brushes

After fingers, the brush is the world's oldest painting tool — and a brush is much more versatile, not to mention less messy. Brushes are made for every application, from the tiniest artist's brush to super-wide wall brushes. Many brushes are intended for specialized tasks, such as the decorative painting techniques that we discuss in Chapter 13.

Figure 5-1 illustrates the qualities of a good brush — one that gives you the desired result with the least amount of work. Price and feel are the best indicators of quality, and you'll need to consider the size, texture, and shape of the surface being finished. Keep these things in mind as well:

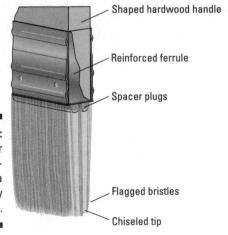

Shaped hardwood handle

Reinforced ferrule

Spacer plugs

Figure 5-1:
Look for these features in a quality paintbrush.

Flagged bristles

Chiseled tip

✔ Check to see that the *ferrule,* a metal band that binds the brush fill to the handle, is made of noncorrosive metal, or rust may develop and contaminate the finish. The ferrule should be nailed to the handle.

✔ Be sure the handle is made of unvarnished wood or a non-glossy material. A handle should feel comfortable in your hand.

Two other things you'll want to keep in mind: the *brush fill* (the materials used to make the brush) and the brush style.

Brush fill

Brush fill, as the brushing material on a paintbrush is called, is the "working" end of the brush. The fill material is very important and falls into two main categories:

- ✔ **Natural bristle** brushes, sometimes called hog bristle or *China* brushes (the hogs are from China), are the best, but you can only use them for oil-based paints because the bristles soak up water and get ruined. Hog bristle has a rough texture that picks up and holds a lot of paint, and the ends are naturally split, or *flagged.* A flagged brush, which looks a bit fuzzy at the tip, allows each individual bristle or filament to hold more paint without dripping and to apply paint more smoothly.

- ✔ **Synthetic** brushes are made of nylon, polyester, or a combination of synthetic filaments. Nylon bristles are more abrasion-resistant than natural bristles, hold up to water-based paints, and apply a very smooth finish. Although nylon brushes can be used with oil-based paints, polyester brushes hold up much better to solvents, heat, and moisture and as such are better all-purpose brushes. The best synthetic brushes blend both nylon and polyester filaments and are an acceptable compromise to a natural bristle brush for exterior oil-based painting.

Regardless of which type of brush you choose, look for a mix of short and long bristles with flagged tips. As the flagging on longer bristles wears, the flagged shorter bristles take over. Bristles should feel full, thick, and resilient. If you fan the brush and tug lightly on the bristles, no bristles should fall out. Pass up brushes that have bristles that are all cut to the same length. Choose brushes with bristles that are contoured or chiseled to an oval or rounded edge. A chiseled tip brush cuts in better around trim, ceilings, and other transitions.

Brush styles

After you know what type of brush fill you want, you need to choose the right style. Brush width (spelled out in inches), the shape of the brush fill (angled or square), and the shape and size of the handle are the most obvious elements of style. As you see in Figure 5-2 and the descriptions that follow, the qualities of the brush fill also vary. As these fill qualities are less obvious, some brushes, such as the *enamel/varnish* brush or the *stain* brush, are simply named according to their intended use.

Figure 5-2:
The brushes
for most
brush-
painting
tasks.

Enamel   Sash   Wall

Here are the four standard brush styles:

- **Enamel (varnish) brushes** are generally available from 1- to 3-inches wide. The brush fill is designed to have superior paint-carrying capacity and has a chiseled tip for smooth application. Use these for trim and woodwork.

- **Sash brushes** look like enamel brushes. They, too, are available in 1- to 3-inch widths, but the handle is long and thin for better control. Although laying paint on flat surfaces may be easier with a *flat* sash brush, an *angular* sash brush is okay for flat surfaces and much better for cutting in (carefully painting up to an edge) and getting into corners.

- **Wall brushes** are designed for painting large areas, including exterior siding. Select a brush according to the size of the surface you are painting, but avoid brushes over 4 inches wide. They can get awfully heavy by the end of the day.

- **Stain brushes** are similar to wall brushes, but they're shorter and designed specifically to better control dripping of watery stains.

Paint rollers

The paint roller is great for most large flat surfaces and is the runaway favorite for painting walls and ceilings. A roller holds a large amount of paint, and that feature saves you time and the effort of bending and dipping. (The only bending and dipping we like to do while painting involves a bag of chips and a bowl of salsa.)

Start with a sturdy roller

When you buy a roller, choose one made with a heavy wire frame and a comfortable handle that has an open end to accept an extension pole. This isn't the time to be frugal. Don't buy economy-grade rollers that tend to flex when

pressure and result in an uneven coat of paint. Choose a heavy, that doesn't flex lets you work with constant pressure.

ller is the standard size roller, but you can buy smaller sizes for hard-to-access surfaces, and there's an 18-inch length if you're painting. Figure 5-3 illustrates the qualities of a good paint roller setup.

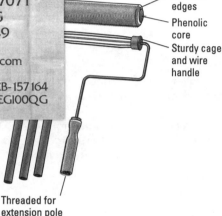

Beveled edges

Phenolic core

Sturdy cage and wire handle

LOOK for these qualities when buying a paint roller setup.

Threaded for extension pole

Then roll up your sleeves

The soft painting surface of a roller is called a *sleeve* or a *cover.* It slides off the roller cage for cleaning and storage. Used properly, a quality roller sleeve leaves a non-directional paint film that looks the same on an upstroke as it does on a downstroke.

Be sure to look for beveled edges on rollers. Rollers with beveled edges are less likely to leave *tracks,* which are lines or beads of paint that may form on the surface at the edges of the roller.

There are two kinds of sleeves you can buy: natural and synthetic.

✔ **Natural sleeves** are made of lambswool and are the preferred nap for oils because they hold more paint than synthetic nap.

Lambswool should not be used with water-based paints because the alkali in water-based paints detans the sheep leather and makes it vulnerable to rot.

✔ **Synthetic sleeves** are usually polyester and can be used for both oil and water-based paints.

The nap length you choose will vary depending on the type of job you plan to undertake. Check out Table 5-1 for pointers on which nap length to use.

Table 5-1	Picking a Nap Length to Suit Your Job
Nap Length	*Job*
¼-inch	For very smooth surfaces like flush doors, plastered walls, and wide trim
⅜- or ½-inch	For slightly irregular surfaces like drywall and exterior siding
¾-inch or longer	For semi-rough surfaces like wood shingles
1- or 1 ¼-inch	For rough surfaces like concrete block and stucco

The worst thing about a cheap roller sleeve is that it sheds fibers. You spend more time picking fibers out of wet paint than you do applying the paint!

Clean a sleeve thoroughly after every job, and it'll last for years. The best core is made of thick phenolic resin. It holds up better to solvents than plastic and is much better than single-use cardboard core covers.

Foam painting pads

Painting pads are rectangular or brush-shaped foam applicators, with or without fiber painting surfaces. Some people find them easier to use than brushes. They do paint a nice smooth coat on trim and leave no brush marks, and the larger pads work well on wood shingle siding. We especially like one that has rollers on the edge to guide the pad when cutting in ceilings and interior trim.

On the downside, pads tend to put paint on too thinly. They do not hold as much paint as rollers or brushes and are not as versatile. Using a pad makes it harder to control drips and to apply an even coat on a large surface. Given the time most people need to develop techniques, it may be best to stick with a brush and roller for most applications.

Power-Painting Systems

If you plan to do a big painting job, you may want to check out the power-painting systems — power rollers (some also include brush and pad accessories) or power brushes. Spray systems are fast, too, and they also have several advantages unrelated to speed that make them desirable for many painting and fine finishing projects. (Spray painting is discussed in-depth in Chapter 6.)

The advantage of power-painting gear is that, after you're set up and adjusted properly, you can paint like crazy, putting out a lot of paint in record speed. If you're facing a major interior paint job, like when you move into an empty house, or if you plan to paint the exterior of your home with a roller, power rolling is definitely worthwhile. You may also get better results. Most people tend to brush or roll out paint too thin, perhaps to make the most of each time they load the applicator with paint. You're less inclined to do that with a power painting system.

Some rollers have an electric pump that draws paint directly from the can. Others are hand-pumped and use air pressure to push the paint from a reservoir to the roller where it seeps out of little holes in the roller-sleeve core and saturates the fabric. The techniques for a power roller and a manual one are the same except that you eliminate the need to load the roller. You just roll away and occasionally push a button or pull a trigger to feed more paint to the applicator. Instead of filling a roller tray with paint, you either fill a reservoir or pump directly from the can.

The principal downside of this equipment (other than the cost) is the increased setup and cleanup time. You also end up with a fair amount of waste every time you clean. Unlike a brush, roller, or rolling pan that can be scraped to remove most of the paint, you have to wash the paint out of much of this equipment.

Brush Techniques

Knowing how to use a paint brush is largely intuitive. Even someone who has never seen a paintbrush and a can of paint can get the idea and figure out how to get the desired results, namely to get the paint on the correct surface. We'll show you a few techniques and tricks, however, that can help you get better results with less fatigue.

It's all in the wrist

Painting techniques can feel awkward at first, but if you use the techniques we describe in this section, you can look like a pro even if you feel kind of weird.

To hold and load your brush:

✔ **Hold the brush near the base of the handle with your forefingers just barely extending over the ferrule.** For detail work, you'll probably want to use your "good" hand, but otherwise swap hands often. Alternating hands takes a little getting used to, but the more you do it, the less fatigued your muscles become and the faster you paint. Changing bodies works well, too.

> ✔ **Dip your brush about a third of the way into the paint and tap it (don't wipe it) on the side of the bucket to shake off excess.** To get the most bang for the buck, fully load your brush. Don't overload the brush but don't shake off any more paint than necessary to get the brush to the surface without dripping. This brush-loading technique lets you paint a larger area without having to move your setup.

To lay on an even coat of paint with a paintbrush:

1. **Unload the paint from one side of the brush with a long stroke in one direction.**

2. **At the end of the first stroke, unload the paint from the other side of the brush.**

   Start in a dry area about a foot away and brush toward the end of the first stroke.

3. **Keep the brush moving and vary the pressure of your stroke to adjust the amount of paint being delivered to the surface.**

   The more pressure you apply, the more paint that flows out of the brush, so start with a fairly light touch and gradually increase the pressure as you move along. If you must press hard to spread paint, you're probably applying it too thinly.

4. **Brush out the area only as needed to spread the paint evenly.**

   Oil-based paint requires more brushing out than latex, but don't overwork the finish, especially when using varnish.

You can minimize brush marks and bubbles with a *finishing stroke* — a light stroke, as long as possible, in one direction and feathered at the end. To *feather* an edge with a brush:

1. **Start your brush moving in the air, lightly touch down, and continue the stroke.**

2. **Slow down near the end of the stroke and, with a slight twisting motion, lift the brush from the surface.**

3. **Continue in the same fashion in an adjacent area.**

4. **Immediately brush the paint *toward* the previous wet feathered edge to *blend* those two surfaces.**

5. **Spread and level the paint with additional strokes and feather a new wet edge.**

   You can't maintain a wet edge everywhere if you're painting a large area, so try to start and finish at corners, edges, or anywhere other than the middle of a surface so that the transition will not be noticeable. To slow drying, avoid painting in direct sunlight or on very windy days.

On a large project, check whether you are applying the correct amount of paint by measuring the area covered with about a quart of paint. The painted area should equal about one-fourth the coverage per gallon that is described on the paint label. In other words, if you paint your entire house with half a gallon of paint, you're spreading it too thin.

May I cut in?

Cutting in describes two quite different painting techniques, both of which are shown in Figure 5-4. In one sense, cutting in refers to the process of carefully painting up to an unpainted edge or an edge of a different color, such as the joint between trim and siding or between a wall and a ceiling.

Cutting in also refers to using a brush or other applicator to get into corners that a roller or larger applicator can't get into, such as where the ceiling and wall meet. Accuracy is not an issue, so work quickly. Just remember to feather the edges and to paint to the feathered wet edges as soon as possible, especially when applying oil-based paint.

Cutting in can get tiring, and beginners tend to tense their arm muscles. To prevent fatigue, put your brush down occasionally and shake out your arm.

Secret weapon: Backbrushing

For some applications, you can take advantage of a roller's speed but you should follow up with a brush — a technique called *backbrushing.* Backbrushing smoothes out roller stipple, pushes out air bubbles, and works the paint into the surface for a better bond. These examples show you when to use this technique

✔ Rollers leave a slightly stippled paint film that's fine for walls and siding but that you may not like on a door or the side of a painted cabinet. A short-fiber pad levels a finish on a door or trim nicely, too.

✔ On exterior surfaces, where a good paint bond to the surface is important, a roller doesn't do as good a job as a brush. Nothing works paint into a surface quite like a brush.

We recommend backbrushing to work spray-applied penetrating and solid-color stains into exterior surfaces.

Backbrushing should be done immediately after the finish is applied and while it is still wet. Dip your brush in the finish just once to condition it, but wipe it against the side of the can to remove excess. You don't need to add finish; just work what's already there.

One final tip — when a project calls for backbrushing, use a team approach — one person with a roller and another with a brush. You'll fly through the job. Don't forget to swap tasks on big jobs to avoid the fatigue associated with each task.

Figure 5-4:
Cut-in up to trim or a ceiling-wall intersection carefully. Less care is need to cut in inside corners or detailed areas on doors that are all one color.

When cutting in carefully up to an edge, remember that you have the best control if you use an angled sash brush. Also, use the edge of the brush, not the face, and follow these steps:

1. **Lay the paint on close to, but not right on, the edge that you want to cut in.**

   Keep in mind that more paint is on your brush when you start a stroke, so apply less pressure and/or stay a little farther away at the outset. For the same reason, apply more pressure and move closer to the edge you want to cut in as you lay on the paint with a long stroke or two. Lay on the paint evenly and uniformly close.

2. **Start a finishing stroke, varying the pressure to *push* the paint that you left on the surface in the first pass right up to the edge.**

   It may take a couple passes, but with practice, you'll be able to apply a finishing stroke in one long stroke.

You may need to reshape a brush that has lost its shape from being used on edge this way. Just dip it in paint and wipe both brush faces several times against the edge of your paint bucket.

Roller Techniques

The goal — getting paint from the can to the surface — is the same for a roller as for a brush. You just get done faster with a roller. The most important thing to remember is that a roller spreads paint so efficiently and easily that the tendency is to spread it far too thin.

The best way to assure that you don't spread the paint too thin is to use a methodical approach:

1. **Load a roller fully by dipping it about halfway into your paint reservoir.**

   Roll the roller very lightly on either the sloped portion of your roller tray or roller screen, depending on your setup. This technique coats the roller surface more evenly while at the same time removes excess that would otherwise drip all over on the way to the surface.

2. **Unload and spread the paint in a limited area (about 10 square feet).**

   On large surfaces, especially rough ones, unload the paint in an "N" or any other three- or four-leg zigzag pattern; then spread the paint horizontally; and make your light finishing strokes vertically. Figure 5-5 shows this three-step zigzag process. Alternatively, you can also roll out the paint in one straight line (or two straight lines next to each other), covering about the same area.

3. **After you evenly spread the first rollerful of paint, reload the roller and unload another pattern that overlaps the just-painted area.**

   Spread the new paint, blend the two areas, and wind up with finishing strokes.

Figure 5-5: Lay on a zigzag pattern, roll it out horizontally, and finish with light vertical strokes.

Normally, you don't need to feather the wet edge when you are rolling on paint because you overlap and blend each section before the paint dries. However, there are a few exceptions.

✔ If you are unable to start or finish an edge at a natural breaking point, such as the corner of a room or the bottom edge of a course of siding, you may need to feather the edge.

✔ When you roll paint onto large surfaces where one painted area must sit while you're working your way back to it, you may have difficulty blending if you don't feather the edge.

✔ Although oil paint takes longer to dry than latex, blending one area with another is harder with oil paint unless you do it almost immediately.

To roll a feathered edge:

1. **Start the motion in the air, lowering the roller to the surface.**

2. **Roll with light pressure until you near the edge.**

3. **Gradually reduce pressure and lift the roller off the surface as you pass into the unpainted area.**

Feather when touching up with a roller. This blends in the newly painted area, which almost always has a slightly different tone than the surrounding area. In fact, feather more than usual: After you feather an edge as described above, use a nearly dry roller to make a few very light passes over the touched-up area and extending at least a foot into the unpainted area.

Using Specialty Applicators

In some applications, using an aerosol or a power sprayer saves so much time or does such a superior job that you should opt for that approach. For the most part, however, you can paint virtually every surface efficiently and well with a brush or a roller. So don't fall for every painting gadget that comes along. Sometimes it's just one more thing to carry around. Take your clue from the pros. They are just as anxious as you are to make a job easier or get a better result, and they use mostly brushes and rollers.

With that caution in mind, however, we like the specialty applicators in the following list and shown in Figure 5-6. We even find some of them to be indispensable.

✔ **Paint mitt:** If you need to slap a coat of paint on a lot of pipes, metal railings, wire or wood fences, spindles, or other hard-to-paint surfaces, consider a paint mitt. They look like furry oven mitts but hold a ton of paint and cover multiple surfaces at the same time. The drawbacks: You'll likely still need a brush, and you can waste a great deal of paint in the cleaning process.

✔ **Corner roller:** This mini-roller, made of foam or natural or synthetic fibers, makes short work of cutting in inside wall corners by painting both surfaces simultaneously. A corner-painting pad does the same thing but uses a 90-degree angled painting pad on a handle to apply the paint. (Refer to Figure 5-3.)

✔ **Mini-rollers:** The long-handled mini-roller has a 1-inch diameter roller sleeve, making it great for getting into tight spaces such as roof overhangs and behind radiators or toilet tanks. Other standard-diameter but shorter rollers get where 9-inch rollers can't go. You can even find a curved mini-roller for round surfaces such as pipe. (Refer to Figure 5-3.)

✔ **Large painting pad:** This firm pad has a fabric-covered painting surface that is very effective for painting rough surfaces such as exterior wood or cement-shingle siding.

✔ **Masonry brush:** This cross between a brush and a pad scrubs paint into very rough surfaces.

✔ **Texture roller sleeve:** This special roller has hundreds of little hooklike fibers for applying textured paint.

✔ **Paint edging pad:** The wheels on this painting pad roll on an adjacent surface (a ceiling, for example) so that paint is applied on the other surface (a wall in our example). The same pad makes quick work of applying paint on baseboard trim.

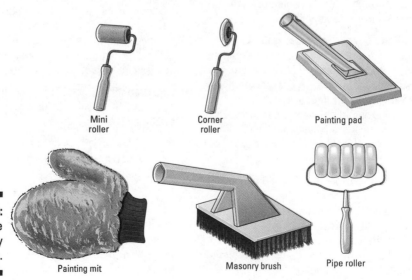

Mini roller

Corner roller

Painting pad

Figure 5-6: Our favorite specialty applicators.

Painting mit

Masonry brush

Pipe roller

Indispensable painting accessories

You need more than a brush or roller to paint. You need to accessorize. We have found the painting accessories listed here to be particularly helpful. (For info on cleaning supplies, see Chapter 7.)

✔ **Swivel/pot hooks:** A must for exterior house painting, a pot hook lets you securely hang a paint can or bucket on your ladder or whatever, and it swivels to let you rotate the can for convenient access.

✔ **Extension poles:** Definitely spend a couple bucks for an inexpensive handle extension that screws into the end of a roller handle. You can roll from floor to ceiling without bending and with less exertion, and you avoid constant trips up and down the ladder. Some poles even have adjustable heads that allow you to attach a paintbrush for hard-to-reach spots or a pole sander for sanding ceilings and walls.

✔ **5-gallon bucket with roller grid:** An alternative to using a roller tray is a 5-gallon bucket with a roller screen, a metal grate designed to fit inside the bucket. The rig is ideal for large jobs because it saves you the time you'd spend refilling the paint tray. The bucket is easier to move around and not as easy to step into. At break time just drop the screen in the bucket and snap on the lid.

✔ **Trim guard:** For painting around windows, doors, and floor moldings, this edging tool is very useful. Press the metal or plastic blade of the guard against the surface you want to shield from the fresh paint. Don't forget to wipe the edges clean frequently to avoid leaving smears of paint.

✔ **Pouring spout:** You know how messy the rims of paint can lids get, right? This plastic spout snaps into a newly opened can. You can pour or paint right out of the can, and when you remove the spout, the rim is spotless. No drips down the side of the can, the label stays clean, and the lid reseals better and comes off easier the next time.

✔ **Aerosol spray-can handle/trigger:** This inexpensive handle/trigger snaps onto any aerosol can. The comfort is astonishing, especially if you have a lot to do, but the real value of the device is that it makes it easier to hold the can at the proper angle. (See Chapter 6.)

✔ **Clamp lamp:** These inexpensive lamps let you direct light where you need it. You also avoid accidental damage to a good lamp that you might otherwise use.

✔ **5-in-1 tool:** The Swiss Army knife of painting tools. It can scrape loose paint, score paint lines for trim removal, loosen or tighten a screw, hammer in a popped nail or other protrusion prior to spackling, and scrape paint out of a roller sleeve.

✔ **Brush comb:** To get a brush really clean, open up the bristles with a comb. (See Chapter 7.)

✔ **Paint spinner:** This paintbrush and roller-cover-cleaning tool makes short work of cleanup and does a great job. For more on this and other cleaning tools and accessories see Chapter 7.

✔ **Paint mixer:** This inexpensive drill attachment does a much faster and more effective job than a paint stirring stick. It's so easy that you actually take the time to stir as often as the instructions say to!

Chapter 6

Spraying Inside and Out

. . . .

In This Chapter

▶ Protecting yourself and the environment

▶ Choosing and using power paint sprayers

▶ Getting the work area ready

▶ Painting!

▶ Spraying paint with aerosol cans

. . . .

*I*f you love toys — oops, we mean tools — then you're going to love paint sprayers. They apply paint, and more of it, many times faster than brushes, rollers, and power rollers do. They're also excellent when you're working on difficult or complex surfaces such as roughhewn cedar, concrete, shutters, fences, detailed roof trim, and wicker furniture. Painting or staining exterior siding usually involves applying the same color of paint to large areas, which makes siding a perfect candidate for spray painting. In this chapter, we explain what you need to know to choose the right spray equipment, to prepare the paint, and to use the sprayer safely and effectively.

Spray equipment requires meticulous cleaning. For a detailed description of that process, make sure that you visit Chapter 7. You can also refer to Chapter 2 for cleanup tips that protect your safety and the environment.

Keeping an Eye on Safety and the Environment

Protecting your own health is a personal issue. If you are particularly sensitive to chemicals or concerned for your health, then by all means go beyond the safety precautions that we suggest as minimums. Play it safe. If you're not sure whether you have good ventilation, for example, then assume that you don't.

Protecting the environment is a public issue. Compressor-driven and airless sprayers *atomize* paint, which means that the paint breaks up into many tiny particles. These extremely small particles float in the air and can be carried for long distances on a breeze, polluting the air that other people breathe and landing on their property. Make sure that municipal ordinances permit the use of spray equipment on exterior projects, and never spray on a breezy day or when parked cars or other buildings are nearby.

Personal and environmental risks also vary according to the type of sprayer and tip you are using. Of the three types of power sprayers that we recommend for homeowners, only the airless system creates significant overspray. You must take precautions to reduce the risk of overspray, or it becomes a health and/or environmental risk.

Paints, stains, and some related products, such as solvents and cleaners, are chemicals. They should not be ingested. Heed the label warnings. Remember that the fumes of poisonous chemicals are poisonous, and the fumes of flammable chemicals are flammable or explosive. Always work in cross-ventilated areas. To protect yourself, take the following precautions:

✔ Always wear a tight-fitting, organic vapor respirator when spraying solvent-based coatings, indoors or outdoors, and when spraying water-based coatings indoors. Masks note on their packaging what they're safe for — read the packaging to determine whether a mask is appropriate for the job you plan to do. Dust masks do not offer adequate protection for most spray-painting applications. You can get by with a dust mask when you're spraying water-based coatings outdoors in good ventilation, but why risk it?

✔ Always wear minimum protection — splash goggles (preferably a pair with interchangeable lenses), gloves, a hat, and clothing that completely covers your skin. Wear these items no matter what type of paint you're using or what the ventilation conditions are.

✔ Wear a painter's hood to cover your head and neck.

✔ Apply protective lotion or petroleum jelly to exposed skin.

✔ Never point a sprayer at anyone in jest. Keep your own fingers away from the tip. The pressure of the spray is so great within a few inches of the tip that you may accidentally inject paint deep into your skin.

Without ventilation, you need a controlled environment with special lighting, switching, and ventilation equipment that does not spark. If you can't ventilate, don't spray. To minimize the risk of fire or explosion, follow these safety tips:

✔ Never spray flammable products in a very hot room or near any source of ignition, such as a spark or standing gas pilot light.

✔ Don't smoke.

✔ Turn off or unplug all sources of ignition, including appliances such as refrigerators, coffee pots, and automatic fans.

✔ Turn lights on or off and put tape over the switches.

✔ Do not activate any electrical switches until the vapors have been cleared.

The Spray-Painting Process

You can't just hook the sprayer up to the paint and start painting. Well, you can, but you really won't like the results. The spray-painting process really has four steps: preparing the work area, preparing the paint, practicing your technique, and, finally, painting the object, all the while adjusting your technique to fit your sprayer.

Why so much emphasis on up-front work? All good painters will tell you that proper preparation makes your painting projects go much smoother. The time you spend up front preparing your work area and readying your paint pays big dividends after you get started painting.

Don't spray-paint when the air temperature is below 45 degrees or above 75 degrees. Don't spray-paint in direct sunlight, either. Too much heat dries the paint too fast, and it won't bond well. If it's too cold, the paint dries too slowly, attracting bugs and dirt, and the gun is more likely to clog.

Prepare the work area

If you're renting a sprayer, plan to do all your preparation work before you pick up the sprayer. Don't forget that the clock starts ticking — and the dollars start adding up — the instant you walk out of the rental shop.

✔ Make sure that the work area is clear and free of tripping hazards or objects that may snag any of the sprayer hoses.

✔ Enlisting the services of at least one helper is a good idea; an assistant can move ladders and drop cloths and otherwise pave the way for you.

✔ Protect nearby surfaces, such as windows, trim, and floors. In most cases, mask off or cover these areas with drop cloths.

Stir and strain the paint (or stain)

Always stir paint well and then strain it to prevent clogs in the tip or at any internal filters. Clogging is the number one complaint about spray-painting, but you can prevent nearly all clogs by simply straining the paint first. Paint suppliers carry a variety of strainers appropriate for different spray equipment. Figure 6-1 shows a typical setup.

Figure 6-1: Strain paint before spraying to prevent time-consuming clogs.

Some paints must be thinned for use with most sprayers. Be sure that you know what your situation requires. Paint that's sprayed on too thick leaves a textured finish like an orange peel, and paint that's sprayed on too thin doesn't cover well and tends to sag or run. To be sure that the paint is the right viscosity, you can buy a *viscometer*. This is a small cup with a calibrated hole in the bottom (or a similar device) that you fill with paint and time how long the paint takes to drain out.

Practice basic techniques first

Painting practice makes perfect painting. Sharpen up your spraying skills with the following techniques:

- ✔ **Start moving the gun before you start spraying and keep the gun moving in long, straight strokes**. (See Figure 6-2.) Sprayers apply paint quickly, so to get an even coat that doesn't run, you must use this technique. Move about as fast as you would brush out a stroke, or 2 to 3 feet per second.

- ✔ **Hold the paint gun nozzle perpendicular to and 10 to 12 inches away from the surface.** Even a slight change in this distance significantly affects the amount of paint being applied: If you move the tip of the gun *twice* as close to the surface (holding the gun 5 to 6 inches), you apply *four* times the paint. Avoid tilting the sprayer downward or upward. Tilting downward causes spitting and results in an uneven application.

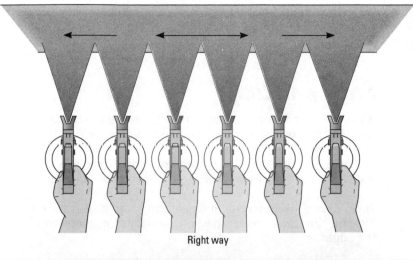

Right way

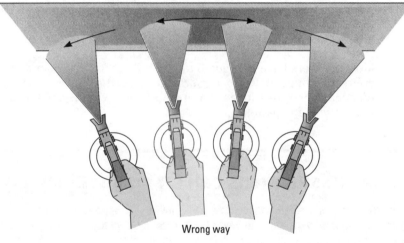

Figure 6-2:
Use long, sweeping strokes and maintain an equal distance from the surface.

Wrong way

✔ **Keep the gun nozzle perpendicular to the surface as you move it back and forth.** The natural tendency is to swing the gun in an arc, which results in an uneven "bow-tie" application, which is fine if you're trying to paint bow ties all over your house.

✔ **Overlap each pass one-half the width of the spray coverage area to avoid leaving light areas or creating stripes.**

✔ **Test and adjust the spray equipment until you produce the pattern that you want.** If the pattern is too narrow, you may apply too much paint to the area, resulting in runs. With a pattern that's too wide, you have to make more than two passes to get good coverage. A pattern that's 8 to 12 inches wide is adequate for painting most large surfaces.

It's better to put the paint on a little light and have to go back and apply a little more than to load the surface with a coat of paint that's too heavy and may sag and dry unevenly. In time, a heavy coat may peel.

Start painting

When you're comfortable and getting the results that you want on cardboard (see the "Practice basic techniques first" section, earlier in this chapter), move on to the real thing. Do the corners and any protrusions first and finish up with the large flat areas. Indoors, for example, paint the two inside corners of one wall and then spray the wall between those two corners before moving on.

Spray corners with a vertical stroke aimed directly at the corner. Move a little quicker than usual, especially on outside corners, to avoid overloading the edges.

After you complete each area (or about every five minutes), stand back and look for light spots or missed areas. Touch up, making sure that the gun is moving before spraying. Keep a brush or roller handy for touch-ups.

Most sprayers have a tip guard to protect you from accidentally injecting yourself with paint. Remove your finger from the trigger and wipe the guards off occasionally — with a rag, not your finger. A paint buildup at the tip may affect the spray pattern.

Special situations call for special techniques

Spraying exterior siding requires that you tilt the sprayer at a *slight* upward angle to cover the underside of each course of siding. Even then, a quick back-brushing along this joint is sometimes needed to get full coverage.

Spraying is an excellent way to apply clear coatings on furniture or cabinets, especially if you use aerosols. The finish covers nicely, without brush marks, and dries quickly. Fast drying is important because people rarely have dust-free environments, and dust sticks to a finish like glue until the finish skins over. The best technique calls for one light *tack coat,* which should be allowed to dry to the touch — anywhere from 2 to 20 minutes, depending on the finish and the humidity. (Check the label for recoating times.) Then apply a thicker *wet coat.* After that dries, apply another fine coat (or *fog coat*) with the sprayer held farther away from the surface.

Some spray applications require *back-brushing* or *back-rolling* — that is, brushing or rolling in the sprayed-on finish to get a more even coat and better penetration. The sprayer, then, is just a fast way to get the paint to the surface. In particular, stain applications on unfinished or previously stained wood should be back-brushed. Back-brushing, which we discuss in greater depth in Chapter 5, also is strongly recommended when applying primers and sealers.

The Tools of the Trade

In the power arena, we recommend three types of sprayers for do-it-yourselfers: the tank sprayer, the airless sprayer, and the newer, HVLP (high-volume low-pressure) sprayer. Figure 6-3 illustrates these types of sprayers. All these sprayers take just a few minutes to learn to operate. Conventional sprayers, which are powered by compressed air, require considerably more skill and training. They also create excessive overspray. For these reasons, conventional sprayers are best left to the pros.

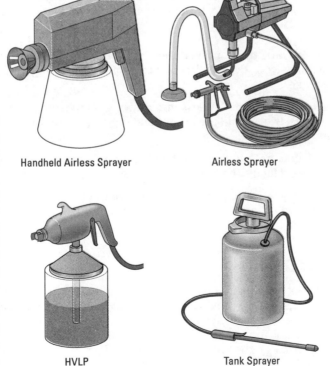

Figure 6-3:
Good spray painters for the do-it-yourself painter include a handheld airless sprayer, a pump air-less sprayer, an HVLP sprayer, and a tank sprayer.

Handheld Airless Sprayer

Airless Sprayer

HVLP

Tank Sprayer

Airless sprayers

Handheld airless sprayers won't win any National Noise Pollution Control award — they are noisy little devils — but they are popular with do-it-yourselfers because of their versatility and moderate price. They range from about $50 to $175. The higher-priced units have more power, more features and controls, and more tip options. With a high-powered unit, you can paint everything from a radiator to the entire exterior of your house.

With most models, you draw the paint from a paint cup attached at the base of the sprayer for small projects. On larger projects, you can draw paint from a backpack tank or directly from the can.

Pump airless sprayers are priced from about $250 for the do-it-yourself models to as high as $900 for "professional" models. These sprayers draw paint from 1- or 5-gallon containers to a spray gun through a long hose. Although you can paint a house exterior with a handheld model, a high-productivity pump sprayer is a better choice. These units pump paint much faster, and the gun is much lighter to hold because no "cup" full of paint is attached to it.

Operating an airless sprayer is not difficult, but you do need a bit of practice to be able to apply an even coat. Here are some tips on using airless sprayers:

- ✔ When using an airless sprayer, keep your finger on the trigger but snap your wrist as you reverse direction to avoid overloading at the end of each stroke.

- ✔ When using a handheld airless unit drawing paint from a cup, keep one hand on the trigger and the other hand under the cup to support the weight.

- ✔ If using a gun, use your second hand to manage the hose, which is sometimes more difficult than handling the spray gun.

- ✔ When buying or renting, ask for a reversible, self-cleaning tip, which flips open to clear a clog without having to be removed.

Tank sprayers

The *tank sprayer* is available in manual pump and battery-powered models. (No, you don't use it for spraying tanks, although . . . .) You can use this multipurpose sprayer to apply oil-based stain to wood decks, fences, and even wood siding. Although you usually need to brush in spray-applied stain (called *back-brushing*), the sprayer does the hard part — getting the otherwise drippy finish onto the surface.

Here are some tips on using tank sprayers:

✔ Never use tank sprayers to spray any liquid that's thicker than water — for example, piña coladas. You shouldn't use them to spray latex stains, but you can spray oil-based stains.

✔ Adjust any available speed control — faster for large surfaces and slower for greater control.

✔ Adjust the spray tip to change the spray pattern — wide for large surfaces and narrow for detail work.

✔ Back-brush as required to smooth drips or work the finish into the surface.

HVLP sprayers

An HVLP sprayer doesn't atomize paint. Instead, it uses a high volume of air at very low pressure to propel paint onto the surface. As a result, you have virtually no overspray and no risk of explosion. You can produce a very narrow spray pattern, and you don't need to cover and mask everything in the room or get dressed up like an astronaut — unless, of course, you're into that sort of thing. Minimum personal protection — splash goggles, clothing, and gloves — is usually all that's required, but use a respirator when using solvent paints or whenever ventilation is questionable.

HVLP sprayers, priced from $200 to $400 and up, are great for small projects and trim painting, indoors or out. They are best used with low to medium viscosity finishes such as lacquers, varnishes/enamels, oils, and stains. On models that claim to handle heavier-bodied finishes such as acrylic latex, you usually must thin the paint. This requirement, combined with the low pressure and relatively small paint cup, makes the HVLP sprayer unsuitable for large projects such as exterior house painting — unless it's a dog house.

Some tips on using HVLP sprayers:

✔ Stop spraying momentarily at the end of every pass.

✔ Control the size of the pattern by moving the gun closer to or farther from the surface, and vary the amount of trigger.

Aerosol paint (also known as spray paint in a can)

Aerosol spraying (with a spray-paint can) is by far the most expensive approach to spray-painting on a per-square-foot basis, but it's worth every penny on the right job. Aerosol paints dry very fast and are great for small, irregularly shaped objects that are difficult to brush, such as toys, some furniture, iron railings, and exterior light fixtures.

A stain-killing primer in an aerosol can is great for touching up water-stained textured ceilings. Brushing or rolling paint on these surfaces can quickly turn some textures to mush.

Paint as wide an area as you can reach area by using side-to-side strokes, starting closest to you and moving away. As you begin each stroke, point the nozzle to the side of the object being painted and start moving toward it. Just before you reach the object, start spraying. Stop spraying as you pass off the other side. Then spray the area again by using top-to-bottom strokes. Several light coats applied this way give uniform coverage without puddling or sagging.

Here are some tips on using aerosol cans:

- ✔ Before you start painting, shake the can for a full two minutes after you hear the *agitator* (a little steel ball) rattling in the can. Spray only at room temperature (roughly 65 to 75 degrees). Avoid spraying continuously; use short bursts instead.

- ✔ Frequently wipe the tip clean to prevent spitting. When you're through painting, turn the can upside down and spray-paint against a piece of cardboard until only clear propellant comes out. Then remove the tip and soak it in lacquer thinner.

- ✔ A spray handle tool that snaps onto an aerosol can makes it easier to control and easier on your finger, too.

- ✔ Remove the tip from an aerosol can before you attempt to clear a clog.

Handy accessories

You can choose from quite a few different accessories that help make your painting project a little easier. Here are several that we recommend for spray painting:

- ✔ **Filters:** Set yourself up with a couple of extra paint buckets and paint screens or filters available at paint outlet stores.

- ✔ **Spouts:** With all the pouring back and forth, buy a couple of inexpensive pouring spouts that snap into gallon-can rims and prevent dripping.

- ✔ **Ear plugs:** Airless sprayers are noisy, especially indoors. Protect your hearing with inexpensive earplugs that conform to your ear canal.

- ✔ **Spray shields:** Use a spray shield on virtually every spray job. Pros use aluminum ones with handles. You can buy inexpensive disposable ones made from plastic or cardboard at paint stores (see Figure 6-4). You also can make your own with some sheet aluminum, acrylic sheeting, or any other semi-rigid, lightweight material and a handle fashioned from a piece of wood. Old slats from a venetian blind work well, too.

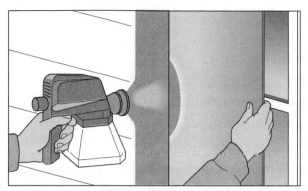

Figure 6-4:
A large
spray shield
keeps paint
off nearby
surfaces.

✔ **Spray pole extension:** It can get pretty foggy when you're using an airless sprayer indoors. Use a spray pole extension to move the working end of the tool away from your face. They are available in sizes from 12 inches to 4 feet. And by extending your reach, this accessory may eliminate the need for constant up-and-down movement on a ladder.

Should You Buy or Rent?

Now the money question: Should you buy or rent your spray-painting equipment? The answer depends.

If you expect to spray-paint only occasionally, consider renting the equipment. This advice is especially true if you are doing a major interior or exterior job where a good spray unit could save you many hours of work. By renting, you can also step up to a professional-quality unit that applies paint faster and better than a do-it-yourself model that you can buy.

Go where the pros go — to paint stores — to get the right equipment and expert advice on using the equipment. Ask to speak to the person who is best informed about the equipment. Describe what you want to paint and what type of finish you are using so that the employee can recommend the best unit and appropriate spray tips for the job. Get a crash course in how to operate a rental unit and ask for any written material on using or cleaning the equipment. Cleaning is complex and important, so a checklist can come in handy. If you don't own or want to buy the necessary respirator, rent it.

Here are some of the most important things that you should know about the equipment before you leave the rental store:

- Filtering/thinning requirements
- How to load paint
- The correct tips to use
- How to start and stop the unit
- How to adjust the paint pressure
- Proper spraying techniques
- How to clear a clog in the tip
- How to troubleshoot the most common spray-painting problems
- How to clean the gun, hose, and pressure unit
- How to remove paint from fur if you accidentally paint the cat

Chapter 7

Cleaning Up the Mess

• •

• •

*W*ith a little planning, cleanup is a relatively simple routine with rewards that outweigh the work — especially if you can talk someone else into doing it! Walking away from a clean work area at the end of a day feels good. You'll appreciate that spic-and-span condition even more the next day. If you have invested money in good painting tools and applicators and you clean and store them properly, they will last for many years. In this chapter, we show you how to set up and clean applicators and power painters. We also explain the procedures for end-of session and end-of project cleanup, including what to do with leftovers and toxic waste.

Planning Ahead for Easy Cleanup

Start the process of cleaning up by limiting the mess you make as you go. Here are some basic tips for making cleanup as easy as possible:

✔ **Protect your skin, your hair, and any clothes that you care about.** Wear the proper protective clothing, such as long-sleeved shirts and long pants, a hat, solvent-resistant gloves, and shoes that could only benefit from a good coat of paint.

✔ **Confine paint-mixing and cleanup to one well-protected area that is child-safe.** Gather all the tools and supplies that you'll need for cleaning — buckets, rags, solvents, and so on — and make a place for them in your temporary "shop."

✔ **Dried paint, even latex, must be removed with solvents, so wipe up spills and spatters promptly.**

✔ **Keep things under control during and at the end of each work session.** A clean work area is safer and much easier to work in. Don't leave paint cans or roller trays on ladders or on the floor where you might . . . oops!

✔ **Plan to finish a painting session at a good stopping point.** For example, if you have cut in an area, plan to finish painting that area and then stop. Don't push yourself. If you work until you're exhausted or right up to dinner time, you're more likely to neglect proper cleanup.

Assembling Your Cleanup Tools and Supplies

Painting cleanup shouldn't be as big a chore as painting itself. Gathering some basic cleaning items will help make cleanup a breeze and extend the life of your painting tools. To make your task easier, set up your "shop" with the following items:

✔ **Solvents:** The proper solvent for cleaning up latex paints is warm, soapy water. The best solvents for cleaning up alkyd paints, enamels, oil-based varnishes, or oil-based stains are mineral spirits or paint thinner. Use denatured alcohol to clean up shellac or other alcohol-based coatings, such as some fast-drying, stain-killing primers. These solvents won't work on brushes that have a buildup of dried paint. For these, you need special brush cleaner solvents or paint remover (or a garbage can). Some paints may require special solvents. Epoxy resin paints, for example, must be cleaned with diacetone alcohol.

✔ **Painter's rags:** If you have a medium to large painting or refinishing task, buy a quantity of absorbent rags. They are usually sold at paint stores by the box or loose by the pound and have many, many uses in addition to paint cleanup.

✔ **Small containers:** Coffee cans and jars (some with lids); clean, empty quart paint cans; plastic paint buckets; or other similar containers can be used to store solvents and paints and to clean brushes.

✔ **Brush/roller spinner:** Buy a brush/roller spinner — a must-have tool for pros who use it to clean their brushes and rollers. A brush/roller spinner works like an old-fashioned spinning-top toy with a forceful centrifugal action that forces excess paint out of the brush or roller. First, clean most of the paint out of your applicator with water or mineral sprits and then put it on the spinner. If it's a brush, force the handle into the spinner clamp or if it's a roller, slide it over the clamp. Then spin the liquid out into a 5-gallon bucket or an empty garbage can and voilà — a shaggy dog spray of the excess appears on the sides of the container. Without removing the applicator, dip the applicator back in clean solvent or water and spin again. Repeat this process once or twice more until the spray is colorless and the bristles or nap are dry.

- **Brush comb and wire brush:** To get a brush really clean, open up the bristles with a brush comb to allow the solvent to get into the heel of a brush where paint tends to hide. Lay the brush on a flat surface and brush the bristles from the heel toward the tip. These tools are also indispensable when trying to restore an old brush with dried paint in it.

- **5-gallon buckets with lids:** Keep one bucket nearby half full of water to rinse out paint rags. Use a bucket instead of your kitchen sink to wash out painting tools. Spin roller covers and brushes inside a bucket to contain the spray. Buckets have plenty of other uses, too, especially if you wipe them out well after each use.

Don't use partially filled 5-gallon buckets when toddlers are around. Small children can easily fall in and drown.

- **5-in-1 tool:** The curved side of this multipurpose painter's tool scrapes paint off roller covers before you clean them up or dispose of them. Paint stirring sticks have a similar curve for the same purpose.

- **Rubber gloves:** A pair of heavy-duty rubber gloves is an essential cleanup accessory. You need to use your hands to work the paint out of the brush, and you don't want to get any more paint or solvent on them than is absolutely necessary.

- **Other stuff:** You may also find that these items come in handy: a trash can, a rubber or wooden mallet, a paint lid remover or a large slotted screwdriver, newspaper, a small drop cloth, paint sticks, goggles, paper towels, a funnel, and a wire brush.

Using the Three-Container Approach

Basically, cleaning an applicator involves these three steps:

1. **Scrape as much paint out of the applicator and into the original paint can as possible.**

2. **Brush or roll out as much paint as you can onto newspaper.**

3. **Clean the applicator in the appropriate solvent (water or mineral spirits) by using a three-container approach.**

By following these steps, you minimize paint waste, do the job better and faster, and use a minimum amount of solvent, which means less water and air pollution — a win-win situation.

The basic idea behind using three containers is that you wash out as much paint as possible in each container before moving on to the next. At each step the brush gets cleaner, and by the time you get to container number three, nearly all the paint is out of the applicator, so the solvent in the third container stays relatively clean and is used as a final solvent-rinse.

Follow this simple step-by-step process:

1. **Wash the applicator in container one, taking time to work the brush or other applicator with your fingers (don't forget your gloves) or by brushing the applicator back and forth on the bottom of the solvent container.**

   This step gets the solvent deep into the applicator, such as the heel of a brush or the foam backing of a pad.

2. **Remove all excess liquid before moving to the next container.**

   With brushes and rollers, the most effective approach is to use a brush spinner. With pads, draw the applicator firmly across a straightedge, such as a paint stick that's held over the container.

3. **Repeat Steps 1 and 2 using container number two and then number three.**

   Blot a pad on an absorbent towel.

4. **When the applicators are completely dry, store them properly.**

   See the section on "Cleaning and storing brushes and other applicators," later in this chapter.

5. **Recycle chemical solvents.**

   Pour all the solvent from container two into container one. Then rinse out container two with solvent from container three, and pour that into container one. Wipe the two empty containers clean with rags or paper towels. Put a lid on container one and let it sit a few days or until all the paint has settled to the bottom of the container. Pour off the now-clean solvent into the original solvent container using a funnel. Scrape the settled paint onto a newspaper and allow it to dry before disposing of it properly.

Although warm soapy water removes most latex paint from brushes and rollers, some paint residue is often left behind, so rinse the tool with a brush cleaner and spin it dry before hanging it up for storage.

Cleaning Up as You Go: Mid-Session Procedures

For your own safety and to make a job run smoothly, keep your work area clean and free of tripping hazards as you work. Did you know that tripping and slipping are the number one cause of falls? Really. We have the government figures to prove it.

Clean paint spills and spatters immediately. Keep a water- or solvent-dampened cloth handy while painting, and be prepared for big spills with a sponge and a container of solvent.

Always consider possible damage to the surface when using solvents to remove paint spatters or spills. Alcohol, for example, dissolves shellac finishes (and livers). Mineral spirits may adversely affect other finishes or materials. If you're not sure, test the solvent in an inconspicuous area first.

If you stop using an applicator for a short time, wrap it in plastic to keep it from drying out. Similarly, keep the lid on paint cans that you aren't using and put them aside so that they won't get knocked over. Brush out roller trays and cover them with a damp rag.

Stopping for a While: End-of-Session Procedures

When you complete the last brush stroke for the day, resist the temptation to drop everything and rush out for a cold beverage. Remove any masking. Check carefully for spatters or drips that you may have missed. If latex spatters have not fully cured, dampen a cloth with denatured alcohol and rub off the paint. Similarly, use mineral spirits (and elbow grease) to remove semidry oil-based paints. On hard, slick surfaces such as glass and glazed tile, use a single-edge razor blade to scrap off dried paint. Porous surfaces are the most difficult because spills get below the surface, so make every effort to protect these surfaces from spills in the first place. Even fresh spills can be nearly impossible to clean unless the surface can be flooded with solvent under pressure. You may need paint removers, sandblasting, power sanding, or other drastic measures to remove dried paint from porous surfaces.

Next, pour paint from trays or paint buckets back into their containers, using a paintbrush to wipe out as much paint as possible. Scrape as much paint as you can from the applicators back into the paint can. Use the rim of the paint can to scrape brushes and a 5-in-1 tool or the curved part of a paint stick to scrape roller covers. Then wrap the applicators in plastic and stick them in the refrigerator until an hour or so before you're ready to paint again. You can also leave a brush in solvent.

If you leave a brush in solvent, keep the bristles off the bottom by attaching a paint stick to the handle with a rubber band so the stick extends below the bristles.

If a brush is overloaded and messy, clean it a little before either wrapping and refrigerating it or suspending it in solvent. Scrape out excess paint, rinse the brush in solvent, and spin out the excess liquid with a brush spinner.

Cleaning paint from your skin and hair

Using warm, soapy water and rubbing — maybe with a scrub brush — is all you need to remove latex paint from your skin. Shampoo and a comb do the trick with hair, although you may need repeated washings and a haircut or two. Although denatured alcohol is a solvent for dried latex paint and some proprietary spot removers work well, don't use these products on your skin or hair.

The only way to get dry oil-based paint off your skin is with solvents. They are toxic and quickly absorbed by the skin, so try to remove paint from your skin before it dries. At that point, the friendlier, natural citrus-based cleaners are effective. Some are general cleaners, and others are specifically made for cleaning your hands and skin. If you do use solvent, follow up with a mild grease-cutting dish soap and rinse well. Use hand lotion or hair conditioner to restore the moisture robbed by any cleaning process.

When your painting tools are clean, replace the lids on paint cans and solvent containers. Drape a rag over paint cans to absorb any paint in the rim and prevent it from spurting out as you tap the lids on. Then clean the work area by picking up trash and dirty rags and taking ladders down or putting them away.

Finishing Up: End-of-Project Procedures

When you complete your painting project, put the room or exterior of your home back in order. I describe these procedures in greater detail in Chapters 11 and 12. At the end of a project, just take the end-of-session cleanup one step further. Break down your temporary shop and store things in their proper places. Dispose of trash, and properly store or dispose of leftover paints and solvents. (See the "Disposing of paint and solvent safely" section later in this chapter.)

Cleaning and storing brushes and other applicators

Thoroughly clean your brushes and other applicators by following the three-container method described earlier in this chapter in the section "Using the Three-Container Approach." Plain water is fine for end-of-session cleanup of latex brushes, but at the end of a project, use soapy water and a brush comb to get solvent deep into the brush and a wire brush to clean and straighten out the bristles. Then fan the brush to inspect for hidden paint. Give the brushes a final rinse in mineral spirits or brush cleaner to remove any residue. When the brushes are clean and dry, put them back in their original sleeve or just wrap them in heavy paper secured with string. If possible, hang brushes for long-term storage, or make sure that they are flat.

Use the full three-container approach for cleaning rollers and paint pads. Place these tools on their edges to dry on an absorbent towel and store them in a plastic bag.

Varnishing is typically a very demanding project, so pay particular attention when cleaning a varnish brush. Use it only for applying varnish when it is relatively new.

Cleaning and storing power rollers, brushes, and sprayers

Power painting is fast; cleaning up the equipment usually isn't. Each unit has specific end-of-session and end-of project cleanup procedures. If you own the unit, read the instructions for cleanup before you use the tool. If you rent a piece of equipment such as a paint sprayer, go over the cleaning procedure with the salesperson and ask for a detailed cleaning checklist. Returning it clogged with paint can cost you plenty.

In general, empty any paint reservoirs and clean them with solvent (water or mineral spirits, according to the type of paint you are using). Then run solvent through the unit. At first, only paint comes out, and that can go into the paint can. When the liquid starts to run clear, direct it back into the solvent container that's feeding the process until the solvent runs clear.

If the system was used for a water-based finish, run a gallon of mineral spirits or a special water-based solvent made specifically for this purpose through the system before storing it. Because mineral spirits is petroleum-based, it doesn't cause rust to develop inside the system the way water can. Recycle solvents as described in "Using the Three-Container Approach."

When the inside of the unit is clean, wash down the outside, especially the spray gun and the hose near the gun where paint tends to build up. Some disassembly is required. Don't take a rented spray gun apart unless directed to do so. Soak the parts in the appropriate solvent and scrub them clean with a toothbrush. When the parts are dry, reassemble the unit for storage. If you end up with extra parts, disassemble the unit and start again.

Don't use needles or anything that might scratch or otherwise damage an expensive spray tip on a power painter. Use soft copper wire or a brush bristle to clear a clog.

Cutting down on waste and leftovers

Avoid leftovers by estimating your needs carefully (see Chapter 1). Avoid waste by storing finishes properly and by recycling applicators, solvents, containers, and drop cloths. Save a little paint for touch-ups but try to get rid of larger quantities. Return any unopened cans of non-custom-mixed finish. Pass unwanted paint or solvent on to others who can make good use of it. Try churches, community organizations concerned with housing, schools, theater groups, or community "swap shops" at waste disposal facilities.

Seal leftover paint in the smallest can possible so that it takes up less room and the finish doesn't dry out. (Buy small, empty paint cans or use ones that you have recycled.) Label unmarked containers with relevant information such as color, sheen, room/location used, solvent, and any special instructions for use. For a better seal, lay plastic wrap across the top of the can before you put the lid on. Tip a paint can upside down momentarily before storing it right side up, or just store it upside down for an airtight seal.

Protect a paper label on a paint can, especially one that describes a custom color or the room in which the paint was used, with wide, clear packing tape.

Solvents have a low *flash point* — the lowest temperature at which a volatile vapor of the solvent ignites when exposed momentarily to a spark or other source of ignition — especially when mixed with some finishes, such as spar varnish. For that reason, store solvents and paint in a locked metal cabinet, away from excessive heat or sources of combustion. Paints should also be protected from freezing temperatures.

Disposing of paint and solvent safely

Oil-based paint and solvent and sludge from chemical removal of oil-based paints (especially lead-based finishes) are hazardous wastes. Never pour these materials onto the ground or into sewer systems. State and municipal governments typically regulate disposal of paints and solvents. Some communities accept oil-based paint in the regular trash collection, but only after it has been allowed to dry. Other communities have special collection sites or collection days.

Municipalities may also regulate disposal of less toxic water-based paints. Small quantities of such paint can usually be poured into an absorbent material, such as shredded newspapers or cat litter, allowed to dry, and tossed into the trash. Large quantities of paint are usually treated as hazardous waste.

If you have used a chemical solvent to remove lead-based paint, you may be required to have the material tested and to have even relatively small quantities hauled away by a licensed toxic-waste hauler.

Part III
Preparing Your Surfaces for Paint

The 5th Wave   By Rich Tennant

"I would try using less varnish remover."

In this part . . .

We're not going to beat around the bush: Properly preparing the surface for a finish is often the most time-consuming, difficult, and least rewarding part of a painting job.

Whoa! If you're thinking, "Fine. Let's skip this part of the work and the book," — don't. Any painter worth his colors will tell you that the key to a successful painting job is preparation. (It's never the fun stuff, is it?)

This part describes what you need to do and how to get it done in the most efficient way possible. The rest is up to you.

Chapter 8

Removing Paint, Varnish, Stain, and Other Finishes

● ●

In This Chapter

▶ Removing finishes mechanically

▶ Removing finishes with heat

▶ Removing finishes using chemicals

● ●

*T*he task of stripping off old paints or varnishes, whether on house siding or a fine piece of furniture, is as alluring as a chain-saw pedicure. Our philosophy: It's an unpleasant task at best, and a job that you should avoid to whatever degree possible. Do only what is necessary to ensure long-lasting, good-looking results. For example, if an existing coating of paint is not peeling or loose, you may need no more than a light sanding to ensure a good bond between the existing finish and the new one. With woodwork, you may want to remove varnish, shellac, or other topcoat surface finishes but not remove the stain.

Preparation on outdoor surfaces that are exposed to weather often involves removing several layers of paint, but only in areas where water has soaked through. If all or most of the finish fails to bond due to age, improper application or preparation, or other reasons, then you may need to remove all the existing finish. (There goes your weekend.)

 Before you begin removing a finish by any method, understand that some hazards are involved. Dust created when a finish is sanded is a health hazard. Chemicals involved in cleaning, refinishing, and removing paint may be toxic or flammable or even present a risk of cancer. Lead-based finishes are particularly odious. Whenever practical, do the removal outside. Always read product labels. Protect your eyes, skin, and lungs from toxic dust and chemicals. Wearing a tight-fitting dust mask (or respirator when fumes are involved), goggles, gloves, and other protective clothing when removing finishes by using any of the methods described in this chapter. (See Chapter 2 and the Cheat Sheet in the front of this book for more important safety information.)

Selecting the Best Paint Removal Method

You can remove paint and other protective coatings in many ways. Each has advantages and disadvantages, depending on the condition and type of finish, the *substrate* (the surface being painted upon), and the desired results.

You have the following options for your interior or exterior paint-removal task.

- ✔ Scraping
- ✔ Sanding
- ✔ Grinding
- ✔ Heating and scraping
- ✔ Chemical refinishing and stripping
- ✔ Sandblasting

Scraping the Loose Coating Away

Scraping is generally the easiest way to remove loose paint or coatings that are flaking, peeling, cracking, alligatoring, or adhering poorly to the surface or previous coating. Inevitably, an exterior paint-preparation task will involve some scraping of peeling paint, especially near joints where water seeps into cracks and gets behind the paint film. Scraping is also often necessary indoors at joints between materials, such as between the rails and panels of a raised panel door. It can be a particularly effective approach for removing paint from metal because in many cases the bond is not that strong.

Working with paint scrapers

The primary tool is the hook-type paint scraper with replaceable blades. Scrapers are a lot less fun than power sanders, but they are just as effective, especially for small areas. Look at the bright side — at least they're quiet.

The secret of using a scraper is to *keep the blade sharp*. Sharpen the scraper when you bring it home from the hardware store — before you use it. Keep a small file handy in your tool belt or painter's apron so that you can sharpen the blade. If you sharpen your blade often enough, it will only take a few quick passes for the tool to work much better. Wear gloves. Then, if the scraper slips, you won't cut yourself in the process. For more involved sharpening, lock the blade in a vise or sharpen it on a grinding wheel.

Although hook-type scrapers are typically pulled toward you, as shown in Figure 8-1, we've found that a back-and-forth or pushing motion works well to chip off thick layers of paint down to the base surface, especially on metal.

Figure 8-1: Apply firm pressure on the working end of the scraper and draw it toward you. A pushing motion may also be quite effective.

To minimize dust, mist the surface with water before you scrape. This procedure, called wet-sanding, is essential when removing lead-based paint.

Contouring scrapers for usage

Flat scrapers are for — you guessed it — flat surfaces. For detailed moldings, furniture, or other irregular surfaces, you need to buy molding or cabinet scrapers. As an alternative, you can make a scraper that conforms to the contour of your molding by grinding an old chisel, screwdriver, or other hardened steel tool into the shape that you need.

A putty knife (with a stiff or flexible blade) is effective for getting into corners. So is an old, wide-wood chisel. Don't use a good chisel because scraping paint quickly dulls the edge and makes it useless for chiseling wood. In other words, borrow your neighbor's chisel.

To minimize cleanup, always lay a drop cloth under the area being scraped.

Unless you have scraped all the paint off a surface, the unscraped paint film will have a hard edge wherever it meets a scraped area. These edges must be feather-sanded, or they will show through the new coat of paint. To feather-sand, keep the sander moving back and forth while applying light pressure. Firmer pressure builds up heat, which tends to peel the sound paint rather than smooth the transition.

Sanding and Grinding to Perfection

Sandpaper is commonly available in standard 9-x-11-inch sheets. Although these sheets may be cut to fit a variety of power sanders and hand-sanding tools, such as rubber sanding blocks, using sandpaper that is precut for specific hand and power sanders is more convenient and sometimes necessary. Abrasive papers come in sheets, rolls, belts, discs, and other configurations. Some have peel-and-stick or hook-and-loop backing — at a premium price. Some papers have prepunched holes to match dust exhaust ports on the pads of power sanders.

Choosing the right texture of sandpaper

The abrasives used in most sandpaper today are aluminum oxide or silicon carbide and range from very coarse to superfine. Although sometimes simply described in terms such as *coarse, medium,* and *fine,* most sandpaper and similar abrasives are numbered — 40, 60, 80, 100, 120, 240, and up. The higher the number, the finer the grit.

Closed-coat papers have more abrasive particles than *open-coat* papers and therefore cut faster, but open-coat papers won't clog as quickly. We usually opt for the open coat to save money. Resin-bonded abrasive cloth "sandpaper" is much more durable (and more costly) than standard sandpaper. Some sandpaper and cloths can be used for wet sanding, which require the use of water or mineral spirits as a lubricant. The lubricant prevents clogging and keeps the abrasive working efficiently longer. Wet sanding is also a recommended approach when sanding paint containing toxic lead.

Don't use mineral spirits or other oils as a lubricant when power-sanding with wet/dry sandpaper. A spark from the tool can ignite the fumes from the oils.

In general, start sanding with the coarsest grit necessary to remove the finish. Too coarse a paper unnecessarily scratches the surface. Too fine a paper doesn't cut fast enough and clogs quickly. You may need to start with 60- or even 40-grit paper to remove thick paint layers from siding, but for a more delicate project, you'd rarely want to start lower than 80- or 100-grit. Switch to progressively finer papers, sanding with the grain until scratches from the previous sandpaper are removed. How fine you go depends on the project. For exterior trim, 80- or 100-grit paper may be fine. For interior trim, you may go as high as 220.

Finishing always accentuates scratches or the transitions between painted and unpainted areas that you have feather-sanded. Scratches are most noticeable when wood is stained, but paint accentuates imperfections, too. Sanding dust makes a project look and feel smoother than it really is, so wipe the surface with a *tack cloth* (a sticky cloth available at paint stores) or any soft cloth slightly dampened with mineral spirits. This procedure reveals any remaining scratches. Priming may also raise wood grain (making it feel rough and fuzzy) and accentuate scratches. If so, sand lightly and reprime any bare spots.

Smoothing the grain with sanding tools

Finishing sanders are the least aggressive machines but are still much faster than hand sanding. You can choose from three types of vibrating actions on a finishing sander: in-line (straight back-and-forth), orbital (little circular motions), or random-orbit (random circular motions). Of the three, our favorite is the newer random-orbit sander, which is nearly as aggressive as a belt sander but much easier to control and which leaves a virtually scratch-free finish.

Next to the disc sander and grinder, the belt sander is the fastest type of sanding machine. It is practical only when sanding large, flat surfaces. If you've never used one before, practice on a scrap of wood before attempting the real thing. Never start or stop a belt sander while the belt is in contact with the surface. Keep the sander moving at all times when it is on the surface or you may sand deep gouges in the surface. Turn the sander on in the air; then slowly lower it to the surface. Go back and forth, overlapping passes. If you are sanding to bare wood, be sure to sand with the grain so that you don't scratch the surface.

Use caution when sanding *veneered wood* (a type of wood that has a core made of a cheaper-type wood, but has a thin layer of a more-expensive wood covering the outside). The veneer is often very thin. You don't want to find out how thin by sanding through it. Some stains that you're trying to sand out may go all the way through the veneer. Use a finishing sander and the finest paper required to remove only as much wood as necessary.

Disc sanders are very aggressive and always leave swirl marks that must be removed with a finishing sander. These sanders require a light touch and a quick hand to keep them moving fast enough to avoid damaging the surface. Some tools accept a metal abrasive disc instead of a paper disc. The nice thing about the metal disc is that when it gets clogged, you can drop the disc in paint remover and brush off the gummy paint residue again and again. Get two or three discs so that you can keep working while the clogged disk is soaking.

Although many power sanders today have dust bags or vacuum ports that draw out most of the dust, you still need to wear a tight-fitting dust mask. When working indoors, it helps a great deal to put an exhaust fan in a window to draw out dust that would otherwise spread throughout your home.

Keep all power sanders moving whenever they are in contact with the surface. Staying too long in one place can cause heat to build-up, resulting in gummy paint that clogs the sandpaper. It also results in uneven sanding or worse: deep depressions.

Try using a sanding pad that is contoured to match the surface you're sanding. If you try to sand by hand or with the corner of a pad sander, you are likely to round over edges or otherwise change the contour of the trim or object you are painting. (Such techniques also waste sandpaper because they often tear the paper or wear it out at one point before the rest of the paper is used.) *Sanding sponges* (flexible blocks of sponge covered in various grains of sandpaper) are great for hand sanding slightly contoured surfaces, or use contoured rubber pads for both hand sanding and power-sanding. You can even make your own: Use a hacksaw to shape a block of polystyrene foam or cut hard rubber with a knife.

Heating and Scraping Oil-Based Paints

Use heat to soften a finish so that you can easily lift the finish from the surface with a scraper. This technique is particularly effective for removing multiple layers of oil-based paint. Heat guns and propane torches, fitted with flame-spreading tips, supply the heat. You supply the scraping.

A torch works a little faster than a good heat gun, but the higher temperatures and flame increase the risk of charring and fire. Although you can wet down visibly charred areas, it's what you can't see that presents the greatest risk. The heat and flame can get into fine cracks and ignite the very dry dust, paper, insulation, and wood behind the siding or within the wall. There it may smolder, sometimes for hours, before igniting. For this reason, never use a torch on siding or trim and always have a fire extinguisher close by. When working outdoors, keep a garden hose or water bottle handy for wetting down any charred areas, and keep an eye on the area for several hours.

Always wear protective clothing. Wear a heavy glove on your scraping hand to protect yourself from possible burns from a misdirected gun or torch, or a hot scraper. Always wear a respirator to protect yourself from toxic fumes. *Never* use heat to soften lead-based paints because the fumes created by the heat are extremely dangerous to your health and the environment. And although some electric heat guns look like hair dryers, they are not — enough said.

To remove paint with heat, move the gun or torch back and forth across a small area until the paint begins to blister. Then immediately scrape off the loosened paint with a stiff putty knife or similar tool. Wipe the edge of the knife across a straightedge such as a board or the edge of a box to remove the goo from the tool. Be careful — the sticky gunk is hot. If you drop some onto your bare skin, you'll invent new words. With a little practice, you can keep the heat moving along with one hand while you scrape with the other, but we suggest that you start by directing the heat well away from the area while you scrape. You're less likely to inadvertently direct the flame where you don't want it, including toward your scraping hand!

Heat from a heat gun or torch can crack glass, especially on cold days. Flame and heat-spreading tool attachments help prevent such damage, but we suggest that you also use a separate heat shield to protect glass that is not easily removable from a window, door, or other frame. Any large, flat, noncombustible material, such as a broad taping knife or a piece of sheet metal, will do. We've even used an old cookie sheet.

Don't bother trying to get every bit of paint off. After you have removed most of the paint, try a chemical stripper to finish the job. It works great!

Removing Clear Finishes with Chemicals

Sometimes a good cleaning/refurbishing isn't enough to bring old natural wood finishes back to life. If the wood has one of the following problems, you may have to remove the existing clear finish but not necessarily strip the color (stain) from the wood:

- ✔ Extensive and random cracking, like the skin of an alligator marks the finish.
- ✔ White hazing or stains from water damage on the surface.
- ✔ The clear finish is peeling from the base coat.

Testing products before using

To remove clear finishes from wood, you need a paint stripper or an antique refinisher. *Paint stripper* (also called a *paint-and-varnish remover*) removes polyurethane or paint finishes. *Antique refinisher* (also sold as *furniture refinisher*) removes shellac, varnish, or lacquer finishes. Both products are available in quart and gallon containers.

To determine the type of finish on the wood, first test the finish in an inconspicuous spot. Pour fingernail polish remover, which contains acetone, or a refinisher on a cotton ball or clean cloth and apply it to the finish. If the chemical does not soften the finish, the finish is probably polyurethane, and you must use a paint remover to strip the wood.

Working safely with chemicals

Many refinishers, strippers, and solvents contain mineral spirits and other chemicals that may be hazardous if improperly used. A little splash of some chemical stripper on you skin can burn. Fumes can make you dizzy or worse — they can steal oxygen from your blood. The best-dressed stripper wears protective clothing, including long-sleeved shirt, long pants, splash goggles, and chemical-resistant gloves. A respirator may also be advisable depending on the product and the ventilation conditions. We know this goes against all natural urges, but always read the warnings on the label of any chemical product you use. See Chapter 2 for important safety and environmental information.

Removing paint and varnish with stripper

Paint-and-varnish removers are expensive, messy, and often toxic. So why are we recommending them? Because this chemical approach is the quickest and easiest way to remove multiple layers of paint or varnish from wood, metal, masonry, and other surfaces. Sometimes it's the only practical alternative.

Strippers work especially well on detailed or irregular surfaces, such as some moldings and furniture, and they get into the pores of rough surfaces. On the other hand, sanding and scraping with or without heat easily damages wood details; and you can't sand or scrape masonry very effectively because tools dull so quickly.

Chemical stripping, most notably a system called Peel Away, is becoming a popular way to safely remove lead paint, especially for siding and exterior trim. This wet process does not produce dust.

Never use torches on lead paint because the resulting fumes are toxic. Although a heat gun under 1100 degrees will not produce as many fumes as with higher temperatures, the scraping associated with this approach produces airborne lead particulates; therefore, avoid heat guns.

Choosing your stripper

The different brands of paint-and-varnish remover on the market vary in numerous ways from the types of finishes the removers effectively remove; to the substance on which removers are safely used (fiberglass, metal, wood, and so on); to consistency (gel, liquid, or aerosol); to the products that neutralize the stripper after the finish has been removed (water, mineral spirits, or a commercial after-wash); to flammability, and toxicity.

Wood strippers come in two basic types. The type you choose depends on the project you are stripping.

> ✔ Of the two types of brush-on strippers, *liquid* and *semi-paste* (also called *heavy-bodied*), semi-paste is the best choice for tough jobs like removing epoxy, polyurethane, and enamel, or when multiple layers of paint or finish must be removed. Use semi-paste or a heavy-bodied remover for stripping vertical surfaces.

> ✔ *Spray strippers* are available in aerosol cans for small projects, and are useful for removing a finish from a difficult-to-reach area like an intricate molding on a wall. When you use spray strippers on a small area, be sure to carefully mask and protect the adjoining surfaces so that no spray gets on them.

The ideal stripper works quickly on your particular finish, doesn't harm the *substrate* (surface underneath), and is nonflammable and nontoxic. In the real world, however, some compromise is usually necessary. Your priorities may differ from ours, but here are the questions that we ask about the product, in order of importance:

> ✔ Will it work on this particular finish? You must be able to answer "yes" to this question.
>
> ✔ Is it safe or good to use on this substrate? Here again, the answer to this question must be "yes." There's no sense stripping something if you are going to ruin it in the process.
>
> ✔ Is it toxic? Methylene chloride, the active ingredient in the most aggressive non-flammable strippers, is so toxic that its use is banned in some states. In recent years, manufacturers have developed low-odor, less toxic alternatives. In general, they take longer (sometimes much longer — 24 hours versus 10 minutes) and are not effective on all finishes. If we know that a non-toxic stripper will, given time, strip the finish, we'll choose it and plan around the time factor.
>
> ✔ Is it flammable? This question is more important when you must use the product indoors or in areas that combine poor ventilation and the risk of ignition from a spark or flame.
>
> ✔ Does it work quickly? If a non-flammable, non-toxic, or more environmentally safe product will work, but requires more time to activate or additional applications, then we use it.

To meet a variety of needs, one leading manufacturer of paint-and-varnish removers has ten different stripping products. To choose the right stripper for your application, consider your priorities, read the label, and consult with a knowledgeable salesperson (though finding a knowledgeable salesperson can be a chore in some stores). If you have a large project or a very special project, invest in the extra time to contact the customer service departments of one or more manufacturers for a recommendation.

Preparing for the task

To make a project easier to strip, remove any hardware or doors. Work outdoors, if possible. Not only is there plenty of ventilation outside, but it's easier to deal with the mess that you may make. Lay doors on a flat surface, such as between sawhorses, for stripping. Remember to place a protective drop cloth under your project.

When you're working on vertical or overhead surfaces, you may be tempted to skimp on the stripper because you are afraid of the messy drips running down the surface. Don't. Instead, protect those surfaces and really lay the stuff on. If you are working on an exterior surface of your house, make sure to protect all areas below your work with plastic. Seal the area with tape if there's a chance that goo may get behind the plastic. If you're stripping cabinets, built-ins, or wall trim, mask the edge of the floor with wide tape and then tape plastic drop cloths over the masking tape.

Paint stripper must remain wet on a surface long enough to dissolve the old finish. Work outdoors if you can, but not in direct sunlight or where a breeze is blowing. Sunlight can dry the stripper before the paint is dissolved. To retard drying, you can also lay plastic wrap or a plastic drop cloth directly on the surface after you apply the stripper.

If you are working with a flammable stripper, extinguish all flames, including pilot lights; provide cross-ventilation; and don't use electrical devices such as fans or switches, which may spark.

Applying and removing strippers

Follow these steps for applying stripper and removing it (hopefully along with the old paint or other finish):

1. **Begin by shaking the container of stripper to mix the ingredients.**

2. **Carefully open the container slowly and cover the lid with a cloth. This permits any built-up pressure to escape.**

3. **Lay on a heavy coat of stripper with a *stripping pad* (an item that looks like a scouring pad) or a soft brush.**

   While it's tempting to "brush" out the stripper like it's paint, don't. Use the pad to apply a generous amount of the stripper while stroking in one direction only. Don't brush back over an area.

4. **Let the stripper work for the time specified on the label.**

   You can't rush the project. While you may be tempted to begin scraping before the stripper has had time to loosen the paint, don't. You'll do more work that way and waste more remover. Be patient and don't scrape until the paint bubbles up from the surface. Let the strippper do the work, not you.

5. **Test the finish with a scraper.**

   Plastic scrapers work best because they don't scratch the wood. You can tell that the paint is ready to be removed when it bubbles and readily lifts off the surface as you gently push the scraper under it. If the paint seems to be unaffected by the stripper after allowing the time prescribed by the manufacturer, try another type of stripper.

If the stripper dries out before all of the finish is softened, apply another layer right on top of the first.

6. **Just keep scraping.**

Gunk, sludge and messy-all-over best describes this part of the job – but we don't know any way around it. Gently push the scraper through the layers of paint, working one area at a time and being careful not to gouge the surface. When stripping vertical surfaces, work from the bottom up. As you remove the sludge, deposit it in a metal container or scrape it into a cardboard box with the flaps cut off. Keep your scraper clean by wiping off the excess into the container.

Premium-grade steel wool is the standard recommended product to use to clean off stripper and paint residue left by scraping, but it can splinter, rust, and leave stains on the finished piece. Two alternatives that we like include bronze wool, available at some hardware stores and marine supply outlets, and green Scotch-Brite scouring pads, available at hardware and grocery stores.

To remove old paint from staircase spindles or other intricate areas, use wads of medium-grade steel wool. To remove the old finish from crevices, twist strands of *premium-grade* steel wool around the grooves or use a length of twine, and use a sawing motion. Check the stripper to be sure that the stripper you are using doesn't react with steel wool or you may end up with black stains all over your piece!

7. **Wash off any stripper residue.**

As you may imagine, a chemical designed to remove paint is not the best undercoat for paint! Paint strippers must be neutralized and removed. Be sure to remove *all* residue with repeated washing and scrubbing.

• Scrub away residue with a stripping pad or brush dipped in warm soapy water if you use a nontoxic stripping gel (often called *water-wash stripper*). Keep in mind that the water may swell the fibers of the wood, raise wood grain, or loosen the glue joints.

• Use mineral spirits or an after-wash product to remove residue if you used a standard chemical stripper, and apply them while the surface is still damp from stripping. Fill a wide-mouthed container with after-wash or spirits so you can dip a piece of fine-grade steel wool into it and then wipe the surface following the grain of the wood. Rinse the pad frequently.

8. **Clean up and remove all the materials that you used.**

Be cautious with these materials soaked in paint chemicals because they can ignite spontaneously. Put all the rags, steel wool, papers, or other materials you used outside to dry in the open air. When they have dried, place them in a metal container that has a tight-fitting lid. For disposal instructions, read the container's label or call your local waste disposal department for instructions about disposal of used or leftover stripper.

Stripping paint from metal

Stripping paint from metal hardware is easy because paint that's applied in the usual way does not typically bond well to metal. Remove the hardware and hold it under the hot water tap and scrape the paint off with a plastic scraper. If necessary, immerse hardware in boiling water with a little vinegar, and the paint will practically fall off. Or you can dip the hardware in a small container of stripper, wait until the finish bubbles up, and use a stiff brush to scrub it off. Wash the hardware with mineral spirits or an after-wash as recommended by the stripper manufacturer. Whatever approach you use, be sure to dry the hardware carefully.

Removing troublesome stains

Oil-based wood stains penetrate deep into wood fibers and so are quite difficult to remove. If the stripper that you used to strip the surface finish doesn't get all the stain out, try one specifically designed to penetrate and remove wood stains.

Certain unintentional stains will come out only if they are in the finish. Some, like black watermarks, are usually too deep to remove by any method other than using oxalic acid. You must apply the acid to an entire section and later attempt to stain that section to match any unbleached areas. Mix about a cup of oxalic acid crystals (the amount depends on the amount of staining) in hot water until no more can be dissolved. Apply this solution to the stained area and let it dry completely. Brush off the dry crystals. Repeat the process, if necessary.

Wear a dust mask, rubber gloves, and splash goggles when mixing or handling oxalic acid.

Chapter 9

Preparing Exterior Surfaces

• •

In This Chapter

▶ Discovering the cause of paint failures

▶ Tackling problems associated with specific types of surfaces

▶ Getting the dirt and mildew off

▶ Caulking and patching

• •

*A*lthough a nice paint job is comparable to icing on a cake, we've never heard the task described as "a piece of cake." However, you can save a bundle of dough by painting or staining the exterior of your house yourself. The amount of work and the cost of materials vary widely according to the size and general condition of your house. To get the most benefit from your money and labor, do the best job that you can by preparing the surface.

Although good-quality paint and proper application techniques are important, surface preparation usually is the single most important factor determining the success of a painting job. This chapter is devoted primarily to the process of preparing the surface and a few additional preparations you should make before you pick up a paintbrush.

Looking at the Preparation Process

Here's an overview of the proper sequence for preparing a house for repainting:

1. **Correct problems that may be causing any premature paint failure.**

2. **Repair or replace any loose, missing, rotten, or otherwise damaged siding or trim.**

3. **Remove any peeling or loose paint.**

   Hand scraping and power-sanding are the usual ways to do this job, but sometimes power-washing, chemicals, or heat are used.

4. **Treat any mildew problem with either a bleach-detergent solution or a commercial house cleaner that contains a mildewcide.**

5. **Prime bare wood or other problem surfaces that require primer.**

6. **Patch nail holes, and seal gaps and cracks with paintable caulk.**

7. **Pressure-wash the entire exterior to remove sanding dust, dirt, and grime.**

Finding Why Paint Fails

If, after five or more years, the last coat of paint on your house is faded, but in good condition, you may be able to simply clean the surface, apply a new coat of paint, and expect it to last for years to come. The same guideline applies if you simply want to change the color of paint that is in good condition. More often, however, paint failures, most notably peeling, are what motivate you to take on such a big task. If you find the cause of the problem, you may be able to prevent it from happening in the future.

Improper preparation (applying paint over dirty surfaces) or incorrect application (spreading paint too thinly) — not poor paint quality — causes the vast majority of exterior paint failures.

Depending on the cause of the paint failure, you may still need to resolve the cause of the failure before you re-side. If, for example, extensive interior moisture and a lack of a vapor retarder have caused paint to peel, re-siding may aggravate the moisture problem. Concealed by the new siding, the old siding and even house framing may rot away, unnoticed, until it's too late. And if you think that it's costly to replace the siding, just wait until you have to replace the wall framing.

So here's a rundown that describes the possible types of topcoat failures, along with suggestions about how to handle each case. We've included some advice and tips to prevent these problems in the future.

✔ **Topcoat failure:** If all or nearly all the topcoat of paint is peeling, flaking, or alligatoring, you must remove the entire topcoat. If you attempt spot repairs, they may last, but new areas will likely fail every year.

How do you prevent the problem from recurring? A good cleaning and preparing the surface before repainting is the answer. If, for example, you are painting over a chalking surface, consider using a paint additive, such as Emulsa-Bond, that improves paint adhesion. Mix the additive with your exterior latex paint according to the manufacturer's directions. If a second coat of paint is needed, apply the paint without an additive. Another way to eliminate peeling due to poor adhesion to a chalky surface is to use a quality latex paint that's formulated as an overcoat for "problem surfaces."

✔ **Patches of peeling paint:** If paint is peeling in limited areas only, assume that you have a localized moisture problem and investigate the source. For example, paint often peels near the clothes-dryer exhaust vent because of repeated steam exposure. To prevent future peeling in this case, extend the vent pipe farther away from the siding to limit moisture contact with the paint.

✔ **Peeling paint on soffits, porch ceilings, or gable end walls:** If paint is intact on the house siding but is peeling on the underside of the soffits (roof overhangs), on porch ceilings, or on gable walls, the problem is usually too much moisture and too little ventilation. For these areas where air doesn't circulate naturally you can purchase simple-to-install round vents, insert the vents, and install continuous ridge vents that extend along the full length of the roof ridge. To increase attic ventilation, install larger gable vents. Or install continuous ridge and soffit vents, which encourage cross-ventilation and provide a path for excess moisture to exit. Before painting any of these surfaces make sure they are clean so the paint can stick to them.

✔ **Peeling paint around windows and doors:** The flat surface trim around windows and doors is another common place for peeling paint, especially on brick and stucco houses. Peeling paint in these spots is generally a sign of poor interior and/or exterior caulking.

To block moisture vapor transmission, use caulk to seal any cracks between the interior trim and either the walls and or the floors. If the trim is painted, use acrylic caulk, which is paintable. Use clear silicone caulk for natural or stained trim. Also remove electrical outlet covers and caulk any cracks between the outlet box and the plaster or wallboard. Install energy-saving foam gaskets between the switch and outlet covers and the electrical boxes to further slow the movement of interior air to the outdoors.

On the exterior, poorly sealed joints are vulnerable to water penetration with the same results. (That water sure is a troublemaker!) To remedy the problem, first use sandpaper or a paint scraper to remove the peeling paint. Then apply a coat of primer on any bare wood. When the primer is dry, use an acrylic latex caulk to seal the cracks between boards before you paint.

✔ **Peeling paint at the base of a wooden porch or columns:** Whenever wood, especially the porous end-grain, sits directly on any flat surface, water gets under the wood and wicks up into the wood, causing the paint to peel. (Here we go again.)

If the problem is severe, remove any rotted wood, stabilize the surrounding wood with a wood hardener, and fill the damaged area with wood filler. If possible, correct the source of the problem by providing the necessary air space. For more information on these and other carpentry repair projects, see *Home Improvement For Dummies*, by Gene Hamilton and Katie Hamilton (IDG Books Worldwide, Inc.).

Otherwise, just scrape away the peeling paint. When the wood is completely dry, seal the peeled area with an alkyd primer. Then seal the joint between the post and the floor with acrylic latex caulk before you paint.

Inspect such areas annually to make sure that the caulk is still in good condition. If the seal fails in one small area, the remaining caulk can trap the moisture under the post, and you will be worse off than if you had never caulked.

✔ **When paint peels down to bare wood:** Moisture migrating through the wall from inside the house is usually the reason, and can be caused by a lack of an adequate vapor retarder in the wall, lack of bathroom venting, or other sources of moisture within the wall.

If your house has large areas where paint is peeling down to the base wood, then you had better sit down. The only solution is to remove all the old paint — down to the bare wood — and apply an alkyd primer, followed by a topcoat of quality latex house paint. The same advice applies when old layers of oil-based paint dry out and cause extensive alligatoring. In some cases, removing all the paint and repainting is so time-consuming and expensive that re-siding is a more practical alternative. Now you know why vinyl siding exists.

When either the top layer of paint or patches of it peels, the solution is not as extensive. Discuss your conclusions with a reputable paint dealer or other painting professionals before you proceed. Then correct the condition before repainting or avoid the application error that caused the problem.

Preparing Exterior Surfaces for Painting

Proper preparation varies according to the type and condition of the exterior surface and further depends on the type of finish you intend to apply. Here are some tips on how to deal with the problems associated with typical exterior surfaces.

✔ **New wood siding:** Just make sure to brush the wood clean, working from the top down. Wait until after you stain or prime before caulking. If you plan to paint or use solid-color stain, set any nails that the carpenters missed below the surface and fill nail holes with caulk.

✔ **Weathered wood siding:** Stain bonds even better to unpainted wood that has weathered. If you plan to paint, sand and/or power-wash the wood to remove any gray weathered surface and to smooth siding that has been exposed to the weather for more than a few weeks. (See the "Saving time by power-washing" section later in this chapter.) In some cases you may have to remove as much as ⅛ inch of the gray, weathered surface to get to the *bright wood* (non-weathered, natural-colored wood). If you are staining, use a wood restorer and/or power-wash the wood to bring the wood back to its natural color so that staining produces the desired color.

✔ **Old painted siding:** Inevitably, you will need to scrape off loose paint, using any one of a variety of scrapers. Then you need to power-sand to feather the hard edges left by scraping (as shown in Figure 9-1), prime any wood made bare in the process, and caulk all joints. Also, set any popped nails, fill the holes with caulk, and spot-prime the siding.

✔ **Hardboard siding:** Pay particular attention to prepping and painting hardboard siding. Because this product is more vulnerable to weather-related failures, a sound protective paint barrier must be carefully maintained. You can easily ruin hardboard siding by neglecting maintenance or by performing the work incorrectly. Follow the special procedures recommended in "Maintenance for Hardboard Siding," a free booklet available from the American Hardboard Association, 1210 W. Northwest Highway, Palatine, IL 60067; phone 847-934-8800. See Chapter 12 for painting guidelines. Here are some of the preparation guidelines:

- **Use a 300-degree steam cleaner (a rental item) or scrub the siding with a very hot detergent solution** if the normal siding cleaning process fails to remove a waxy coating or oily grime.

- **Lightly sand glossy finishes** to remove the sheen (called scuff sanding), but sand, scrape, or cut into the surface only as much as is necessary to correct existing problems. Replace or fill badly damaged areas.

- **Don't set nails** or you will break the factory-applied protective coating.

✔ **New cedar and redwood:** Cedar and redwood bleed tannin when the wood is new. They should be washed with a general cleaning detergent and water solution (see "Scrubbing the Entire House Down" section, later in this chapter) before being primed with a stain-blocking alkyd primer. For more information about treating cedar and redwood, contact the California Redwood Association or Western Wood Products.

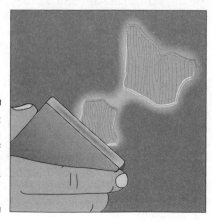

Figure 9-1:
Feather the edges of scraped areas by sanding.

✔ **Concrete and masonry:** Unfinished, fully cured concrete can be finished with concrete stain or paint after cleaning it with a power-washer to remove dirt, stains, and any residue from old sealers. If you are repainting use the same type of paint: latex or oil. Although scraping or sanding small areas of peeling paint off concrete or masonry surfaces is feasible, doing so dulls scrapers and chews up sandpaper very quickly. If you have a large area consider sandblasting or stripping with a chemical remover, which is discussed in Chapter 8.

Clean out cracks with a shop vacuum or blow out dust with compressed air before caulking the cracks. Do the same when using a concrete patch and mist the surface before applying the patch.

✔ **Stucco:** In many cases, a masonry cleaner — available at any janitorial supply store — is all you need to renew a stucco surface. Hose off the loose dirt and while the surface is still wet, apply the cleaner to lift the remaining dirt. Then scrub with a stiff brush. If the stucco still looks dingy, consider having a stucco contractor *redash* the finish, a process in which the contractor can either spray or brush a new cement surface onto the stucco. For information on patching, repairing cracks, and caulking joints on stucco, check out *Home Improvement For Dummies*.

Power-washing stucco, especially old stucco, is risky at best. The force of the water can blast the finish off, turning a simple cleaning job into a major repair.

✔ **Glossy finishes:** Paint does not bond well to glossy surfaces, including painted ones. If a cleaned painted surface still shines, it must be dulled. Sanding is a surefire approach, but it's time-consuming and especially difficult on detailed areas of trim, windows, and doors. Brush-on deglosser, available for both oil- and latex-based paints, is a much easier way to dull the surface — just be sure not to spill any on your personality. For an extra precaution, you can also mix a boxing additive in the paint.

✔ **Ferrous metal railings, siding, and so on:** Clean the metal to remove all dirt, grime, and oil before priming with a rust-inhibiting (direct-to-metal) primer. Follow the paint manufacturer's cleaning guidelines. Generally, you can use a 50-50 vinegar and water cleaning solution for all metal except galvanized steel. New galvanized metal should be cleaned with mineral spirits before being primed with special galvanized metal primer.

Rust often occurs under the paint, causing a bumpy finish and stains. Eventually the corrosion flakes off with the finish. There are two basic approaches to preparing rusty metal for paint. You can eliminate all rust by sanding, grinding, or sandblasting. Or, when it is impractical to remove every last spot of rust, you can simply use a wire brush, to scrape off only the loose, flaking rust and then treat the metal with a chemical to neutralize the corrosion. Results with chemical neutralizing will vary, so always apply rust-inhibiting or rusty metal primer on bare metal. You also can apply paint conditioners, such as Penetrol, to rusty areas before you apply any paint. Such conditioners seal the rusty areas and provide a better paint bond.

- ✔ **Aluminum or vinyl gutters:** Avoid painting aluminum and especially vinyl gutters, if possible. If you do paint aluminum or vinyl gutters, scuff-sand for better bonding.

- ✔ **Mill finish aluminum storm and screen windows and doors:** You can topcoat the exterior face of mill finish aluminum storm and screen windows and doors with 100-percent acrylic-latex paint to match trim colors. However, you must remove oxidation (corrosion) with sandpaper or a wire brush and apply a primer specifically for aluminum or galvanized metal. Don't get paint into the tracks or on the glass or screen sash.

- ✔ **Aluminum siding:** Generally, a very good cleaning is all that aluminum siding needs before you paint.

Scrubbing the Entire House Down

The secret to a long-lasting paint job is cleanliness. The ideal time to clean is after you have completed scraping, sanding, spot priming, and caulking — and taken a long nap. Allow two to three days for drying before you paint. In addition to the many commercial cleaners available, you can make two widely recommended homemade cleaning solutions:

- ✔ For general cleaning, mix ½ cup of laundry detergent or trisodium phosphate (TSP) in 1 gallon of water. Scrub with a stiff brush and rinse thoroughly with water.

- ✔ To remove mold, mildew, algae, and lichen, mix 1 quart of fresh household bleach and 2 ounces of TSP detergent, or a phosphate-free substitute, with 3 quarts of water. Spray on with a garden sprayer. If necessary, cover the area for about an hour to prevent it from drying out. Rinse well with water. Repeat as necessary.

Saving time by power-washing

Washing your house may seem like an insurmountable job, but an electric or gas-powered washer has to be one of the more useful and labor-saving machines a homeowner can get his or her hands on. Plus, they're just plain fun to use.

Small electric power-washers (or *pressure-washers* as they are also called) go for as little as $150. Gutsy gas models are two to four times that. You can also rent a really killer unit for about $65 a day. If you rent such a washer, you may want to share the rental cost with a neighbor, because cleaning the entire exterior of two houses in a day is entirely possible.

Virtually risk-free uses of a power-washer include preparing concrete and asphalt surfaces for protective coatings, and restoring a slimy green or severely weathered wood deck to its original beauty. However, other applications may present risks, both to you and to your house. For example, if you have an old house with little or no insulation, loose-fitting windows, or very old siding, especially wood shingles, you may want to skip the power-washer and wash the house by hand instead. If you're not comfortable with the risks of power-washing, you can get the job done with nothing but some elbow grease, a bucket of cleaning solution, and a scrub brush.

Handling a power-washer

Power-washers usually have a control to vary the pressure of the water stream, called psi (pounds per square inch). For most cleaning projects, especially on wood, 800 to 1000 psi is adequate. On less vulnerable surfaces, you may go up to a maximum 1500 psi. Be sure to read the operating instructions of the power-washer or have a rental unit demonstrated.

The jet of water spraying from any power-washer can be lethal. Exercise good judgment when using a power-washer, and most importantly, never use it around other people or pets. If you are on a ladder, keep one hand on the ladder and be prepared for the considerable kick that occurs when the trigger is pulled or released.

Depending on the application, some products may be used with power-washers that meter chemicals into the water stream from detergent bottles or through siphon hoses. Be sure to read the label. Many solutions have chemicals that can damage the washer and/or put your health at risk when used with a power-washer.

Preparing the site and using safety precautions

High-pressure water finds its way into any unsealed opening in its path, so make sure that you protect everything you do not expect to spray. No matter what you are washing — siding or deck — follow these basic guidelines:

- ✔ Wear rain gear, especially boots and safety goggles.

- ✔ Use drop cloths or large sheets of cardboard to catch paint chips.

- ✔ Test pressure adjustment, spray pattern, and working distance on an inconspicuous area, like your neighbor's house.

- ✔ Practice your spray angle by holding the sprayer to the surface until you get the even results you want. Overlap passes for even cleaning.

- ✔ Don't swing the wand in an arc; you will get uneven results because you are closer to the surface in the center of the arc.

Battling mildew stains

A brown, gray, or black stain on siding or trim may simply be grime, or it may be mildew. To test whether a stain is grime or mildew, try washing the stain away with water and a detergent such as Spic and Span. If the stain does not wash away with water and detergent, the culprit is probably mildew.

Because mildew is a fungus growth, it thrives on moisture and dirt, so keep the siding open to the sun and air. Don't store firewood or other materials close to the house. Prune tree branches that shade the house. If you have recurring mildew problems, power-wash the house exterior once a year and apply a mildewcide solution every two to three years.

Handle bleach and mildewcide solutions with care. Read label warnings. Always wear protective clothing, especially neoprene gloves and goggles.

Cleaning chalking surfaces

Some exterior paints, such as those used on aluminum siding, intentionally chalk for self-cleaning. Wipe the surface with the palm of your hand. If the paint color comes off on your hand, the paint is chalking. If the siding comes off, painting won't help. Scrub off the chalk with a strong solution of water and Spic and Span, or TSP detergent (or a non-phosphate TSP alternative) and water. You also can use a commercial wood cleaner to remove the chalked paint. Water pressure alone doesn't do the trick.

As you scrub the surface, work from the bottom up to avoid streaking; rinse frequently with clear water; and allow the surface to dry before painting.

Cleaning stucco and other masonry

Efflorescence, mold and algae, lichen, and stains from chalking paint or rusting metal are all problems that you should attend to before you paint masonry, which includes surfaces such as stucco, brick, and concrete block.

First, eliminate the sources of the problems. Overhanging trees can cause mold and algae; and a deteriorating chimney cap can allow water to penetrate behind the brick and cause efflorescence. Rusting may result from the use of various metals reinforcing materials in masonry construction, such as wire mesh or steel structural materials such like over windows and doors. Even when the metal is not visible, the rust stains may bleed through to the surface. If the paint on siding above masonry is chalking, it washes down onto the masonry and stains the surface.

In most cases, you need to scrub the surface with a chemical cleaner. See the introduction to this section for cleaning solutions to use for general cleaning and for removing mildew, mold, and lichen. For efflorescence and other stubborn stains, try the following solution, which is made from products available from your local hardware store. Mix 1 cup of 10 percent muriatic acid in 1 gallon of water. Heavy stains may require up to 1:1 solution, but the risk of damage to the surface is increased. Scrub with a stiff brush and rinse thoroughly with water. Strong acid solutions must be neutralized with a 1:10 ammonia-water solution to stop the etching.

Always add the acid to the water or it will spatter. The acid vapors can also burn your lungs. Keep a safe distance from the acid by using a long-handled brush to scrub the surface. Wear protective gear, including a respirator, heavy neoprene gloves, and splash proof goggles, and read the label for additional handling instructions.

Sealing Cracks and Holes with Caulk

Filling cracks and holes in the trim and siding of your house before painting not only makes the paint job look better, but it also makes the paint last longer. Cracks and holes in any surface collect water, which eventually causes the paint to peel.

Caulk is a substance designed to seal a joint between two surfaces and to fill small holes. Make sure you use top-quality caulk outdoors. It needs to withstand extreme temperature changes and, unlike us, to remain flexible for 30 to 50 years. When caulking joints between dissimilar materials, make sure that the manufacturer recommends the caulk for both materials. If the area is to be painted, the caulk must be paintable. If you have any doubt about the suitability of a caulk for a particular application, contact the manufacturer's technical service department for a recommendation.

The best time to caulk is after you complete scraping, sanding, and priming. Caulk adheres better to primed surfaces, and the gaps, cracks, and holes are more evident.

Scrape away any peeling paint that's adjacent to the caulked areas. If that exposes any bare wood, then recaulk all cracks between any two nonmoving materials. Let the caulk cure a few days before power-washing the exterior.

Don't caulk the horizontal joints on siding where the siding courses overlap. The cracks between two courses of siding provide ventilation points to let moisture escape from the siding and from inside the wall. In fact, one of the often-recommended cures for a moisture problem involves inserting numerous wedges between siding courses to create a larger gap through which moisture can escape. For the same reason, don't try to fill the joints between courses with paint.

Patching Surface Cavities Before Painting

Fix small holes in the siding with an exterior patching compound, available in a premixed form (much like interior spackling compound) and in a dry powder form that you mix with water. Either type is effective. Just make sure that the package states that the patching compound is for outside use.

To patch holes and depressions in siding of any kind, follow these steps:

1. **Clean the hole or depression that you plan to fill.**

   Roughen the area that you want to patch with 80-grit sandpaper for a better bond.

2. **Fill the area with the patching compound.**

   Apply the compound to the hole or depression in one direction and then smooth it in a direction perpendicular to the first so that it's level with the original surface.

3. **Allow the compound to become hard and sand it smooth.**

   Compound shrinks, so a second coating may be necessary. Be sure to remove the dust from sanding the compound before you apply a second coat.

To repair large cracks and damaged trim, first remove any rotten wood with a chisel. Use a two-part polyester-based compound, similar to auto-body filler, to make the repair. Two-part fillers come with a thick paste base and a small tube of hardener. Mix the hardener with the paste according to the manufacturer's directions. The filler sets up quickly (within 3 to 5 minutes), so mix only the amount that you can use right away, and clean your tools immediately after use.

Use a putty knife to apply the compound to the damaged area and level it with the surface. This filler doesn't shrink as much as premixed exterior fillers, but you may still need to apply several coats to fill a large hole. When the filler hardens, it's suitable for rasping, sanding, or drilling.

At the point when the compound has set firm but is not completely dry, it can very easily be shaped or smoothed with a Surform tool or rasp.

Use auto-body fillers or two-part polyester-resin fillers for aluminum siding in a similar way. But before you apply the filler, drill numerous ⅛-inch-diameter holes in the patch area. When the compound is applied, it locks into the holes for a better bond. You can also cover damage with a new piece of siding. Just cut the top flange off so that the patch fits under the course above and embed it in adhesive caulk along the top and sides.

Although you can use the same procedure for vinyl siding, replacing a course of damaged vinyl siding is easy. For more information on these and other siding and stucco repair or replacement procedures, check out *Home Improvement For Dummies.*

Chapter 10

Preparing Interior Surfaces

. . . .

In This Chapter

▶ Starting with a clean surface

▶ Gathering tools and other materials

▶ Making room to work

▶ Repairing and prepping walls, textured surfaces, and woodwork

▶ Priming, sealing, and caulking

▶ Sanding and preparing wooden surfaces

. . . .

Skip this chapter if you enjoy repainting every couple of years. If you don't, read on.

Most interiors will look better if all you do is slap on a fresh coat of paint. However, you get results that are even more striking and a longer lasting paint job if you take special care in cleaning and preparing the surfaces. Preparation includes making minor repairs to the walls, ceilings, and woodwork and scraping and sanding to remove any loose paint. To make the preparation and painting easier, you need the right tools and a clear space to work in.

If you need to remove the existing paint due to peeling, paint buildup, lead abatement, or other reasons, refer to Chapter 8, and then come on back here; we'll wait for you. If you need to make significant drywall or plaster repairs, refer to *Home Improvement For Dummies,* by Gene Hamilton and Katie Hamilton (IDG Books Worldwide, Inc.).

Cleaning a Room for Painting

Unless you know that you will be undertaking messy repairs or surface preparation work, start work with a thorough cleaning. The goal is to strip the room of all dirt and cobwebs (hidden in ceiling corners) and clean the baseboards, windows, and door casings. A vacuum with a crevice tool can catch the cobwebs and dust. And while you're at it, vacuum up dust and dirt around radiators and heating ducts. Open the windows to remove all dirt and debris from inside the sill. And clean any closets while you're at it.

Due to environmental concerns, some states ban the use of TSP (trisodium phosphate). If walls and woodwork have dirt or grease, wash them with a sponge and a phosphate-free household cleaner. You may have to wash some dirty areas more than once to get them thoroughly clean. Then rinse the surfaces with clear water and let them dry.

Solving Kitchen and Bath Problems

Paint's number one enemy in a kitchen is grease. It clings to walls, ceilings, and cabinets. (Your number one enemy, at least if you're counting calories, is a gallon of fudge ripple ice cream.) Use your favorite household cleaner to remove grease from walls, ceilings, cabinets, and other woodwork. Keep in mind that wood cabinets don't like harsh detergents or water. Work quickly and dry the surface immediately. If you intend to paint cabinets, they need special attention (see "Repairing and Preparing to Recoat Painted Wood" later in this chapter).

In addition to the dust and dirt you may find in any room, bathrooms often have mold or mildew stains. These living critters thrive on warm, moist surfaces. Give the bathroom the same general cleaning that you would any other room, but if you just wash away mildew stains, they will return. To kill mildew, try a solution of 1 part household bleach and 3 parts water. Sponge or spray the solution on and let it sit for at least 15 minutes. Repeat the process if necessary until the stain is completely gone.

Bleach is not good for painted surfaces, so after it has done the deed on the mildew, stop the bleaching action by rinsing the surface well with a neutralizer such as clean water or a vinegar and water solution.

Bleach is caustic and splashes easily, especially when working overhead. It also can ruin your clothes, bath linens, and your day. Wear goggles, rubber gloves, and your spouse's clothes.

Selecting Prep Tools and Supplies

When all the surfaces are clean, the next step is to repair any dings and fill holes so that they will not be visible under a fresh coat of paint. Don't assume that paint will hide imperfections. In fact, the opposite is usually true. For typical plaster or drywall repairs, you need only a few basic tools.

> ✓ **Putty knife:** A putty knife is useful for minor scraping of loose paint and for applying spackling compound, wood fillers, or joint compound to nail holes and other small imperfections.

✔ **Taping knife:** A 5- or 6-inch-wide taping knife is the standard tool for applying reinforcing paper tape over drywall joints and plaster cracks and for spackling nail dimples and small holes.

✔ **Caulk gun:** Get a caulk gun with a quick release button that stops the flow of caulk when you press it.

✔ **Spackling compound:** Available in very small cans, premixed spackling compound fills nail holes and other minor imperfections.

✔ **Joint compound:** This product is available in two premixed versions (regular and lightweight). The lightweight is faster drying but does not dry as hard, so we suggest the regular type. Joint compound is also available in powder form. Although much less convenient, you get longer lasting results patching cracks in plaster if you use the dry mix compound with perforated paper reinforcing tape.

✔ **Reinforcing tape:** There are two types. *Self-adhering fiberglass mesh* is convenient and easier to use for do-it-yourselfers that have little taping experience. Although some people claim it is stronger, pros rarely use it. *Paper reinforcing tape* is superior for repairing cracks in plaster.

Clearing the Way

If you've ever moved, you know what a great opportunity it is to follow up on those New Year's resolutions to get rid of unnecessary possessions and cut down on the clutter. Well, pretend you're moving as you empty a room for painting. The idea is to clear the room as much as possible so that you have free and easy access. Move out all the furniture that you can. You may want to leave that tank of a sofa bed or other large pieces that may ding your walls or woodwork when you move items out or (worse) back in after you paint. Just make sure that everything remaining is in the center of the room and out of the way. You need room to move a ladder around and enough floor space for your paint setup — and make sure that you can reach the entire ceiling, too.

Go through the following checklist to get your room ready for the big makeover.

✔ Take down pictures and other wall hangings. If you plan to return them to the original location when you're done painting, leave the picture hooks in place. If it's time for a change, carefully pull the nails straight out at the same angle they went in. If you have plaster walls, twist them out with a pair of pliers to avoid chipping out the plaster.

✔ If it's a very large room, stack the furniture in two areas with space between them. In a smaller room, pile everything in the center, at least three feet away from the walls. Cover all furniture with plastic drop cloths.

✔ Remove any area rugs. Put plastic drop cloths under your paint supply and mixing area, but cover the floor with quality canvas drop cloths, which are less slippery to walk on than plastic ones.

✔ Minimize the amount of tedious work painting around electrical switch plates and receptacle covers. Remove them and place a strip of wide masking tape over the switches and receptacles to protect them. Also remove or lower light fixtures. Keep all the small parts together in a shoebox or similar container.

✔ If you're painting any doors, mask the hardware or remove it. It takes less time to remove and replace hardware than it does to paint around it, and you eliminate unsightly goofs and don't waste time cleaning paint off hardware.

✔ Even if you're painting during the day, you need good electric lighting and may need power for tools, so plug an extension cord into a nearby room or hallway and bring power to the room.

Before you remove outlet covers or light fixtures, shut off the power at the circuit breaker. Remember, wall receptacles and lights are usually on different circuits. Double-check that the power is off by using a neon circuit tester or plugging in a lamp or other electrical device that you know is working. Place tape over the breaker as a reminder to others that the power is off.

Smoothing the Walls

After you take down all the pictures and remove or cover the furniture, it's time to repair damage to the walls. Some defects are all too obvious, like door knob puncture. Other trouble spots seem to show up only when you thought that you were done with the preparation work and are all geared up for painting. The best way to spot all the problems is to shine a bright light across the wall at a sharp angle (called *side lighting*) and to mark areas that need attention with a lightly penciled circle.

Note: Major wall and ceiling repairs are beyond the scope of this book. If you have a hole that's bigger than a football, check out *Home Improvement For Dummies*.

Making minor drywall repairs

Typically, you have a few minor dings or nail holes that you need to repair. Buy a small container of spackling compound and apply it with a putty knife. When it's dry, sand the patch smooth with fine sandpaper on a rubber or padded sanding block. Because spackling compounds tend to shrink, you may need to add another coat to fill a remaining indentation.

Another situation you may face, called *popped nails,* describes an all-too-common problem with drywall installation in which the nails, which were originally set below the surface *(countersunk)* and concealed with joint compound, pop out enough to make a bump or even break the surface.

Popped nails are generally caused by the movement of framing lumber that is of poor quality or too wet; by the installer's failure to hold the drywall against the studs when nailing it; or by the use of nails that are the wrong kind or size.

Whatever may cause these nails to pop up to the surface, there is a four-step solution to correct this problem.

1. **Secure the drywall tightly to the framing with new nails or, better yet, drywall screws, one on each side of the popped nail, as shown in Figure 10-1.**

   On walls, studs are vertical, so drive fasteners above and below the popped nail. On a ceiling, you can usually tell which way the framing is running by the line of popped nails or by tapping lightly. A tap sounds hollow between framing and more solid on the framing.

Figure 10-1: Press drywall against the framing as you drive two fasteners on each side of the popped nail.

2. **Drive the popped nail back where it belongs.**

   Because the new fasteners will be doing all the work, the popped nail should stay put this time. Both the new fastener and the popped nail should be driven so that they are just below the surface but do not break the paper facing of the drywall.

3. **Apply two or three coats of joint compound to conceal the fasteners and dimpled areas around them. See Figure 10-2.**

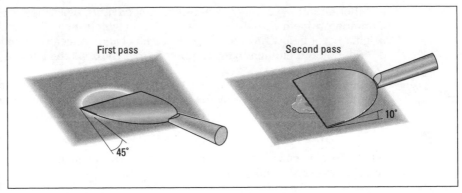

Figure 10-2:
Apply two or three coats of joint compound with two strokes perpendicular to each other.

First pass

Second pass

45°

10°

Scoop a glob of compound onto a 5- or 6-inch taping knife. Apply it to the wall with the knife held at about a 45-degree angle to the surface. Then draw a clean knife across the patch in a direction perpendicular to the first pass and with the knife nearly flat against the wall. Allow the compound to dry (anywhere from a few hours to overnight, depending on the humidity) and apply another coat.

4. **When the compound dries, sand the area smooth with fine sandpaper on a sanding block.**

Surface cracks at the joint of corners may be due to the buildup of taping compound or paint. These hairline cracks are in the excessively thick material and do not extend through the reinforcing tape itself. To repair these surface cracks, fold a piece of sandpaper over the blade of a 6-inch taping knife or over the corner of a block of wood and carefully sand away the excess material. Do not sand through the reinforcing tape. Clue: If you see daylight, you've sanded too deeply.

Repairing cracks in plaster walls and ceilings

Back in the years B.D. (before drywall), one common way to form walls was to put plaster directly onto wooden slats or a wire mesh (called lath backing). If you have an older home with plaster walls, you can apply spackling compound over small holes with the same technique we describe in the precious section. For minor cracks, which have the nasty habit of reappearing in a year or two (sort of that *déjà vu* all over again thing), try this method, which we picked up from the nation's leading plaster and drywall manufacturer.

For starters, use *paper* reinforcing tape and *dry* joint compound (the kind you mix with water, not the premixed stuff). This combination, the manufacturer says, offers the greatest strength and surface bonding. We tried it on a ceiling that had cracked repeatedly, and to date, no cracks have reappeared.

We make no such guarantees for your cracks, but here's what we did:

1. **Scrape out any loose or protruding materials by dragging a can opener or old screwdriver along the crack; then blow out or vacuum the dust and mist the crack with water.**

   Misting helps to prevent the dry plaster from sucking all the moisture out of the patching material and may improve the bond. It may not be necessary, but it's easy to do . . . and every little bit helps!

2. **Mix Durabond 90 or a similar dry joint compound in a large plastic bucket with water according to package instructions.**

   One of those premixed joint compound buckets you have left over from the last attempted repair should do nicely!

3. **Use a 6-inch taping knife to apply a bed of compound all along the crack.**

4. **Embed perforated paper reinforcing tape into the wet compound and scrape the taping knife along the tape to level the material and squeeze out the excess, as shown in Figure 10-3.**

   Do not attempt to scrape out every bit of compound from under the tape or the tape won't stick. Just make it smooth and level.

5. **When the first application is dry, scrape off any loose bits of dried compound with your taping knife. Then apply another smoothing coat of compound over the tape.**

   If you have a 10-inch knife, use it, otherwise use the 6-inch knife to smooth on a thin, 10-inch-wide coat.

6. **When the second coat of compound dries, scrape off any loose bits of compound and sand lightly with a pole sander.**

   Be careful not to sand into the reinforcing tape or you will make it fuzzy, and you don't want fuzzy tape now, do you?

   When sanding, put a fan in an open window. Open another window in a nearby room. Set the fan to *exhaust,* and no dust will migrate to other parts of the house.

Figure 10-3:
Apply compound over the crack and embed the paper tape. Apply a second smoothing coat (left); then apply a final smoothing coat (right).

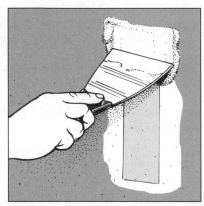
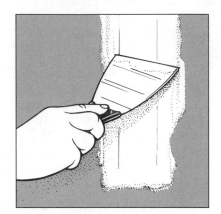

7. Repeat Steps 3 through 6 for a third, hopefully final, coat that is a few inches wider than the second.

Dry compound dries faster and harder than the ready-mix variety you may be familiar with. When you use dry compound, cleaning tools is easier if you wash them off while the material is still wet.

You can't expect to cover a patched area with a single topcoat of paint. Your best bet is to prime the patched area only with the finish paint and, when that's dry, apply a topcoat over the entire surface.

If your plaster walls or ceilings have large structural cracks or large holes, or sections are sagging or have come loose from the lath backing, check out our coverage of these repairs in *Home Improvement For Dummies*.

Repairing and Preparing to Recoat Painted Wood

Woodwork is one of those "details that make a difference," as designers describe what distinguishes an ordinary room from an extraordinary one. Woodwork is designed to catch the eye and if it doesn't look good, the whole room can look shabby even if the walls and ceiling are perfect. In this section, we describe how to make your woodwork look new again.

If the wood is chipped, gouged, or otherwise damaged and you plan to paint, you can make an easy, invisible repair by using a two-part polyester resin compound as follows:

1. **Clean out any loose material and scrape off any finish so that the patching material will bond better.**

2. **Mix the hardener (part one) with the filler (part two) as directed and apply it with a putty knife.**

   Generally, overfill the hole.

3. **Use a rasp or Surform tool to shape or level the material as soon as it sets up hard but before it cures (dries) completely.**

4. **When the material is fully cured, sand the patch to smooth and blend it in with the surrounding area.**

5. **Apply a primer to the patch and any bare wood before you paint.**

Making paint stick to paneling and cabinets

Getting rid of dark paneling is complicated by the fact that when you pull it off, the adhesive remaining has ruined the drywall underneath. For this reason, many folks turn to paint. Factory finished wood cabinets and paneling require special preparation for painting. To assure that the paint adheres properly to factory-finished panels or to waxed or varnished board paneling, take these steps:

1. **Clean the wood especially well to remove dirt, grease, and wax.**

   For paneling, use a solution made of equal parts of household ammonia and water. For cabinets and paneling that are beyond cleaning with a mild detergent solution, try a solvent such as mineral spirits.

2. **Take the shine off the surface with a chemical deglosser or by sanding lightly.**

   If you sand the wood, put an exhaust fan in the window of the work area and open a nearby window outside the room. The fan prevents sanding dust from going anywhere but outdoors.

   Use a chemical deglosser and/or sand lightly, but remember to apply paint within a half-hour or the deglosser loses its effectiveness. Apply a thorough coat of deglosser on varnish or polyurethane finishes.

3. **Wipe the surface well with a *tack cloth*, a sticky cheesecloth for removing sanding dust that's available where paint is sold.**

   The oil in tack cloths may interfere with proper adhesion of latex finishes. If you're planning to use latex, just use a cloth slightly dampened with mineral spirits or water.

4. **Finally, prime the wood.**

   Mix a bonding additive to your primer or use an alcohol-based primer-sealer or other special bonding primer, tinted to the approximate color of the topcoat. See Chapter 4 for advice on choosing the additive, primer, and topcoat.

If you're planning to paint cabinets, remove the handles or pulls so that you don't have to paint around them.

Toiling with wooden windows

The amount of work required to prepare windows for painting can vary from a good cleaning to everything short of replacement. In this section, we take a look at the most common problems and their solutions.

One problem that you may encounter is a sash in a double-hung window that has become stuck. You can solve this problem by using a *paint zipper,* a serrated tool designed to cut a paint film between the formerly movable sash and its channel.

Improper painting technique also contributes to another window problem — peeling paint where the wood meets the glass. Failure to create a paint seal between the gloss and the wood allows condensation and window-cleaning chemicals to seep into the joint. To remove loose paint, follow these steps:

1. **Scrape or sand such areas to remove loose paint.**

   Wrapping the sandpaper over the edge of a putty knife makes it easier to sand up close to the glass without scratching it.

2. **Apply a stain-killing primer to water-stained wood before applying the topcoat.**

   Avoid this problem in the future by using proper window-painting techniques, which are described in Chapter 11.

When old-fashioned double-hung windows need painting, you should also replace ropes (or replace an old-fashioned rope-and-pulley system with a more modern counterbalance mechanism). To do so, you must remove the sash. This and other window repairs are covered in greater detail in *Home Improvement For Dummies.*

Dealing with doors

Some doors require a significant amount of prep work. Often, taking them down and working on a sawhorse is easier than working with a hung door.

To remove a door for such work (or for painting later), follow these steps:

1. **Slip a wedge loosely under the latch side of the half-open door, especially a heavy exterior door.**

2. **Tap out the hinge pins.**

    Insert a nail into the bottom of the barrel — you may need to remove a snap-on cover – and tap it partially out with a hammer. Then use a screwdriver to tap it out the rest of the way from the top of the barrel. Always remove the lower hinge pins first. As you remove the upper hinge, grasp the door to prevent it from falling, and pull it straight away from the hinges.

Whether you remove a door or not, we find that it's easier to remove the lock set than to paint around it (or over it!). Designs vary. With one type you must depress the *locking spring* and pull off the handle; with another you need to loosen a screw in the face of the *rose* (the trim around the knob) and unscrew the handle. Then remove the two screws (if any) that hold the locking mechanism in the door. Finally, unscrew the strike plate from the jamb.

Making Final Preparations

If you've read the other sections in this chapter, you're probably getting anxious to paint. However, don't make the mistake of thinking that skipping things like priming and sealing, caulking cracks, back-prepping, and masking saves time and work. On the contrary, in the long run you're just creating more work for yourself.

Priming and sealing

Some people don't include applying a primer or sealer in their definition of painting. Priming and sealing are processes that fall somewhere between tasks that are clearly preparation and the actual job of applying a topcoat of paint. Perhaps it's a matter of semantics, but we tend to think of priming and sealing as preparation when they're associated with these spot repairs, and as painting when those jobs involve new construction. (The president's press secretary couldn't have done any better fence sitting than that!)

Spot priming improves the bond of the topcoat to surfaces such as bare wood and metal. It also seals the surface of unfinished or patched areas so that they will absorb topcoats to the same degree that surrounding areas do. If you try to just topcoat, the patch area will have less sheen than the area around it, making the patch more noticeable. This advice applies to patches and repairs to drywall, plaster, and trim. Therefore, spot prime these areas, being careful to feather the edges of the paint into the surrounding areas.

See Chapter 5 for feathering and other painting techniques. For information on how to prepare previously wallpapered surfaces for paint or wallpaper, refer to Chapter 15.

Sealing cracks with caulk

Caulk covers a multitude of sins and prevents many problems from occurring. *Caulk* has a consistency like thick toothpaste, which makes it easy to spread and fill small holes and narrow cracks. When it dries, it becomes firm but remains flexible, and can tolerate movement between materials that expand or contract or otherwise move in relation to one another. You can find a caulk for virtually every combination of materials; but if you're painting, choose a quality paintable acrylic latex caulk or a siliconized acrylic latex caulk. Buy it in cartridge form to fit in a caulking gun.

Cracks show up better after priming and caulk adheres better to primed wood, so complete any priming before you caulk. For a neat job, caulk all joints. Caulk all the joints between trim and wall surfaces to prevent penetration of moisture vapor into walls.

Cut the tips of two tubes of caulk. Cut a very small opening in one tube and use it for narrow cracks at nearly all joints between the woodwork and walls or between different trim members such as window stops and frame joints. Cut the tip of the second tube with a larger opening for caulking wider cracks.

Apply caulk by squeezing the trigger as you either push or pull the tip along the joint. Use as little caulk as needed to fill the crack, or the excess will spread out onto surface and become visible. Use a wet fingertip to fill very small holes and to smooth the caulk. Allow adequate curing time according to label instructions before you paint.

Backprepping

You'll hear a few terms in painting that include the word *back,* such as *backpriming* (priming the back side of siding and trim), *backbrushing* (brushing out paint that has been applied with a sprayer or roller), and, "Oy, my back is killing me." For the lack of a better term, we use the term *backprepping* to describe the process of taking a final look after prepping is complete to catch and correct any missed problems.

Imperfections show up best lighted from the side. Shine a bright light across the surface, as you did in the initial inspection. Look for drips, brush bristles, roller fuzz, or other surface irregularities left by the last painter. Check any patched areas to be sure that you feathered the edges of the finish to blend.

Masking saves time

Take a little time to mask areas that you don't want to paint. For masking windows, see Chapter 11. The materials available go far beyond masking tape. Here are a couple that we like:

- ✓ **Painter's tape:** This blue tape, available in various widths and in disposable dispensers, is specially designed for masking. It seals well but comes off much easier than regular masking tape.

- ✓ **Pretaped masking paper or plastic:** The self-stick edges adhere to surfaces such as the tops of window and door trim for a straight painting edge. The paper or plastic, which ranges in width from a couple inches to many feet, drapes the surface. The seal is not as reliable as that of painter's tape.

Don't use regular masking tape, which has too much adhesive, making it harder to remove. Paint bleeds under regular masking tape more easily, creating a rougher edge.

After you apply painter's tape or other masking systems, keep these tips in mind:

- ✓ **Press the edge with a putty knife, a block of wood, or another hard material to seal the edges.** This prevents paint from bleeding under the tape.

- ✓ **Remove masking tape as soon as the paint has dried to the touch.** Generally, you should wait three to four hours but not more than 24 hours. It's especially important not to leave the tape on any longer than 24 hours if the sun might bake the tape on or if the tape might get wet.

- ✓ **When you remove the tape, slowly peel the tape back at an angle away from the painted surface.** Do this to avoid peeling off the freshly applied paint with the tape.

When you plan to paint walls and ceilings, consider masking any or all of the following areas:

- ✓ The tops of base moldings
- ✓ The tops of windows and door casings
- ✓ The tops of chair rail moldings
- ✓ The tops of baseboard heating trim
- ✓ Heating or air conditioning grilles that you cannot remove
- ✓ Around the base of any wall- or ceiling-mounted light fixtures

Pretaped paper or plastic systems are handy when it comes to protecting the area below a chair rail molding if you're not painting it the same color as the wall above, or for covering the face of baseboard heaters.

When painting or finishing each of the following areas, follow these masking recommendations:

- ✔ Mask hardwood flooring at baseboards when painting baseboards
- ✔ Mask baseboards when finishing or painting flooring
- ✔ Mask all hinges and other hardware when painting doors and windows
- ✔ Mask walls when painting baseboard heating trim

Sanding stripped or unfinished wood

Sanding is no one's idea of fun, but you must smooth new wood or wood that has been stripped of its finish before you can apply a stain or finish. Sand out any imperfections such as deep scratches, tooling marks, or an overall rough or fuzzy surface. In addition to removing imperfections and making the wood look and feel smooth, sanding also takes off a very thin top layer of wood, enabling stains and other finishes to penetrate more evenly.

Start with 120-grit (fine) paper. If you need to remove deep scratches, start with 80-grit (medium) or even 60-grit (coarse). Work your way up to at least 150-grit, and preferably 220-grit, making sure at each stage that all scratches left by the coarser grit sandpaper are removed. Most do-it-yourselfers switch to the next finer grit paper or stop sanding long before a professional would.

Smoothing by hand or with a power sander

Whenever possible, use a sanding block or pad that conforms to the shape of the surface being sanded: flat for flat surfaces, concave for outwardly curving profiles, and so on. Holding the sandpaper in your hand usually produces uneven results because you exert more pressure in some places than you do in others. Just as foam sanding pads are available that conform to irregular surfaces for hand sanding, accessory pads are available that conform to gently curving surfaces for some finishing sanders. If you have a lot of detail work to do, such as when refinishing the moldings in many rooms, you may want to purchase a profile sander, which has a variety of rubber sanding block attachments to conform to irregular surfaces.

An *electric palm sander* and its more aggressive cousin, the *random orbit sander,* are both finishing sanders that make smooth wood faster — a lot faster — than sanding by hand. These power sanders are ideal for smoothing flat surfaces such as wide baseboards and tabletops. A palm sander costs $30 or more but is well worth the investment. You not only save time and effort but also do a better job. Somehow, when you're hand sanding, you usually decide a lot sooner that the surface is smooth enough.

Exercise extreme caution when sanding veneered furniture or cabinets, especially when you're power sanding. Wood veneer is thin, sometimes very thin. You often don't have a clue that you're about to sand too far. Suddenly the material under the veneer, such as particleboard, just appears. Staining doesn't help to disguise the damage, and sometimes it just makes the damage stand out like a sore thumb. Also, keep in mind that sometimes what appears to be wood veneer is either a photographed plastic film or a very convincing plastic laminate — and neither can be sanded.

Knowing when enough is enough

To better gauge when you should move on to the next finer grade of sandpaper, try these trade secrets:

- Make a series of *light* pencil marks across the surface and sand the area until the pencil marks are all gone.
- Sidelight the surface to make imperfections more evident.
- Cover your hand with a sock or a pair of pantyhose and wipe it over the surface. The sock or hose will snag on rough spots.

The rule is to follow the grain of the wood as you sand. This means that you sand along the length of a board, rather than across it. If you sand across the grain, you will scratch the surface. However, if you must remove a lot of wood to get out deep scratches, start sanding on a *diagonal* to the grain until the imperfections are gone. Then sand with the grain until you remove all diagonal scratches.

Getting furniture-quality results

To achieve a super-smooth surface on a beautiful door, cabinets, or other wood that is new or has been stripped of its finish, try the following furniture maker's method for your final sanding:

1. **Wipe down the surface with water or denatured alcohol to intentionally raise the grain; it will feel peach-fuzzy.**

2. **Sand the fuzzy surface until it's smooth.**

3. **Repeat wetting and sanding one or two more times. With most woods, you will find that the grain no longer raises after repeated sanding.**

Another trick that furniture makers use is to apply a liberal coat of a clear *sanding sealer,* a liquid product available at hardware stores and paint outlets that you brush or roll on before the final sanding.

Sanding to a super smooth surface with open-grained woods, such as oak, is especially difficult. You need to fill the wood pores. Woodworking specialty shops and mail-order outlets sell special grain fillers in a variety of wood tones for the purpose. Apply the filler by rubbing it on with a rag across the grain. As it starts to dry, rub off the excess, at first across the grain and then with the grain. Press hard at each stage to force the filler into the open-grained surface. Filling the grain is not necessary if you are planning a wax finish because the wax itself will do the job nicely.

Use sanding sealers and filler only *after* you apply stain.

Part IV
Painting and Finishing, Inside and Out

The 5th Wave   By Rich Tennant

"Honey— can you toss me the bug spray, quickly? I think I disturbed something in the gutter."

In this part . . .

Now's the time to reap the rewards of all your preparation. Painting and finishing goes fast and with every brushstroke things start looking as they did in your mind's eye.

With a general understanding of painting materials, tools, and techniques, this part walks you through the actual process of painting your house. On the outside, from the siding to windows and doors; on the inside, from the floor to the ceiling and everything in between. And if you want to give your projects a special touch, turn to the chapter on decorative finishes. You'll be amazed by what you can do.

The Color Wheel

The color wheel, a tool for artists and designers (and you), contains 12 basic colors from which all others are derived. Paint colors are complex formulas that typically contain many colors. You're not likely to choose one of these pure colors for the walls of a room or the outside of your house. The color wheel can help you, however, to understand the relationships between colors (shown on the next page) and ultimately help you choose the colors that work to create the effects you want.

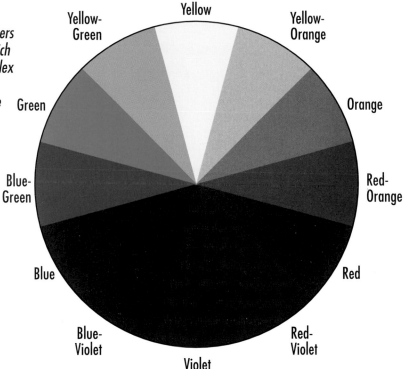

Make Your Own

You can find color wheels in art theory books, but a hands-on approach — crafting your own — makes the learning a lot more fun and the understanding more intuitive.

Starting with a blank piece of white paper, draw or trace a circle. Using the three primary colors (red, yellow, and blue), dab a bit of each color on the perimeter of the circle, spacing them equally around the circumference. With the paint still wet, mix an equal part of two primaries and place a large dab of that secondary color between those two primaries. Do the same for the other two pairs of primaries and then follow the same principal to mix and locate the tertiary colors.

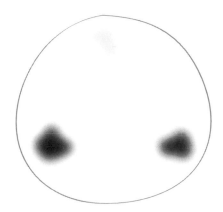

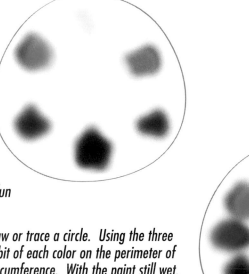

All the Colors of the Rainbow and Then Some

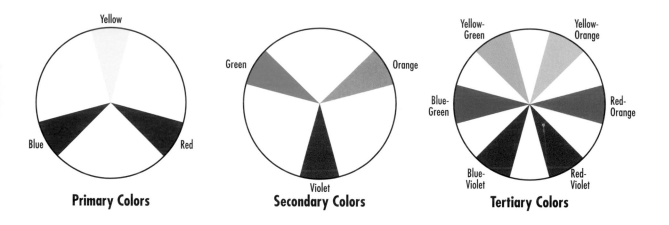

Primary Colors

Yellow
Blue
Red

Secondary Colors

Green
Orange
Violet

Tertiary Colors

Yellow-Green
Yellow-Orange
Blue-Green
Red-Orange
Blue-Violet
Red-Violet

Harmony Guaranteed: Related and Complementary Colors

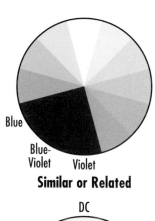

Blue
Blue-Violet
Violet

Similar or Related

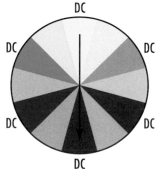

DC
DC
DC
DC
DC
DC

Direct complementary

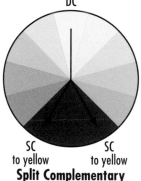

DC
SC to yellow
SC to yellow

Split Complementary

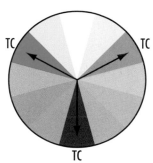

TC
TC
TC

Triad complementary

Use the color wheel to quickly determine colors that go together. Related colors blend well together. Complementary colors provide increased contrast in varying degrees. Harmonious colors fall into four general categories:

Similar or related colors fall next to each other on the color wheel, such as blue, blue-violet, and violet. Analogous color schemes make use of similar colors.

Direct complementary colors fall directly opposite each other, such as yellow and violet, red and green, or orange and blue, and are always good choices for two-color schemes.

Split complementary colors include any one color and the two colors adjacent to its direct complementary color. Because two of the colors are only one color apart on the wheel, they would also be considered similar colors. You could use these colors on the larger elements in a room like the walls and floor, while the third color would make an attractive accent color.

Triad complementary colors are any three colors equidistant from each other on the wheel, such as yellow, blue-violet, and red-violet. Any two, or all three together, work well.

The Effects of Color

Light

Dark

Warm

Cool

The color that you paint a room impacts the perceived size of the room — and doing it with paint is a lot cheaper than other decorating changes and certainly easier than moving walls and ceilings. Cool colors (those toward the blue end of the color spectrum) tend to make a room seem larger. Warm colors (the beiges, reds, and golds) make a space seem smaller and more intimate. Similarly light colors, which reflect more light than dark colors, make a room feel more spacious.

Photo: © Crandall & Crandall   Design: Susan White Design

Decorative Painting

Ragging

These two pages show how a little creativity in the way paint is applied can go a long way in making a room look spectacular.

Photo: © Crandall & Crandall   Design: Rathfon Designs

Photo: © Crandall & Crandall   Design: Kitchens Del Mar

Pickling

Martin Senour Paints 1-800-MSP-5270

Stenciling

Finishes

Photo: © Crandall & Crandall   Architect: Powell Design Group   Trompe L'Oeil: The Wall Works

Photo: © Crandall & Crandall   Design: Judy Ramazzina

Color Wash

Sponging

Martin Senour Paints 1-800-MSP-5270

A combination of techniques: Ragging and stenciling

Each project is uniquely yours and the best thing about many of the techniques is that they are simple to do and very forgiving.

Common Paint Problems

Alligatoring: Paint film can crackle in an alligator pattern when an inflexible coating, such as alkyd enamel, is applied over a more flexible coating, such as latex primer. This problem can also result if you apply a topcoat (finish coat) before the primer has dried. And sometimes alligatoring simply happens as paint ages and loses its elasticity. Remove all the paint; apply primer; and apply a new topcoat. See you later, alligator!

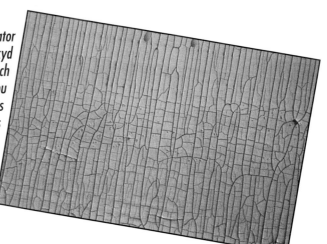

Blistering: Bubbles in the paint surface result when moisture tries to escape through exterior walls, when you paint in the direct sun, or when rain or dew falls on the surface too soon after painting. Locate the source of moisture; perhaps your roof leaks or you don't have or use a bathroom fan. Blistering may also happen when insulation is blown into the exterior walls of an old house. (This insulation lacks the paper facing or plastic sheeting that typically covers insulation and blocks moisture from flowing through the wall from inside.) Painting the interior walls with a vapor-retarding paint, careful caulking around baseboards, and sealing outlets with foam gaskets help stop moisture. Remove blisters by scraping and sanding. Apply primer and a topcoat.

Excessive chalking: Powdering of paint is a result of weathering. Chalking is a normal self-cleaning quality of some paints, but excessive chalking indicates that a poor-quality paint or an interior paint was used. Power wash or scrub residue off with a stiff-bristle brush and garden hose. Apply a primer and topcoat. Scrub stained masonry with a detergent solution or have it acid-washed.

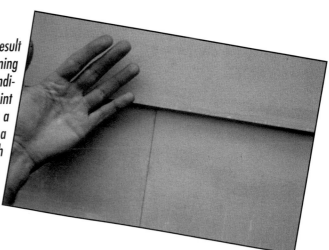

Cracking/flaking: Nothing says "Paint me" more than cracking paint that chips off in flakes. Latex paint can crack if it dries too quickly as a result of being applied in cold or windy weather. Poor surface preparation, failure to apply primer to bare wood, spreading the paint too thin, or poor-quality paint are other causes to consider. Scrape and sand to remove loose paint — or to bare wood, if necessary. Apply primer to bare surfaces and then apply a topcoat.

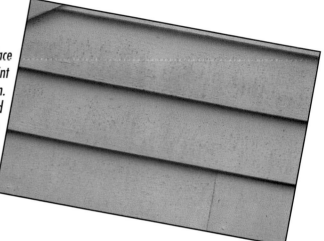

Mildew: Black spots may appear on the paint surface due to dampness and a lack of sunlight. Poor-quality paint or not using a mildewcide additive aggravates the problem. Recurring mildew may also be due to failure to kill and remove the mildew prior to repainting. Remove all the mildew with a household bleach/water solution, using a 1-to-3 ratio, or power wash with a commercial cleaning product containing bleach. Rinse. Apply a topcoat.

Nail-head rusting: These stains are caused by the failure of the galvanized coating (a rust-preventative treatment) on nails due to sanding or chipping or by improper use of non-galvanized nails. (They must be driven below the surface with a nail set [countersunk] and then filled.) Sand and countersink nail heads, wash off stains, and seal with acrylic or paintable silicone caulk.

Peeling: Paint can peel in one layer or several layers. Causes include inadequate preparation, caulk failure or leaks, interior moisture that gets trapped behind oil-based paint as it seeks drier outdoor air, blistering that was not remedied, or the application of alkyd paint over a damp surface. Correct the problem and then scrape, sand, prime, and paint as needed.

The World of Wallpaper

In the clean design of this bedroom, bold vertical stripes heighten the ceiling and the border nicely outlines the space.

Thibaut Wallcoverings & Fabrics

Thibaut Wallcoverings & Fabrics

Here the warm floral pattern on the fabric and walls create a striking contrast with the painted wainscoting in this dining room.

Chapter 11

On the Outside Looking In: Painting the Exterior of Your Home

*Y*ou've done your homework and you chose just the right finish and color for your house exterior. You've worked hard to repair and prepare the surfaces. But now you're having a hard time keeping your enthusiasm, we know. Your house, which didn't look all that bad to start, now looks terrible, stripped of shutters and other decorative touches and scraped and sanded everywhere.

Well, cheer up! Now comes the relatively easy part — applying the paint. The work goes quickly, and seeing the house transformed before your eyes is very satisfying. This chapter guides you through this final stage, starting off on a safety note.

Focusing on Exterior Safety

Exterior house painting presents a special set of safety issues relating to ladders, stinging insects, incoming power lines, and physical endurance. We discuss those concerns in this section, but don't forget to refer to Chapter 2 for general safety information (especially on ladders) that applies whether you're working indoors or outdoors.

Using ladders safely outdoors

When painting a house exterior, you can reach the top sections of the job by using ladders of various heights. In addition to the standard step and extension ladders, many special-purpose ladders are available. Some ladders can be used as both stepladders and straight ladders or even as scaffolds.

As tedious as it is to have to stop repeatedly so that you can move the ladder, never try to overreach. When using a stepladder, the trunk of your body must remain entirely within the rails of the ladder. If you use an extension ladder, a good safety practice is to crook the elbow of your free arm around the rail of the ladder (for example, your left arm around the left rail), and reach out with the free arm only as far as this grip allows.

Always open a stepladder fully and lock the braces in place before climbing on it. Don't lean an unopened stepladder against a wall.

Set up your extension ladder so that the bottom is the proper distance away from the house wall — approximately one-fourth the working length of the ladder. Ladder rungs are spaced 1 foot apart, so just count the number of rungs from the bottom to the point where the ladder rests against the house to determine its *working length*. Divide that number by four to determine how far from the wall the bottom must be positioned.

Take time before you start a big job to make sure your ladders are in good operating condition. In most cases if a ladder is bent, cracked, or otherwise damaged, it should be taken to recycling (aluminum) or discarded. Use a spray lubricant on all moving, metal-to-metal parts, but be sure to wipe off any lubricant that gets on the rungs.

Several ladder accessories can make your work easier and safer. Although an accessory from one manufacturer may work for a ladder made by another, your safest bet is to buy ladders and accessories from the same manufacturer. You may find some of the following accessories helpful:

- A *stabilizer* (or *stand off*), shown in Figure 11-1, serves several purposes. It gives the ladder more lateral stability, and it allows you to center a ladder over a window so that you can paint the entire window without moving the ladder. In addition, if your house has roof overhangs, it stands the ladder off the wall so that you can safely paint the overhang without bending backwards.

- *Scaffolding* allows you access to a wider area. You can use two ladders to support a scaffold plank (see Figure 11-1). The equipment is available at tool rental outlets. A wood or aluminum plank sits on a pair of *ladder jacks,* which hook onto the rungs of each ladder. Although this setup is relatively safe at low to moderate heights, we don't recommend it for second-story work. Without guard rails or fall-arrest protection, such as a safety harness, you could fall. These protections just aren't feasible for do-it-yourselfers.

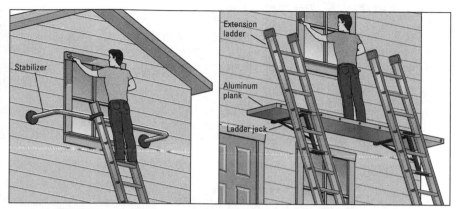

Figure 11-1:
A stabilizer spans windows and positions you to paint roof overhangs safely, while a ladderjack scaffold lets you paint a wide area.

✔ *Automatic levelers* let you quickly set an extension ladder with secure footing on uneven surfaces. Without them, you need to dig out the area under a rail or build it up with lumber — which takes more time. Avoid unsafe jury-rigged setups, such as stones or too small wood blocks.

More safety reminders

Use extreme caution around electrical service lines, especially if you are using an aluminum ladder. Don't forget to look for them when moving a ladder. Also make sure that you get help moving a heavy extension ladder so that you are in full control of it, and not the other way around.

We're warning you now: Expect bees, wasps, or bats to fly out of cracks in the roof soffits. Keep one hand on the ladder so that when you're startled you're less likely to fall. You can't run, so protect yourself with a long-sleeved shirt, long pants, and a hat or painter's hood. Tap suspicious areas with a broom handle before you get too close, and use wasp spray that you can aim from a safe distance.

Don't assume that you have good ventilation just because you're outdoors. There may be little or no air movement on an inside corner of a house. If you're working in such areas with products that suggest application in "a well-ventilated area," wear a respirator.

Don't overdo it on a hot day. Drink plenty of water (or, better yet, a sports drink) and take breaks to avoid heat exhaustion.

Weather Permitting

Coordinating an exterior paint job with the weather and your schedule can be quite difficult in some parts of the country. First, you must wait for warm weather to allow a house to dry out after winter and early spring. Most paints and other finishes require that the temperature be at least 50 degrees and preferably above 60 degrees Fahrenheit. Next, you need at least a couple days of sunny weather to dry the house after any rain or power-washing. You need another good day if you are priming. Finally, you need a nice day to apply the topcoat; an ideal day is one with temperatures between 60 and 85 degrees Fahrenheit and no wind.

Some differences between latex and alkyd (oil-based) finishes may affect your decision of when to paint. While most alkyd finishes can be applied even if rain is expected within a few hours, don't try it with latex finishes. And if the surface is already damp, latex can be applied on a slightly damp surface, but you're asking for paint blisters if you try it with an alkyd.

Whatever type of paint you use, allow the specified drying time between coats — or more if the weather is cool or humid. If the topcoat is applied over a primer too soon, paint failures, such as alligatoring and blistering, will occur.

 Follow the sun — when painting, that is. The best time to paint a surface is after it has been warmed by the sun but is no longer in direct sunlight. If you paint a hot surface, the paint dries too quickly. Then, as you go back to adjacent areas, you end up brushing over paint that has begun to dry. The result is distinct *lap* or brush marks. Painting in the direct sun may also cause a variety of more serious failures, including cracking, flaking, blistering, or wrinkling — and that's just on the back of your neck; direct sun isn't good for the paint, either.

 Avoid painting or applying any surface coating outdoors on a breezy day. Windborne mold spores, pollen, dirt, flying bugs, and other types of debris lodge in the wet paint. The wind may also dry latex paint too fast, causing the finish to crack or flake.

Planning Your Painting Sequence

In most cases, you should paint the body of the house first and then make another pass to paint the trim, windows, and doors. (As you paint the trim, you automatically cover any areas on the trim that were inadvertently painted with siding paint.) Use a large brush, roller, or sprayer on the body of the house. For the trim, however, use a smaller brush, such as an angled sash brush, that helps you paint with more precision. Paint from the top down to minimize touch-ups for those inevitable drips or other goofs.

Time is money to the pros, so they plan their ladder moves carefully. They plan their work by painting everything within reach at one time: siding, trim, gutters, and all, even if they are using different colors or types of paint. The harder the setup, the more advisable this approach may be. This technique is a no-brainer if you are using scaffolds or trying to maneuver around shrubs and level the ground to properly set up a 30-foot extension ladder so that you can access a roof peak. But at lower heights, with less setup, follow the siding-first rule.

Making Last Minute Preparations

Once you get the brush out, you don't want to stop to remove light fixtures or hardware or take time to tie back a bush that's in the way. Before you start to paint, make sure that your path is clear and that you have removed everything in the way. See Chapter 9 for more final preparations steps.

To avoid paint drips on screens in storm windows on combination storm windows, remove them or slide them in their tracks so they're concealed. If there's a screened porch, take out those screens that are removable and drape plastic drop cloths over those in place.

Always place drop cloths below the area where you are painting. This task takes only a moment and may save a great deal of cleanup time. Use canvas drop cloths or buy heavy paper drop cloths to cover walks, drives, porches, and patios that abut the house. Plastic drop cloths are slippery when walked on, especially when they're wet.

Tooling Up for the Job

To apply paint or stain, choose from any of the paint application tools, including brushes, pads, and rollers. Refer to Chapter 5 for a description of the applicators and tips on buying and using them. For information on choosing and using spray equipment, refer to Chapter 6. The applicator that you need often depends on what you are painting and the type of finish you are using.

The paint pad, for example, is especially appropriate for painting siding because the top edge of the pad paints the bottom edges of the siding while the face of the pad paints the face of the siding. A stain brush holds watery stain better than a paint brush. If a roller cover is sized to suit the siding, laying the paint on with a roller can save a great deal of time. If you use a roller, go back with a brush to get the undersides and to remove the stippled texture left by the roller.

To thin or not to thin

Today's paint is ready to spread right out of the can, but when it is sprayed it requires thinning. The temptation is to overthin the paint, but you can avoid this problem by following the directions on the label.

Mineral spirits (paint thinner) is the best solvent for thinning alkyd paints, enamels, or varnishes. Use water to thin latex paint, but not necessarily tap water because if the water has heavy minerals, the colors will shift. In that case, use distilled water to thin latex paint.

Carry sandpaper, a scraper, a wire brush, wood putty, a putty knife, and caulk so that you can clean and patch any defects that you missed during preparation. Don't forget painter's rags to wipe off spatters and other goofs.

Invest in a pair of painter's pants or overalls so that you don't ruin your good clothes. They have convenient loops and pockets that allow you to carry all that stuff up the ladder. The tight-knit canvas clothes are made tough and snag-proof for climbing, and they are also designed to soak up paint spills so that paint doesn't reach your skin.

Spreading It On

You'll find an amazing amount of useful information on the paint label including its coverage rate per gallon, which varies by the job. Some of the variables are the condition of the old paint and the porosity and texture of the surface. Rough or dry surfaces absorb more finish than a smooth, sound base coat of paint. Most inexperienced painters tend to apply too little paint. Don't try to stretch the paint. Follow the spread rate suggested by the manufacturer, which is intended to provide full protection of the painted surface and to provide good *hide* (coverage) of the old paint color.

Be sure to mix paint well before you use it. It's difficult to do this in a full container even if you use a paint-mixing drill accessory. There may also be slight differences in color between the paint in one can and another, which won't be noticeable until after its too late (when it dries on the house). To overcome this problem, painters use a mixing process called *boxing* and you should, too. Mix at least two gallons together in a large container; then when you have used about a gallon, add a new gallon, and so on.

Before you carry that large can of paint up a ladder, think about the mess it will make if it falls. You're better off pouring about a quart of the paint — or just enough to cover the area within reach of the ladder — into a smaller can.

Priming the Surface

On most unpainted exterior surfaces, the standard procedure calls for a primer coat, followed by two topcoats of paint. (See Chapter 4 for information on choosing these finishes.) We also recommend this procedure for any painted surfaces that required significant scraping and repairs. However, you may be topcoating only because the surface is dull or because you want a new color or because your spouse has "suggested" that you do so. If that's the case and the existing paint is sound, a single coat of a "one-coat" acrylic latex paint applied properly offers adequate protection and coverage.

You can apply quality latex paints over any oil- or latex-painted surface that is in good shape. If the paint is sound, you generally need to prime only scraped or repaired areas. You can also use a stain-blocking primer in lieu of regular primer to seal knots in board siding or trim and to cover stains that you cannot remove, such as rust from nails.

The solution for rusty nailheads is not difficult, but it sure is tedious. You'll be tempted to just set and fill the holes, paint over them, and hope for the best. Unfortunately, the corrosion continues, and rust stains will probably bleed through the topcoat. The only right way to correct this problem is to use an awl or other pick to remove any caulk or glazing compound wherever rust stains are visible and set any nails that are exposed. Then use a stiff-bristle artist's brush to coat nailheads with a stain-blocking, rust-inhibiting metal primer before covering them with caulk or exterior spackling compound.

If you're applying latex paint over a glossy paint, play it safe and prime the entire house, even if you have sanded or treated the existing finish with a deglosser. A primer also may be required for hardboard siding (see Chapter 9 and "Painting hardboard siding" later in this chapter). As a general rule, use an alkyd primer and a latex topcoat when repainting.

Be sure that your primer is appropriate for the surface you're painting. Cedar and redwood, for example, usually require an oil-based primer to seal the surface so that tannin stains don't bleed through the topcoat. Also make sure that the primer and topcoat are compatible. How do you know? By telling your supplier what you are painting, by reading the label, and (although not always necessary) by using the same brand of primer and topcoat. To make it easier for the a colored topcoat to cover a primer, have the paint dealer tint the primer to the approximate color of the finish coat.

If you already have three or more coats of oil-based paint on the house, use alkyd house paint. Using latex may cause the old paint to lift off the substrate.

Painting Your (House) Body

Although your siding is certainly the largest area to paint, the work goes surprisingly fast, even if you are using a brush. And with a sprayer, you'll be moving so fast that you have to be careful not to bump into yourself! This is your reward for doing such a good prepping job.

Painting wood siding

Here are some tips for painting wood siding:

✔ **New or untreated wood siding:** New wood siding should be coated as soon after installation as possible. Untreated wood requires a primer and two topcoats, if painting, or two coats of stain. Previously untreated or bare redwood and cedar may bleed tannin through a paint finish unless the surface is sealed with an alkyd primer/sealer (preferably two coats) before applying a 100-percent latex topcoat.

✔ **Rough lumber:** Airless spraying works best for painting or staining rough surfaces, but the finish should be brushed as it is applied. Backbrushing, as this techniques is called, gets paint into areas that the roller misses and works the finish into the surface. Brushing also results in a more uniformly stained surface and gives you the chance to brush out drips and runs. New rough-sawn wood may snag roller and pad fabrics, but if the wood is already painted, you can use a roll and backbrush.

✔ **New, smooth wood:** Some new siding that is installed with the smooth side out doesn't accept stain well and sometimes is even too shiny for paint or *solid-color* stain, which is like thin paint. If you plan to use stain, you can have the wood siding installed with the rough side out. The smooth, sometimes shiny planed surface (called *mill glaze*) doesn't provide enough "tooth" for paint or solid color stain to grab onto. Sand off the mill glaze with 100-grit paper and then stain or paint. If you plan to use a *penetrating* stain, you can also let such siding weather for six months to a year and save the sanding work.

Painting hardboard siding

You can topcoat previously painted hardboard siding if the finish is clean and in excellent condition. The American Hardboard Association recommends using an alkyd primer if you are painting over the original factory finish or if you are unable to determine when the existing finish was applied. After cleaning and making any repairs (see Chapter 9), you need to use an alkyd primer to spot-prime any areas where the existing finish was removed.

Choosing finishes for decks

Unfinished decks usually require annual applications of a protective coating. A clear water repellent (also called a *water sealer*) prevents the problems associated with the constant wetting and drying of wood by helping it to maintain a more even moisture content. Some water repellents contain mildewcides; none block damaging ultraviolet (UV) rays. Semitransparent stains with "UV protection" limit the effects of UV radiation to a small degree. Some clear wood finishes also contain UV-blocking particles. Solid-color stains and paints offer the greatest UV protection, but solid-color stain wears on walking surfaces, and paint is likely to peel.

Stained and painted areas should be renewed every two to three years. Clear water repellent or, even better, a water repellent with UV-blockers can be applied over a semitransparent stain as a maintenance coating between stain applications.

Decking, railings, and steps may call for different finishing. Stained or natural wood should get annual water repellent coatings and restaining as necessary. Decking needs abrasion-resistant stain and should not be painted. Even railings are easier to maintain if stained rather than painted. Some woods accept paint better than others do. Redwood, for example, is better than pressure-treated Southern Pine.

You can treat the largest deck in a matter of minutes using a low-pressure garden sprayer or similar tool (see Chapter 5). For best results, follow up with a bristle-type pad on a long handle.

Apply quality latex paint approved for hardboard siding, paying special attention to grooves and drip edges. A brush gives the best results. If you use another applicator to lay on the paint, we recommend backbrushing. Two topcoats are always recommended, and two coats are required for satisfactory spray applications.

Painting aluminum siding (and gutters)

We usually think of aluminum siding as maintenance-free, but the finish eventually fades and ages. Refer to Chapter 9 for cleaning and other paint preparation tips.

However, if you're happy with the color but the finish looks dull, try cleaning the siding with a wood-cleaning product designed to renew wood decks. Another approach that works wonders is to apply a coat of Penetrol, which is a paint conditioner. Buy a pint and test it in an inconspicuous spot. Often it will renew the luster so that you don't need to repaint. If Penetrol does the trick, apply it with a sponge or paint pad over the entire surface. If you do decide to paint after all, Penetrol provides an excellent base.

Some painting experts say you only need to apply a good-quality, light-colored, acrylic latex paint. Perhaps that's true, but you can improve your chances of success by first applying a high-quality sealer-primer, such as those used for hardboard siding. Or if you want, you can skip the primer but mix a bonding additive, such as Emulsa-Bond, to the first topcoat of paint to improve paint adhesion to the existing paint. (Add 1 quart of bonding additive to 1 gallon of paint.) A bonding additive helps latex paint adhere better to chalky surfaces. Don't add Emulsa-Bond to the final coat. It's just not necessary, and it can cause variations in the amount of sheen.

If you have made repairs that expose bare metal, you must spot-prime those areas with a special primer formulated for aluminum or galvanized metal. Despite claims to the contrary, our experience is that if you try to topcoat bare aluminum without this primer, the paint peels off.

Don't lean ladders against aluminum siding (or against any freshly painted siding, for that matter) unless you pad the top of the ladder rails with taped-on rags, foam-rubber ladder mitts, or other ladder accessories designed for that purpose.

Painting vinyl siding

Vinyl siding does not have a surface coating of paint. The color is continuous through the material. Painting eliminates one of the primary advantages of this siding material, namely that it is maintenance-free. Nevertheless, if you can't stand the color, or it has become dull with age, painting is an option.

Always use light colors when painting vinyl siding. Dark colors cause excessive expansion and contraction, resulting in paint failure and buckled siding. Use a high-quality sealer-primer or a bonding additive, as recommended for aluminum siding in the previous section.

Painting concrete, brick, or stucco

Generally speaking, you can paint brick, stucco, concrete, or concrete block with exterior latex paint after you clean the surface to remove accumulated grime. (See Chapter 9 for more information about cleaning these surfaces.) Use a finish with a satin sheen to make cleaning easier.

Think twice before you tamper with unpainted brick. Removing paint from brick is nearly impossible (see Chapter 9). Use water-repellent sealer or stain, which offer some weather protection but don't peel.

Ask a paint dealer or stucco contractor about painting stucco in your area. Typically, you can paint stucco with an acrylic latex product. Some masonry, especially highly alkaline surfaces such as stucco, should be sealed with an alkali-resistant masonry primer. Moisture from the ground and from the interior of the house rises to the exposed portion of the foundation and escapes harmlessly when the foundation is unpainted. If you do paint it, make sure that you use a water-based product that allows moisture vapor to pass through. Use a sprayer, long-nap roller, or rough-surface painting pad/brush, to paint a masonry surface.

Seal the joint between the foundation and the house with caulk. Uncaulked, this area is a major source of energy loss and cold drafts.

Painting Trim, Windows, and Doors

Although it's important for the body of a house to look nice, you should pay special attention to the trim, windows, and doors. These elements attract the most attention and are the most vulnerable to paint failure because of all the joints where water can enter if the seal fails.

Roof and wall trim

After you prime all bare wood, apply caulk along all open seams between trimboards. Allow the caulk to dry the amount of time specified on the label before applying a topcoat. Brushes are best for applying paint to most trim. Generally a 2½- to 3-inch angled sash brush is all you need, But if you have a lot of wide trim, you may want a 4-inch square brush, a pad, or even a mini-roller.

Windows

The outer surface of a window is painted to provide weather protection. Some double-hung windows have removable *sashes* — the operable part of a window. If this is the case for the window that you're painting, remove the sashes by following the same procedures that you use for cleaning the windows, or consult the owners' manual — if you can find it. Lay the sash flat on sawhorses or a workbench to paint it.

Here's the gameplan to follow: Begin in the center and work out. This approach ensures maintaining a "wet edge" on all the surfaces so that you have smooth transition and no lap marks. The problem of painting the window trim and frame first is that those areas will be is tacky by the time you finish painting the sash. Here's the sequence to follow:

1. **Begin painting the wood next to the glass using an angled sash brush.**

2. **Paint the stiles and rails of the sash next.**

3. **The window frame and *casing,* or trim, come next.**

4. **Open the lower sash to paint the exterior windowsill last.**

Do not paint the edges of the sash. When these surfaces are painted, they tend to stick to the frame. This advice is especially important when you're painting windows with a sash that slide in vinyl channels. Even a little paint on the edge of the sash can make it stick shut. Instead, seal these areas with a clear penetrating wood sealer to prevent moisture entry into the sash.

If you're painting the window sash while it's in the frame, use a dry brush, one that has very little paint on it, to coat the outside edge of the sashes. The dry-brush method prevents paint from running into the crack between the sash and the exterior stops, where it may cause the window to stick. Also move the window sash frequently as it dries to prevent the window from sticking. If the window does stick from paint runs, try using a butter knife to cut through the paint that glues the sash to the exterior stop. Years of paint buildup here may require a more aggressive tool, such as a serrated *paint zipper.* Touch up, if necessary.

To form a moisture shield between the glass and the sash, overlap the paint about ⅛ inch onto the glass. If you have a steady hand and a quality angled sash brush, apply the paint freehand and wrap a clean cloth over the tip of a putty knife to clean off any mistakes. For the rest of us mortals, mask the glass before you paint or use reasonable care and plan to use a razor scraper after the paint has dried. If you decide not to mask, you can use a trim guard to protect the glass, but don't push too tightly against the glass or you won't get the desired overlap.

If you leave masking tape in place and it gets wet or the sun bakes it on, it is nearly impossible to remove. Apply masking tape when you are ready to paint, not before, and remove the tape before you move on to the next window.

Recognizing that the previously mentioned approaches are all difficult tasks, Wagner, a manufacturer of painting tools, invented a nifty solution called Glass Mask. This product is a protective film that you apply around the perimeter of the glass and then paint without worry about getting some on the glass. When the paint dries, you use the built-in scraper that lifts off the film but automatically leaves the ⅛-inch overlap.

Entry doors

Choose a semigloss or high-gloss alkyd-based paint for doors, which get a lot of use and abuse. Latex enamel also holds up well. If the door was previously painted with a high-gloss paint, use a deglosser to dull the finish and clean the surface. If a wood or metal door has never been painted, or if bare wood or metal is exposed by sanding, apply the appropriate primer.

You're much less likely to have drips and runs if you take a few moments to remove the door and lay it flat on sawhorses. Use plastic food containers, shoeboxes, or the like to keep all the parts together.

Make sure that you paint the bottom and top of a wooden door. If you don't, moisture enters the door and may cause it to swell or warp. A convenient mini-pad paint applicator lets you paint the bottom edge without removing the door.

Use a 2-inch- or 3-inch-wide brush to paint a door. If the door has a flat surface (called a *flat* or *flush door*), as opposed to a raised-panel surface, paint it with a brush, pad, roller, or sprayer. A roller typically leaves a stippled finish that may not be acceptable on surfaces when viewed up close, so if you use a roller for speed, plan to backbrush with a brush or pad.

If the door is paneled, use a brush and paint the panels first. Then paint the horizontal cross pieces *(rails)*, and finally paint the vertical pieces *(stiles)*. Paint with the grain as you do when sanding. To minimize applying too much paint in a corner, brush out of a corner rather than toward it. Check over your work as you proceed and brush away any drips. As you paint, check often for drips and excess paint in inside corners and brush out the excess paint before moving on. Refer to Chapter 5 for information on paint applicators and techniques for using them.

Garage doors

Paint failure is common on wooden garage doors, especially raised-panel ones, which have many joints where water can enter. Of course, run-ins with bicycles, basketballs, and Buicks don't help. After you remove all the loose paint and degloss the surface with deglosser or by scuff-sanding, prime any bare wood or hardboard panels. You must use an alkyd primer on hardboard panels, so plan to use it on the whole door. For extra protection and better bonding, mix Emulsa-Bond into the first topcoat. After priming, carefully apply a thin bead of paintable caulk to the sides and bottom of each panel where it meets the door's stiles and rails (the vertical and horizontal members of the frame). If the existing finish is in good condition, you can just apply one topcoat to the cleaned and caulked door. If the door needed scraping, repairs, and sanding, finish the primed door with two topcoats.

Shutters

If the weather is iffy and you don't want to risk painting the siding or trim, and if you have removed your shutters and put them in a garage or other protected area, now is the time to paint them. Before you do, however, make sure that you will not obscure any label or other identification. Hardware stores sell tack-like numbers, which you can apply to the shutter, that correspond to numbers on the window frames to help you put shutters back in the right place.

After you have made any necessary repairs, scrape off loose paint, feather-sand your shutters, and then prime any bare spots. If you have a paint sprayer, there's no better time to pull it out than now. Spray the louvers first at a slight upward angle so that you can paint the upper portion of each slat. Then spray the entire face, including the frame. Two or three light coats are better than a single heavy coat, which can drip and run. Do the back first. Check both sides frequently for drips and runs, both as you paint and as the shutters begin to dry. Brush out drips with a dry paint brush.

If the shutters are held in place with metal hinges or other brackets, these should be painted, too. See the following sidebar for tips on painting exterior metal.

Taking care of metal railings

Today's iron railing posts are usually made with square tubing rather than solid metal. Water, salt air, acid rain, and air pollutants all can cause corrosion. In the majority of cases, rust begins where the railing posts are embedded in concrete. If you do nothing else but scuff-sand and recoat the bottom 2 inches of your railing every year, touch up any chips as soon as you notice them, and repaint the entire railing every five to eight years, the railing will last indefinitely.

Major repairs that involve sandblasting and refinishing of iron are best done by experienced metalworkers. Never try to sandblast iron yourself.

The rusting process starts immediately on bare metal, so paint the railing *immediately* after sanding, scraping, and making other repairs. Always use a rust-inhibiting primer and paint on ferrous metals, as described in Chapter 4.

Penetrol, a multi-purpose paint additive, also makes an excellent sealer — and sealing is essential to prevent further corrosion. Apply it over the rust before you paint, and add it to your primer to improve bonding. Treat any visible rust with a rust-neutralizing chemical. See Chapters 8 and 9 for more on removing finishes and exterior preparation.

More tips on painting ironwork:

- Never paint when the relative humidity is above 80 percent, and certainly not in the rain or fog or on a wet or damp surface!

- Don't paint ironwork in direct sunlight — it dries too quickly for optimum bonding.

- Don't paint if the temperature is expected to fall below 50 degrees Fahrenheit within 24 hours.

- If you use a sprayer or roller for a primer, follow up with a brush to work the paint into the surface and create a better bond.

- Two coats of primer are better than one.

Winding Things Up

Before you store painting tools and equipment, make one final inspection, making sure that you didn't miss spots or overlook drips. Be sure to remove all masking tape. If it bakes on or gets wet and dries, it can be nearly impossible to get off.

Cleaning up the yard

Yard cleanup is minimal if you are careful to use drop cloths during both preparation and painting stages. Be careful not to contaminate the ground with paint chips, especially if they contain lead.

We've found it helpful to use a shop vacuum to pick up paint chips that escaped our drop cloths. If you're careful and hold the nozzle just above the ground, you can pick up paint chips and sanding dust without sucking up too much soil or an occasional chipmunk.

Removing drips and spills

While drips and spills are fresh, you can immediately wipe them up with water (for latex) or mineral spirits (for alkyd paints). Use denatured alcohol to clean up alcohol-based coatings, such as some fast-drying primers.

If the paint has dried but not fully cured, you may be able to use denatured alcohol on latex paints or mineral spirits on oil and alkyd paints. Several commercial products, such as Goof-off, are available to soften latex paints. You may need an abrasive pad but be careful; abrasives can dull a glossy finish.

On glass and other relatively non-porous surfaces, you're often better off to let the spatter dry and scrape it off with a fingernail or a razor scraping tool. Use caution to avoid scratching the surface. A little paint spatter is much better than a ruined pane of insulated glass.

For fresh spatters and spills on masonry and other porous surfaces, flood the surface with water or thinner and scrub, scrub, scrub. Repeat the process as needed, using clean thinner each time. If the paint has dried, try a paint-and-varnish remover (see Chapter 8).

Chapter 12

Interior Motives: Painting the Inside of Your Home

. . . .

In This Chapter

▶ Painting a room in sequence

▶ Teaming up to paint a room

▶ Finishing woodwork, cabinets, and furniture

▶ Applying paints, stains, and clear finishes

▶ Using oils and varnishes

▶ Sprucing up hardware

▶ Reviving tired wooden floors

. . . .

A room that starts out needing just a coat of paint may soon look quite a mess after you complete the preparation work in Chapters 8 and 10. The room at this point is devoid of furniture, artwork, curtains, and the other decorating touches that soften and give a room character. It may display patched drywall, sanded and filled woodwork, indications on the wall where pictures formerly hung . . . and, of course, work lights to show it all off. You have little cause to worry that *Architectural Digest* is going to show up with a photographer. In fact, you're lucky if even *Better Hovels and Gardens* shows up. After you finish all the heavy and dirty work, you're ready for the fun part — the room transformation that we promise you in Chapter 1. So get your painting duds on, dust off the top of the paint can before you open it, and start to work.

Note: For those of you about to embark on painting a room who may be thinking that a chapter with the title "Interior Motives: Painting the Inside of Your Home" is *just* the place to start, sorry. This chapter is for people who do their "homework." See Chapters 3 and 4 for information on choosing finishes and colors; see Chapters 5, 6, and 7 for the scoop on choosing, using, and cleaning up paint applicators; and see Chapters 8 and 10 for guidelines on the all-important preparation work. We'll wait here for you to catch up.

Painting in the Right Sequence

Ceiling, walls, woodwork (including windows, doors, and moldings), and then the floor is the usual top-down sequence to follow when painting a room. Of course, it's quite common to paint only the walls and the ceiling and to just give the trim a good washing, thanks to the durability and scrubability of trim paint. (And you don't have to paint your carpeting just because it's last on our list!)

You're probably unlikely to question the sense of painting or refinishing floors last; and, clearly, you're more likely to spatter paint on a wall while painting a ceiling than the other way around. However, you do have room for some flexibility in determining the sequence for painting the walls and woodwork.

The argument for painting the walls before the trim is that you're more likely to spatter wall paint onto the trim while rolling paint on the walls than the other way around.

On the other hand, if you wish to paint the trim first, go for it! Painting walls without messing up the trim is relatively easy to do. If you get wall paint on the trim while rolling or *cutting in* the walls (refer to Chapter 5), it's relatively easy to wipe off; and gloss trim paint does cover flat wall paint much better than the other way around. You may also find that cutting in, around already painted trim, by using a brush or edging pad on the wide wall surface is easier than brushing the narrow edge of the trim — we do.

 If you're planning two coats on the trim, you may want to paint the first coat before you paint the walls so that it's dry by the time you apply the second coat. If you have a lot of trim to paint, you may want to paint the windows right after you roll the ceiling. Then break from that meticulous small-motor-skill work for some big moves with a roller on the walls before going back to finish the doors and baseboard. Are you dizzy yet?

Painting Ceilings and Walls

Interior ceiling and wall painting is a project that's best divided into two — cutting in and rolling. (Having two people do the work is also nice — especially if you're not one of them!) One person uses a brush to cut in, or outline, all the areas that a paint roller can't cover without getting paint on an adjacent surface. The other member of the team spreads paint on the ceiling and walls with a roller. If the ceiling and walls are the same color, you can cut in both at the same time. Otherwise, work on the ceiling first. (For a detailed description of these techniques, see Chapter 5.)

Working as a team

If you're painting with a partner, have the person with the brush, who we'll call the *outliner,* start first by spreading a two-inch band of paint on the ceiling, all around its perimeter. Lap marks result if the cut-in paint dries before you blend in the rolled area with the cut-in area, so don't let the outliner get too far ahead of the roller. (*Hint:* You both want to be in the same room.) You also want the roller to roll over as much of the cut-in band of paint as possible. The textures that a brush and a roller leave are quite different.

The outliner and the roller both must observe the top-down rule and paint in the following sequence:

1. **The outliner paints the ceiling molding, if any, and then cuts in a band of paint on the ceiling along the short wall.**

2. **The roller follows the outliner, rolling the ceiling as soon as it is cut in along one wall.**

3. **The outliner cuts in a band of paint on one wall at the ceiling and down the wall at two corners; the roller is then free to begin that wall.**

4. **The outliner cuts in around any windows and doors on that wall and then any other areas the roller can't do, such as around light fixtures or behind radiators.**

5. **The outliner completes the wall by cutting in the wall at the baseboards.**

6. **The roller follows along, usually at a pace that makes the outliner feel as if one is being pushed along.**

   (The outliner says, "You missed a spot," but refuses to say where.)

7. **The process continues in this manner until all the walls are done or the divorce papers are served.**

For a perfect paint job, follow the brush and roller techniques in Chapter 5. To apply paint to broad, flat surfaces such as walls and ceilings, use a 9-inch roller and either a shallow roller pan or the bucket-and-grid setup. (See Chapter 5.)

Before you use a roller, wet the paint-roller sleeve with water (for latex) or paint thinner (for alkyd) and spin or wring out the excess. Wetting the sleeve gets rid of new roller "fuzzies" that can drive you crazy if they get onto a newly painted wall. Expect your first few rolling attempts, however, to drip and run all over the place if you don't get *all* the excess liquid out before you actually start painting. Use a brush/roller spinner (see Chapter 7) or squeeze out the liquid and then roll the sleeve back and forth on an absorbent towel.

Start painting by *carefully* rolling a band of paint to smooth and blend in the cut-in areas while you still have a wet edge, as shown in Figure 12-1. Now you have a nice wide band so you won't unintentionally spatter the adjacent surface as you roll the rest of the ceiling. Then work your way across the narrow dimension of the room in three- or four-foot-square patches. By choosing to work across the narrow dimension and by starting each row at the same wall, you maintain a wet edge and spread the paint into new areas without creating noticeable lap marks.

Figure 12-1:
The outliner keeps ahead of the roller, cutting in ceilings and baseboards first and then windows, doors, and wall-mounted fixtures.

Attach a *pole extension* to your roller. You find that this device enables you to do the work with less neck strain, less bending, and without the need for ladders, staging, stilts, or platform shoes.

Rolling paint on the walls

To roll walls, keep these tips in mind:

✓ **Begin in a corner at the upper third of the wall, painting a three- or four-foot-wide area at a time until you reach the bottom.** Smooth your work out by rolling lightly from the ceiling to the floor with a dry roller. Continue to work your way down the wall in this fashion. (You may need to nudge your partner to cut in some baseboard out of sequence so that you can keep working.)

Textured or "popcorn" ceilings

You may or may not find that you can roll paint onto a *textured* or "popcorn" ceiling. The texture easily disintegrates if it gets wet unless you previously painted it with an oil-based paint that seals the surface (and even then, you must be careful). If you do roll such a ceiling, use a long nap roller and roll on alkyd-based paint in a single pass (or two at the most). Come back for a second coat if you must, but don't roll back and forth or the texture starts coming off the ceiling. That leaves you with a big, fat Redenbacher mess, wishing that you'd taken the following advice: Use an airless sprayer to paint textured ceilings.

One brand of airless sprayer even has a right-angle attachment that directs the spray upward while you hold the unit level. Spraying, however, requires more protection — draping windows, doors, and woodwork to protect them from over spray and using a moon suit, painting hood, respirator, and goggles to protect your body. See Chapter 6 for more information on spray equipment, preparation, and spray application.

Use an aerosol stain-blocking primer on water-stained textured ceilings before you paint the entire ceiling.

✔ **Don't skimp on paint.** If you tend to roll paint too thinly, using the zigzag approach (as we describe in Chapter 5), apply a single ceiling-to-floor vertical stripe of paint per roller of paint, smoothing with a dry roller every three or four feet.

✔ **Step back and observe your work frequently from several angles, checking for lap marks or missed spots.** Adequate lighting is important here. Deduct points for painting over windows and electrical outlets.

Enhancing and Maintaining the Natural Look

Unfinished wood collects grime, stains easily, and generally gets shabby in short order unless it is protected with a finish. So whether your project involves new unfinished wood, or wood that you've stripped (Chapter 8) and prepared for finishing (Chapter 10), the next step is to apply a protective coating.

Staining wood on purpose

New wood or wood that has had its finish stripped will accept a coloring in the form of oil-based stains, water-based stains, non-grain-raising (NGR) dyes, and products that blend stain and protective coating in one application. Of course, you can also forgo stain for the natural wood tone.

All woods accept more stain on the ends of boards (called *end grain*), which are more porous that the faces and edges. Some woods accept stain unevenly even on the face, however, because the structure of the wood is such that some areas are much more porous than others are. Clear wood toner or conditioner evens out the surface porosity on softwood like pine and fir so that when stain is applied, you'll get more uniform results and avoid dark blotches that look like muddy footprints.

Whenever it's humanly possible, test the stain on a wood scrap or on an inconspicuous area, such as the back of a piece of molding or the underside of a table.

Applying stain

The application technique you use depends on the type of stain. You'll get more even results if you wipe on a penetrating stain, but pigmented stains, wiping stains, and water-based stains are better brushed on. You should also brush on products that combine a stain and a durable polyurethane finish in one application.

The pigment in the stain settles to the bottom of the can after several hours. For a more uniform stain job, stir the stain well before you start and at regular intervals. Stain is also harder to remove from your skin than paint, so rubber gloves are a must.

If you do get stain on your skin, the most effective way to get the color out is with a clear "natural" stain of the same brand. We always keep a can of natural on hand (pun intended). Then wash your hands with a hand cleaner or straight dishwashing liquid and just a touch of water.

Coat all wood surfaces, including the insides of doors and drawers, to prevent the wood from warping due to an uneven absorption of moisture on a finished and unfinished side.

The process for staining wood is the same whether the wood is new or stripped:

1. **Pour a small amount of stain into a wide shallow container, such as a paint roller tray.**

2. **Dip a clean folded cloth or a brush into the satin and squeeze or tap out the excess.**

3. **Apply the stain to a small area at a time. Use long, continuous strokes with the lumber's grain (that is, along its length).**

4. **Even out the application by wiping the entire surface with your stain rag without dipping it, and then again with a clean, dry cloth. If you're using a brush, tip-off the area with a dry brush.**

   Repeat the application for a darker tone.

Assembly-line staining and new woodwork

If you're adding new trim or molding, or installing ceiling beams, you can get the job done without time-consuming cutting in, without having to work overhead, and without needing to protect walls, ceilings, or other surfaces.

First, lay all the unfinished trim across two sawhorses. Next, using the sponge- or cloth-wiping method described in the steps in the section "Applying stain," wipe the stain on the pieces. Then cut and nail the pieces of trim in place. After you install the trim, use a small brush to touch up at cut ends. Mix a small amount of stain with wood putty that accepts stain, and use it to fill the nail holes.

You may also be able to apply an initial coat of polyurethane before installing the trim. Keep in mind, however, that after you seal the wood, you can't touch up with stain. So cut the pieces to length, check the fit, and touch up cut ends. Install the trim and, instead of using stained putty to fill nail holes, use suitably colored wax filler sticks when the final coat of polyurethane is completely dry.

Protecting Wood with Clear Finishes

Interior and exterior stains and transparent finishes are formulated for interior, exterior, or interior/exterior use. Stains intended for interior applications offer little or no protection and must be top-coated with a protective finish. When stain has dried for 24 hours, you are ready to apply that finish.

Generally, it's a good idea to stick to the original finish — applying oils to furniture or cabinets that have been oiled, for example. However, each finish has its characteristics and special qualities. Oils, polishes, and waxes generally are the best for enhancing the beauty of the wood but offer less protection. Polyurethane tends to mask the natural beauty of the wood but is the runaway favorite in terms of the protection it offers against water. It is an excellent choice for floors. Wooden kitchen floors, unheard of years ago, are now very common thanks to the protection that polyurethane and other synthetic finishes offer. The most popular options are described in Chapter 4.

The two most popular, easy-to-apply finishes are alkyd-based oils, such as Danish oil and tung oil, and polyurethane varnish.

Wiping on oils

Tung and Danish oils, available in most paint departments, protect the wood while bringing out its natural or stained color. They are alkyd-based and have hardeners in them that make them more like rubbing varnishes than true oils. The advantage is that they offer more protection than penetrating oils and they are easy-to-apply, wipe-on finishes. The instructions on some products say to apply the oil and then let it dry; others tell you to apply the oil and then buff it with a clean rag. You can't go wrong by following the manufacturer's instructions, but we've have had great success with the following approach:

1. **Using a clean cotton rag, gently rub one or more coats of antique oil or tung oil into the wood.**

   As when painting and staining, apply an oil finish on detailed areas first and leave the flat, most visible surfaces for last.

2. **As soon as the first coat dulls (about an hour), apply a second, light coat.**

3. **After about 20 minutes, lightly rub down the finish with your oiling cloth but without adding any more oil.**

   The goal is to even the finish, not to remove or add to it. Use an especially light touch at the edges so that you don't wipe off the finish. Allow the finish to dry overnight.

4. **Then sand the entire surface very lightly by hand with 220-grit or finer sandpaper and clean it carefully with a tack rag before applying the next coat.**

5. **Repeat this procedure the next day for maximum protection.**

To give the wood additional protection from liquids and abrasion, and to give it a sheen that would put a smile on your grandmother's face, you can apply a paste wax with a soft cotton cloth. When it dries to a haze, buff it with a clean cotton cloth, flipping the cloth often to expose an unused portion.

Brushing on polyurethane varnish

Some wooden doors and woodwork just seem too beautiful to paint, and a clear polyurethane finish, applied correctly and maintained, will enhance and preserve that natural beauty.

The three most important elements of a smooth, streak-free varnish coating are the right brush, the right brushing technique, and properly thinned varnish.

Use a top-quality brush for varnishing and use it only for varnishing. A China bristle brush and a nylon/polyester brush with flagged tips are both good choices. Condition the brush before you use it: Dip it in the appropriate solvent for the finish you are using, wipe off the excess on the edge of a clean can, and brush it out a bit on a piece of clean wood.

You get a smoother finish by applying several thin coats of varnish rather than one or two heavier ones. Varnish is self-priming and is usually thinned with an equal part of solvent (mineral spirits) for the first coat. This thinning maximizes penetration into the wood. Subsequent coats must usually be thinned, but to a much lesser degree. Straight out of the can, the coating is so thick that it tends to show brush marks; if the coating is too thin, however, it will sag and drip. Always thin a finish in a separate container so that you can add finish or thinner to achieve the desired results without affecting the finish in the original container. Experiment by adding small measured amounts of thinner to a measured amount of finish as needed until the finish seems to brush on without streaks or brush marks. (Write your "formula" on the paint can label for future reference.)

To avoid creating bubbles in the finish, never shake or use an electric mixer to stir polyurethane. Use a paint paddle with slow movements, lifting the sediment from the bottom into the rest of the finish.

If you're tempted to varnish the exterior of your door, too, don't — at least not until you turn to Chapter 11 and read about all the extra maintenance work that you'd be signing up for.

Brushing with strokes of a genius

Your brush stroke is important for a smooth finish. Hold the brush loosely with your fingers just onto the *ferrule* (the metal part). Dip it into the finish no more that halfway up the bristles. Then tap the brush on the edge of the can to shake off the excess. Although this technique is standard practice with paints, too, the reasons for doing it with varnish are different. With paint, you are just trying to get the maximum amount of finish on the brush without dripping on the way to the surface, and wiping the brush on the can removes half the paint on the brush. With varnish, you also tap to fully load the brush without dripping, but you avoid wiping the brush on the edge of the can for a different reason — to prevent the formation of tiny air bubbles in the finish — bubbles that even Lawrence Welk would hate.

Paint must be brushed out or agitated to become more fluid so that it spreads evenly. Polyurethane, on the other hand, should be applied with as few strokes as possible so that you don't cause air bubbles in the finish. Working quickly is also important. If the finish begins to set up before you have done the *tipping off,* which we describe later in this section, you will leave brush marks. Always start with more time-consuming detailed areas and save the flat, most visible areas for last. When you are working in corners, lay the finish on a distance away; and then, with less finish on the brush, apply finish in the corner and brush outward.

Ideally, you brush a flat surface, such as a door, from one end to the next. However, you can't brush across the starting edge without wiping finish off the brush and sending it dripping down the edge. A good compromise technique is to start with a backstroke a few inches from one edge, lifting the brush just as it leaves the edge. Then brush in the other direction, starting just inside the wet edge. As you near the far edge on your long stroke, raise the angle of the brush from the typical 45-degree angle until it is nearly perpendicular by the time it leaves the surface. Repeat that for the next area, slightly overlapping the edge of the previously finished area.

You're less likely to end up with runs and sags if you varnish on a horizontal surface rather than a vertical one. So, remove a door and all its hardware for varnishing. If you need to varnish both sides of a door, screw short blocks of wood into the hinge mortises and into the lockset hole so that they each protrude an inch or two beyond one face of the door. Apply varnish to that side first. Next, after your final tipping off, turn the door over so that it rests on the support blocks. Then finish the other side and all edges.

After you complete an area, such as the face of a door, tip off the entire surface with an unloaded brush, beginning in the area where you first applied the finish. As the term implies, use only the tip of the brush, and brush from one end to the other in long, very light strokes.

If, despite your best efforts, you discover a drip after the finish dries, scraping it off with a very sharp chisel is better than sanding it off. After you scrape off the drip, sand the area lightly with 220-grit paper and touch up with a small amount of finish.

Burnishing and waxing a polyurethane finish

If polyurethane has a drawback, it is that it looks plastic, especially when compared to a fine oiled or waxed piece of woodwork. Most professionals burnish a polyurethane finish with a dry cloth, 0000-grade steel wool, or a very fine abrasive pad to take off the plastic-looking shine. Then, for a more natural luster, they apply a final wax coating as described in the section, "Wiping on oils." Waxing, however, has a couple drawbacks. Assuming that you want to maintain the wax luster, you have to wax a couple times a year and periodically remove the wax buildup. Perhaps more importantly, you may not be able to apply a maintenance coat of polyurethane over a waxed surface without stripping the finish back to the bare wood — a job you definitely want to avoid.

Don't try the wax-over-polyurethane trick on floors or stairs. The resulting finish can be treacherously slippery, especially in socks. If you don't like the glossy look on floors, use a satin finish and burnish the final coat with a coarse cloth.

Scuff-sanding between coats

Don't put away the sandpaper just yet. In addition to sanding before you finish wood, you often need to sand between coats. Sanding removes fine particles of dust and any brush marks and assures a good bond between subsequent coats.

Use only the finest aluminum oxide or wet-and-dry sandpaper for this task. *Always* sand with the grain and use a sanding pad that conforms to the surface. Dampen the surface with water during this process. The watery liquid with undissolved, fine abrasive particles lubricates the surface and speeds the cutting action of the sandpaper. Use 0000-grade steel or bronze wool for hard-to-sand areas.

Some finishes react with steel wool and leave tiny black stains in the wood. Always test on a wood scrap. If you have any problem, try bronze wool.

Wipe the surface clean with a tack cloth and inspect it carefully by shining a bright light at a sharp angle across the surface. Recoat when thoroughly dry.

Although the label on some finishes, such as polyurethane, may say that the finish can be recoated without between-coat sanding; the timing is critical. You must wait until the previous coat is hard enough so that it won't soften or return to a liquid state when the subsequent coat is applied, but you can't wait so long that a bonding problem develops. And it's not just a matter of watching the time. The humidity level and the amount of air circulation also affect the drying time, and these factors are variable. The best bet is to wait until each coat is thoroughly dry and sand before applying the next coat.

Painting Woodwork

In painting wood windows and doors, moldings and floors, make sure that you keep your work area clean and that it is free of drafts and airborne dirt to prevent dust and lint from settling on the wet paint. Turn down the thermostat to prevent the furnace from cycling on, which causes dust-laden drafts.

Getting professional results depends on good prep work as described in Part III. If the wood is bare, apply a primer. (For information on choosing a primer, refer to Chapter 4.)

If you're painting over already painted or varnished woodwork, prepare the surface as described in Chapter 10, and apply the one or two coats of paint, always sanding between coats. If the finish has a glossy sheen, sand it or use a deglosser (as described in Chapter 9 and 10).

If enamel is too thick, it sags and leaves brush marks. We like *Penetrol* for thinning alkyd enamels and *Floetrol* for thinning latex enamels. Don't add the thinner to the paint can. Instead, pour the paint (in the amount that the directions suggest) into a new container and then add the thinner until you get the right consistency. Thicken the mixture with more paint or thin it with more Penetrol. (For more information on Penetrol see our discussion of additives in Chapter 4.)

Working on windows

You want to paint windows from the *inside out*. That means that you paint the operational part of the window, the *sash*, first. Then you paint the frame and the casing. (*Casing* is the molding or trim on the top and sides of a window frame.) Paint the interior windowsill (called the *stool*) last. While you're working on the sash, paint any interior horizontal and vertical dividers (called *muntins*) before you paint the *stiles* and *rails* that make up the frame of the sash.

The two most common window styles are the *double-hung,* in which two sashes slide vertically in channels, and the *casement,* in which the sash has hinges on the side and cranks opens outward. In many modern double-hung windows, you can easily remove the sash and should do so for painting so that you don't get any paint in the channels. Sometimes even the slightest bit of paint on plastic channels makes the sash difficult to slide — or even totally inoperable. For the same reason, don't paint any previously unpainted surfaces. Coat these surfaces instead with a clear, penetrating wood sealer to prevent moisture from entering the sash. Set the sash on a surface at a comfortable working height. (A surface about 36 inches high works for most adults.) Because most tables are 30 inches tall or lower, you need to prop up the table or the window to avoid back strain — or find a four-foot-tall painter.

Taking an orderly approach to double-hung windows

Paint older-style double-hung windows in place. If someone's painted the upper sash shut or the pulley/counterweight system needs repair, consider correcting the problem *before* you start painting. Inevitably, these repairs damage the finish, so now is the best time to take care of the situation. When you're actually ready to paint, just follow these steps:

1. **Reverse the positions of the lower, inner sash and the upper sash, leaving both slightly open, as shown in Figure 12-2.**

2. **Using an angled 1½ -inch sash brush (see Chapter 5), paint the lower exposed portion of the outer sash.**

3. **Return the upper and lower sashes to their normal positions but don't close them completely.**

4. **Paint the remaining portion of the outer sash and the entire inner sash.**

   Don't paint the outside sloped portion of the window (called the *sill*). This area is an exterior surface, and you must paint it only with an exterior paint, typically while painting window exteriors.

5. **Switch to a wider 2½-inch angled sash brush to paint the casing.**

6. **Start by cutting in the casing where it meets the wall (see Chapter 5) and then do the stops, which form the inner edge of the channel for the inner sash, finishing with the face of the casing.**

Figure 12-2:
Reverse the sash on a double-hung window to paint the lower half of the outer sash first.

7. **Paint the stool next.**

8. **Wait until the sash dries to paint the window channels.**

    Slide the sash all the way up to paint the bottom half of the channels and, after the paint dries, slide the sash all the way down to paint the upper half. If unpainted metal weather-stripping lines the channels, don't paint the stripping.

To save all the waiting, we often paint the lower half of the window channels before we start painting the walls and ceilings so it can dry while we cut and roll. As soon as the channels are dry, we stop rolling and do the upper half of the window channels.

As you're painting around the glass, lay the paint on in the middle of the area you're painting rather than starting in a corner. Then, with less paint on the brush, work from the corners out, dipping your brush into the paint you initially lay down as necessary.

Use a *dry brush* (one with very little paint on it) to coat the vertical, outside edges of the sash. The dry-brush technique prevents paint from running into the crack between the sash and the stops, where it may cause the window to stick. Move the sash as soon as possible to break any paint bond in these cracks before it dries completely. If, despite your best efforts, the sash does stick, use a serrated tool known as a *paint zipper* (available at paint and hardware outlets) or the tip of a utility-knife blade to cut through the paint that binds the stop to the sash. For more information about painting windows (and doors), see Chapter 11.

Working on casements from inside out

Follow the same inside-out procedure for casement windows, with one exception — paint the outer edges of the sash first so that they can start drying ASAP. You can't close the window until it's completely dry. If you close a casement window before the paint dries, you need a jackhammer to open it. Start by opening the window part way so that you can remove the operating mechanism from the sash. After you paint the outer edges of the sash, cut in the glass perimeter, and then paint the face of the sash. Next, crank the window wide open to access and paint the frame. Finish by cutting in the casing and painting the frame and the face of the casing.

You need to overlap paint onto the glass slightly, especially on the lower third of each pane, to prevent water that condenses on cold glass from soaking into the wood behind the paint. This process causes the paint to peel and eventually leads to woodrot.

Doing doors

Doors take a lot of use and abuse, so for best results, choose a durable finish that has a semigloss or gloss sheen. Semigloss or gloss will make cleaning easier and hold up to frequent cleaning (see Chapter 4). Inevitably, you need to lay down at least two topcoats to get a uniform appearance. If the current finish on the door consists of a glossy paint, use a deglosser to dull the finish (see Chapter 9).

Leave doors hanging on their hinges while you paint them so that you can paint both sides at the same time. You can remove most modern lock sets in less than a minute (and replace them in under two), so removing them for painting is easier than masking; but make sure that you do one or the other.

You must seal all surfaces of new doors to prevent moisture from entering the door and causing it to warp. This step is critical for a solid-wood door and solid-core veneered door. We even recommend sealing for less warp-prone hollow-core doors (the most common lightweight interior door). If you're not planning to take the door off, slip a mirror under the door to see if the bottom edge is painted. If not, either use a mini-painting pad that enables you to paint the bottom edge; or remove the door from its hinges, apply a sealer, and rehang the door to paint the rest of it.

Rolling a flush (flat) door

Paint a *flush door* (or a flat door that isn't paneled) with a brush, pad, or roller (with a ¼-inch nap or foam sleeve). If you use a roller, however, backbrush immediately with a wide brush or pad to smooth the roller stipple. This texture, which rollers impart, works well for walls and ceilings but isn't attractive on doors or wood trim.

Doors with a luan mahogany veneer have a rougher texture than do those with a birch veneer. Although you can never get a mahogany door as smooth as you can a birch door, sanding between coats helps, especially if you're priming and painting a new door. After painting the door itself, paint the doorjamb and casing, beginning at the doorstop and working out.

Raised panel doors

Paint a raised panel door, shown in Figure 12-3, with a brush and paint with the natural grain of the wood. Painting around the panels is time-consuming, making a *wet edge* difficult to keep. (See Chapter 5 for additional information on *cutting in* and the importance of a wet edge.)

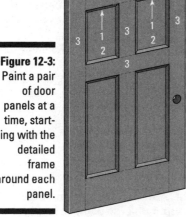

Figure 12-3: Paint a pair of door panels at a time, starting with the detailed frame around each panel.

One commonly recommended approach says to paint all the panels first. But this approach works only if you cut in carefully and avoid getting paint on the faces of the stiles, muntins, and rails that frame the panels. If you get paint on a stile, for example, while painting the first couple panels, the paint may set up before you're ready to paint the rest of the stile.

For most painters, the best approach is to paint the top pair of panels and the stiles, muntins, and rails around them. Then move to the next lower pair of panels, and so on. Using a paint conditioner keeps the wet edge longer, makes the paint go on more easily, and improves its bond — all-important qualities for door painting.

Making transitions

In painting a door frame that's a different color on each side, apply one color up to, but not including, the face of the stop on the in-swinging side of the door. Paint the same color on the in-swinging face of the door but not on any edges. Make the final cut along the outside edge of the casing and wall and then finish painting the face of the molding.

Getting up close to baseboards and other molding

Put away the roller, hot shot — time for some precise paint brushing. Choose a *sash brush* or brushes that match the dimensions of the woodwork that you're painting. An *angled brush* that's comfortable to hold at various angles works best, because painting trim, balusters, or a fireplace mantle can sometimes require the flexibility of a contortionist. Get up close to whatever you're painting, whether doing so means lying on the floor to paint baseboards or climbing a ladder to reach areas higher than shoulder height.

 In painting woodwork, use a paint box with the sides folded down to hold the can of paint and a couple rags, one of which you dampen with water (for latex) or paint thinner (for alkyd) to wipe up drips or splatters.

Finishing Touches

Before you pack away the paint and equipment, remove any masking tape and check carefully for places needing a touchup. Look for paint drips, too. Paint drips and runs take time to form, and despite your best efforts to keep checking back on just-painted surfaces, you may find some. You must wait until they dry completely before you scrape off, sand smooth, and retouch them with paint.

If you have paint on the glass in windows or doors (and you probably do), use a single-edge razor or a razor scraping tool to carefully scrape it off. Before you scrape the paint off the glass, score the paint with the point of a utility knife and then scrape up to the scored line. Doing so prevents you from accidentally peeling paint off the wood. If you're trying to maintain a ⅟₁₆-inch overlap onto the glass (see the "Painting windows" section in this chapter), hold a wide taping knife against the wood as you score, as shown in Figure 12-4.

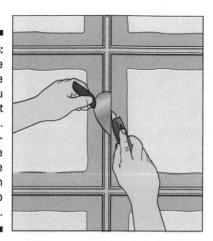

Figure 12-4:
Score the paint line before you scrape paint off glass. The taping-knife guide reserves the ⅟₁₆ -inch overlap onto the glass.

Be careful while you're scraping glass. Hold the razor at a low angle with its entire edge on the glass and work slowly to avoid scratching the glass.

Next, reinstall hardware, fixtures, and outlet covers that you removed in preparing the room. If you haven't done so already, clean, polish, lubricate, or otherwise spruce up these items before reinstalling them. In some cases, you may want to invest in new replacements. Inexpensive finishing touches, such as new cover plates, can really make a difference.

Move the furnishings back last and please — *watch out for the trim!*

Chapter 13

Decorative Finishes

. . . .

. . . .

*T*he power of paint to transform a room, to add character and style, to camouflage problems, and to draw attention is never more evident than when you use decorative painting techniques. You've probably seen the work — stenciled borders, painted walls with wallpaper-like textures and patterns, and "antiqued" woodwork — but may not have realized how much fun and how easy some of these finishes are to produce. The basis of virtually all these techniques is the use of *broken color,* a term that decorators use to describe the application of one or more colors over a different-colored background, allowing some of all the colors to show.

In this chapter, you see that anyone — yes, even you — can introduce subtle color and texture to virtually any interior surface in your home. All you need are off-the-shelf paints, other finishes, and a few specialized applicators. You can bring character and style to your ceilings, walls, floors, doors, special features, woodwork, or cabinets, by using decorative painting. These techniques can disguise imperfections, such as gouges in wood floors, downplay or camouflage an unattractive element in a room, such as a radiator, or alter your perception of a room's scale.

Decorative painting encompasses a couple dozen well-known, defined techniques and hundreds of variations. In fact, projects often involve more than one technique, such as spatter painting on a sponge-painted surface. When applied, each technique or combination of techniques results in one-of-a-kind creations that are derived from the combination of colors, sheens, and application tools that you choose, and how you use them. The resulting finishes are sometimes called *faux* (French for "false") because many fool the eye into believing that a material is other than what it really is. For example, wood graining or marbleizing (also called marbling) can make metal look like wood or wood look like marble. The effects are limited only by your imagination — and your desire to continue reading this chapter.

Use an old grocery list or bookmark to mark where the color insert starts. Check it out to see several examples of the decorative finishes found in this chapter displayed in their full glory.

Bring Your Vision to Life

The colors and finishes that you choose determine the success of a decorative painting project, so be sure to check out Chapter 3 for information on selecting colors and Chapter 4 for additional advice on choosing a finish. As usual, the better prepared the surface, the better the results are, so spend some time in Part III. There you can find information on cleaning, removing old finishes, sanding techniques, and applying primers and sealers.

The tools and supplies required vary with the technique and the project. You'll likely need the standard stuff, such as ladders, drop cloths, safety gear, a free weekend, and some very specialized applicators and tools. Many of the applicators and other tools are everyday objects, such as cheesecloth, sponges, and hair combs, whose quality does not really affect the results. With other tools, quality makes all the difference — both in the results and the amount of effort required producing it. With a couple of exceptions, it pays to buy top-quality brushes that are designed for the specific application, such as a stenciling brush or a wall stippling brush.

What about the paint? Oil or latex? You can use an oil- or water-based coating. To a degree, you can base your choices on the same factors that you consider when choosing paint for any painting project — ease of use, durability, flexibility, color retention and other characteristics. Check out Chapter 4 for more information.

Oil-based systems (primer, base, glaze, and varnish) are the traditional decorative painting mediums. After all, decorative painting has been done for hundreds of years, but quality latex paints have come into their own only in the last 10 to 20 years. Although oil-based paints are still more durable than latex paints, some latex decorative finishes can and should be protected with durable alkyd or acrylic varnish.

Despite the odor, difficult cleanup, and other disadvantages, an oil-based system may still be a good choice for beginners because its longer drying time means that you have more time to work the paint. That time is stretched if you add an extender to the paint. On the other hand, you have to wait longer between coats. Latex dries more quickly so the project moves right along, but you can get into trouble if you try to do too large an area or don't practice the technique before you start so that you can work at a good clip. We know that it's hard to believe, but some folks actually skip practicing and jump right into the painting (hey, we've done that). When you really need slower drying time with latex glaze, just use a tinted glazing medium and don't add latex paint, which slows the drying time. Other methods include: using an acrylic-gel retarder, cutting down on air circulation, painting on a humid day, or running a humidifier. The point: Dry air means faster paint drying.

As you may know, some surfaces require special paints for best results. For example, use fabric paint on fabrics, and ceramic paint on glass and china. If you are painting any atypical material, ask for advice at your craft or paint store.

As with other do-it-yourself projects, start with modest-sized projects and use the simplest and quickest techniques, such as sponging and ragging. Don't choose a room with vaulted ceilings or your kitchen cabinets for your first decorative painting project. Instead, choose surfaces like walls or the woodwork in a smaller room. That way, if you don't like the results, you can simply paint over and start again. Of course, the ultimate way to refine your painting techniques is to practice on someone else's house.

Decorative painting is so much fun that you can get carried away. If you don't want your family and friends wondering whether you have gone off the deep end, heed the following advice: Although you can decoratively paint almost any surface, including glass, tile, fabric, and the kitchen sink, don't do them all! A little bit goes a long way. Remember, too, that these techniques are usually most effective when the effects, color differences, and textures are subtle. In other words, don't use fluorescent colors, and rethink the idea of zebra-striped cabinets.

Exploring Decorative Techniques

Surprisingly, only a handful of basic tools and procedures are used in most decorative painting techniques. For many of the techniques in this section, you start with a completely opaque, smooth, nonporous surface called the *base*. For the base, apply a coat of slightly thinned satin, eggshell, or semi-gloss latex paint. For other techniques, you don't want to obscure the surface. For example, if you are pickling or whitewashing woodwork with an attractive grain pattern, you probably want the grain to show through the finish. Right? (This is where you nod your head up and down.)

After you apply any base, you apply one or more coats of a semi-translucent finish, called a glaze or a wash. *Washes* typically refer to water-thinned latex paints, and *glazes* refer to oil-based finishes. However, a wash can also be any very thin, watery glaze, water-based or oil-based. So don't get hung up on terminology or embarrassed about asking for clarification when discussing a project with your paint or craft dealer.

There are many "recipes" for glazes, and the combination of ingredients can affect the texture, drying time, workability, and appearance of the result. Part of the fun is experimenting. Don't worry. You can't blow up the house — at least we don't think so. The simplest formulas call for using a commercial glaze (also called *medium* or *scumble*), which is a clear liquid that's colored with standard interior house paints, universal colorants, (the stuff they use and sell to color paint in paint stores) or artists' paints. This glaze mixture is sometimes thinned for certain techniques, most notably colorwashing (see "Colorwashing or glazing for a natural look," later in this chapter). You can also use straight paint or thinned paint as a glaze, but such finishes usually lack the depth and translucent character that makes these techniques so appealing.

You can apply and work with the glaze by using a special applicator, such as a sponge or lint-free rag, in one of two basic ways — an additive or subtractive approach.

- ✔ Using the *additive* approach, you add each glaze to the previous coat, leaving some of the color below showing. If you use a sea sponge, this technique is called sponging *on;* if you use a wad of muslin, the technique is called ragging *on.*
- ✔ Using the *subtractive* approach, you apply the glaze with a brush or roller and then use a sponge or rag to partially remove the glaze to reveal the color below. The techniques are then called, respectively, sponging *off* or ragging *off.*

Generally, the additive approach is easier for beginners and for people working alone. The subtractive approach often requires good timing, and if you are not careful, you can easily muddy the colors, which is fine — if you're a catfish.

Some projects require one additional step — a protective coating. To protect surfaces subject to wear, moisture, or dirt, such as kitchen cabinets and wood and concrete floors, or to make such surfaces easier to clean without damaging your fine painting work, apply one or more coats of varnish, typically an alkyd- or water-based urethane.

Applying the base coat or ground

To produce a completely opaque base, you usually need to apply at least two base coats on top of sound paint. And if you're painting an unfinished surfaces such as wood or drywall, apply primer first. Use regular interior latex or alkyd paint.

When the project is furniture or cabinets, leave a texture-free surface. To achieve that, thin the paint to a creamy consistency, use a top-quality brush, and apply the paint by using good brushing techniques, such as those described in the section about applying polyurethane in Chapter 12.

Although you can use contrasting colors, using complementary colors and similar tones is safer. Use eggshell, satin, or semigloss finishes; flat sheens are too absorbent.

Applying the glaze

A glaze medium gives you more drying time than paint alone, so you have enough time to apply and work the paint. A glaze also gives the paint the body that it needs to hold its tooled shape (ridges created by a comb, for example). Leveling is normally considered a good paint quality because you don't usually want to see brush marks, but it is not a desirable quality for a glaze. You want the patterns that you create when applying and tooling a glaze to hold their shape. You also want whatever color that you exposed in the layer below to remain visible.

To make a glaze, mix four parts clear glazing medium with one part paint. Add more glazing medium to make the finish more translucent and to slow the drying time for some of the more time-consuming techniques like marbling. Extenders or acrylic gels, made for latex systems only, slow the drying time and thin the glaze.

Subtractive techniques require that you work quickly. With most of these techniques, do large sections, not an entire room, at one time so that you avoid lapping problems or noticeable changes in your technique, which can vary from day to day. If possible, work with a partner. Apply the glaze with a wide brush using a crisscross approach — up and down, left to right, and up and down again. For large surfaces, such as walls, use a roller in the usual fashion. Limit yourself to a 4- to-5-square-foot area at a time, more or less depending on the complexity of the tooling required and whether you have a partner. The glaze is workable for only 10 to 20 minutes.

Depending on the applicator (sponge, comb, stiff brush, or crumpled plastic) and how it is used, the glazing effect is subtle and random, or pronounced and highly patterned.

Whatever the approach, be careful not to build up too much glaze on the inside corners. The tendency is to *double-coat,* the result of applying glaze first while doing one wall and then again while doing the adjoining one.

One sure way to avoid the problem of double-coating is to mask the corners of two opposite walls with low-tack painter's tape and glaze the other two walls one day and let them dry completely. Then unmask the corners and reuse the tape to mask the corners of the completed walls before glazing the other two walls.

Sealing the finish

If a surface that you decoratively painted with latex paint is subject to a lot of use or abuse, apply a protective coating. Modern polyurethane varnish is superior to old oil-based varnish in virtually every way, including less *ambering* (yellowing) because of age and exposure to ultraviolet radiation. It is a very durable, very clear finish. Clear acrylics, on the other hand, are generally less durable and somewhat cloudy, but they do not amber. Acrylics, therefore, may be the best choice for use over white or light pastel colors; polyurethanes may be best over wood graining.

Follow the thinning and application guidelines spelled out in Chapter 12. Water-based urethane is more difficult to apply without leaving brush marks, so apply it with a roller if possible and tip off the finish immediately with a nearly dry, top-quality varnish brush.

In addition to the protection that sealers offer, they also make the surface reflect more light. This feature may be desirable on the walls of a relatively dark room or on a piece of furniture that you have painstakingly smoothed and painted to perfection, but not on a distressed piece of country furniture. Remember that the shinier the finish, the more the imperfections show. Use a gloss finish if you want to maximize the reflective qualities, and use satin for less reflection. To minimize or eliminate any shine, burnish the final coat with a coarse cloth or steel wool (or just use a slipcover if you want to hide the thing altogether). For wood surfaces, you can also apply a wax to the surface after it is burnished. The resulting sheen is less plastic-looking and more like oiled or waxed wood.

Achieving the Look You Want

You may become so inspired by a decorative painting process described in this book that you immediately start looking around your house for something to paint. But here's a better idea: First find a room, a special architectural feature, or piece of furniture that needs help, and *then* choose an appropriate painting technique that appeals to you. You can choose from dozens of techniques, and because you can use many of them together — with great results — there's hardly a limit to what you can do.

Always try out a technique on paper or another suitable surface until you are comfortable with the technique and happy with the pattern or color mix that you are able to achieve.

In this section, we describe step-by-step procedures for the most popular decorative finishes, beginning with those that are considered among the easiest to do. Before you begin your decorative painting, gather up some general supplies such as plenty of cleaning cloths and rags, solvents, drop cloths, safety gear, ladders, and so on, as explained in Chapter 5. Additional tools and supplies that you use to apply and work the finish depend entirely on the painting technique.

Sponging glaze on and off

Sponging, the process of applying or removing a glaze with a natural sea sponge, is one of the simplest painting techniques and is suitable for both large- and small-scale projects, and is shown in Figure 13-1.

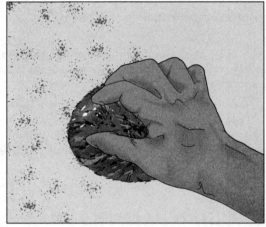

Figure 13-1:
The sponging technique.

You can sponge a light tone or color over a darker tone or color. Or you can sponge on one or more tones of the same color or different colors over a base. The more water or thinner that you add to the glaze, the more transparent the glaze will become.

Here's how to sponge on a glaze:

1. **Dip a dampened sponge in glaze and squeeze out all the excess. Blot on paper to make sure that you have the right amount of paint to produce the results you want.**

   Err on the dry side. You can always add more glaze to the wall if you've used too little paint. But if you use too much glaze, you won't see the sponge texture, and it's harder to remove it without muddying the texture.

2. **Use a light touch to dab the paint onto the surface without squeezing the sponge.**

   To keep the pattern random, keep turning the sponge as you dab, and overlap each imprint. As the sponge gets drier, increase pressure as needed so that you apply the same amount of paint.

Sponging off produces a more subtle effect. It's best done with a helper, but if you work alone, just work smaller areas at a time. If you want, you can follow sponging off with sponging on, allowing full drying between steps. Here's how to sponge off a glaze:

1. **Have your partner apply a glaze with a roller or by using the criss-cross brushing method described in the section "Applying the glaze."**

2. **Dip a sponge in water (or turpentine for oil glazes) and squeeze out the excess.**

3. **Dab the surface by using the same technique as for sponging on (described in the preceding set of steps), working from top to bottom and turning the sponge often.**

   Rinse the sponge in solvent as it becomes covered with paint. Wring out the excess solvent, blot on paper, and continue sponging. Work in 2-foot-wide, ragged-edge strips on large surfaces, being careful that each successive strip just touches — and does not overlap — the preceding one.

Ragging and rolling patterns on

Ragging and rag rolling are two of the better-known techniques in a broader category known as cloth distressing, which also describes the wardrobe of messy painters. You use crumpled or rolled rags made of various types of cloth like cheesecloth, muslin, and burlap, to apply or remove glaze by dabbing or rolling, respectively. The additive process is easier, but the subtractive approach produces more interesting results. Ragging is often done with a dark glaze over a light base boat, a combination that produces a greater depth. Bright, contrasting colors, however, also can produce exciting results. How much glaze you apply or remove is determined by how hard you press as you dab or roll the rag. As always, experiment first and then use consistent pressure when painting the surface.

We prefer to use oil glazes for cloth distressing. Be sure to thin the glaze about 10 to 15 percent with mineral spirits. Rags should all be the same material, free of seams, hems, buttons, zippers, pocket protectors, and so on. For rag rolling, also make the rags the same size (about 2 feet square for large surfaces). You will notice differences in the finish if you use rags of different sizes. An old cotton sheet works well, but you can also experiment with less porous materials or even nonporous ones, such as plastic. Have plenty of rags on hand and replace them when they become so saturated that they no longer produce the desired pattern. Ragging is shown in Figure 13-2.

Figure 13-2:
Cloth-
distressing
technique.

To rag on, follow these steps:

1. **Soak a rag in glaze and squeeze or wring out excess.**

2. **Open the rag up and lay it loosely in your painting hand with as many creases and folds as possible.**

3. **Holding the rag loosely, lightly dab it against the surface.**

   After every dab, rotate your wrist or arm or reposition the rag in your hand. Work from the top down, in 2-foot-wide, ragged-edge strips on walls or narrower strips for smaller surfaces. Step back from your work (look out for the paint can). You should not be able to see individual imprints. Fill in as needed to achieve a uniform pattern.

4. **If you want, repeat ragging with a darker-toned glaze.**

To rag off, follow these steps:

1. **Have your partner apply a glaze with a roller or by using the criss-cross brushing method described in the section "Applying the glaze," earlier in this chapter.**

2. **Dip a cloth in turpentine, wring out the excess, and fold the rag into your painting hand, using the same technique that you do for ragging on. (See Step 2 in the preceding set of steps.)**

3. **Dab the surface, using the same technique that you do for ragging on. (See Step 3 in the preceding set of steps.)**

   When you find that you are applying as much paint as you are removing, dip the rag in the solvent once and wring it out.

To avoid a noticeable transition, dab a just-dipped and wrung-out rag a few times on paper before you go back to the painted surface. Also, avoid changing or completely rinsing out rags in the midst of a surface.

Rag rolling produces a repeating vertical pattern. To rag roll on, here's what you do:

1. **Saturate a rag with paint and squeeze out the excess paint.**

2. **Fold two opposite sides of the rag toward the middle, or just fold it in half. Then roll the rag into a loose cylinder in a paint roller tray.**

3. **Starting at a corner of a room or just to the side (not on) of a lightly penciled plumb (vertical) line that you've made by using a level, roll the rag vertically, up or down the surface, whichever seems to produce the most uniform results.**

   You can make a wavy edge by steering the cloth a little to one side and then the other as you roll, but keep the pattern vertical.

4. **Repeat all steps, making each successive strip just barely meet the previous one.**

With cloth-distressing and most other decorative painting techniques, you can also create a striped wallpaper-like pattern by masking off vertical strips of any desired width and applying a glaze to only every other strip; or apply a glaze of a different color or tone to every other strip.

Spattering on color tones

For most paint jobs, you try *not* to splatter paint all over the surface, but not with this decorative technique. *Spattering* is the technique of splashing small droplets of paint from a brush (or toothbrush) onto a wall or other surface. It can work well in conjunction with other techniques, such as sponging, or on its own. Although you can spatter an entire wall, it is very time-consuming and so is usually reserved for smaller projects such as a fireplace mantle. However, you can rent spray equipment with a tip designed for spatter-painting large areas. For more information on spraying paint, see Chapter 6. Given the nature of the technique, cover everything that you don't want spattered, including yourself, your eyeglasses, and any curious pets.

To spatter in limited areas or only specific shapes, use masking tape or stencils to control where you paint.

Use artists' acrylics or oils, or latex paint. Thin the paint to the point where it spatters easily and produces drops that are the size you want but don't thin it so much that the spatters drip down the surface. Spatters are good, drips are bad. (That's a direct quote from Jackson Pollock, I believe.) Experiment on paper. Base and spatter paint colors are entirely up to you. Use two or more colors, contrasting or complementary. Spattering couldn't be more simple. Here's the basic technique:

1. **Dip a stiff-bristled paintbrush into the spatter paint and shake off the excess.**

2. **Hold a stick about a foot away from the surface you are painting and tap the brush against it.**

   The brush stops and the paint flies. As usual, paint from the top down.

   When you're painting large surfaces with this or any decorative technique, frequently step back and check out your work from a distance so that you can make timely touch-ups.

3. **Switch to a toothbrush or other very short, stiff-bristled brush. Hold it sideways to the surface and draw your thumb or a knife blade across it toward yourself.**

4. **Repeat Steps 1 through 3 for subsequent colors or tones.**

Colorwashing or glazing for a natural look

Colorwashing and glazing are painting techniques in which a glaze is applied in a way that allows the color below to show through. More often, however, the term colorwashing applies to techniques that use a particularly watery glaze or diluted paint. Following are two basic approaches, depending on the look you want:

- **Transparent glaze:** To simply add depth to an existing wall color, apply a uniform amount of glaze, brush it out, and then use a very soft, dry brush to remove as many brush strokes as possible.

- **Textured result:** To add texture and depth, apply glaze in varying amounts and use a brush, rag, sponge, or similar tool to remove varying amounts of glaze.

  - Using a cloth produces the subtlest effect, but sponge imprints and brush strokes can both be softened by using a long, soft-haired badger brush.

  - You can use oil or latex glaze, but oil glaze gives you more time to work the glaze, which is a plus, especially for beginners.

No matter what type of glaze you use, colorwashing is a two-person job when done on walls or other large surfaces. Figure 13-3 shows color washing.

Figure 13-3:
Color-washing technique.

Creating texture by combing and dragging

As a general category, *dragging* refers to a number of painting techniques in which a stiff brush, comb, or similar tool is dragged across a glaze to reveal a color below. When a comblike instrument is used, it is called *combing*.

Comblike instruments include tooth trowels, hair combs, or pieces of soft plastic or stiff rubber that you have cut with a utility knife. Combing produces a variety of interesting patterns, which seem to be especially effective on small- and medium-sized projects. Some popular patterns for this subtractive technique include the following:

- Simple, vertical patterns which looks like striped wallpaper
- Moiré, which is a wavy vertical or horizontal pattern or a combination of the two
- Small repeating patterns, such as the basket weave, in which alternating squares are combed vertically and horizontally, or fan shapes, which are made by holding one end of the comb in place as you rotate the other

To comb a surface, follow these steps:

1. **If you are using a regular pattern, such as a basket weave, you may want to pencil light guidelines to keep you from wandering off level (horizontal) or plumb (vertical).**

2. **Have a helper apply a glaze over a dry base coat in a limited area defined by the guidelines.**

3. **Draw the comb across the surface.**

For a vertical pattern, drag the comb from the top down and don't overlap. For a cross-cross pattern, follow-up by combing horizontally. For a basket weave pattern, comb a vertical square and then a horizontal one, continuing to alternate patterns in a row across the top of the project. Start the next row with a horizontal square and then alternate with the vertical pattern across the row. For a fan, hold one end of the comb in one spot and swing the comb in a semicircle; start the pattern at the bottom and work up, as shown in Figure 13-4. Warning: If you have trouble combing your hair, you might want to skip this technique.

Measure the width and length of the project and adjust the width of your comb so that the resulting pattern contains only full-sized squares. For example a 36-x-48-inch surface might have six 6-inch-wide columns and be 8 rows tall.

Figure 13-4:
Overlap alternating courses of fan-shaped patterns for a dramatic overall pattern.

To drag a surface with a stiff brush, follow these steps:

1. **Apply a glaze with a brush or roller over a limited area, a 2-foot wide top-to-bottom stripe on a wall, for example.**

2. **Take a dry stiff-bristle brush and drag it down the surface from top to bottom.**

3. **When you reach the bottom, wipe or brush the paint off the brush onto a towel or rag. Then repeat Step 2. As you work your way across the glazed area, try to just meet, not overlap, the previous stripe.**

Experiment with a variety of brushes until you get the look you want. Special dragging brushes are available that produce a more pronounced pattern. You can also experiment by cutting alternating rows of bristles from an old paintbrush.

Reviving Wood with Special Finishes

You'll find woodwork decorated with paint finishes in every style and color spanning the rainbow. We chose finishes we think are particularly easy to create, so we hope you're tempted to give them a try. Maybe it's for some cabinets you want to rejuvenate or wood trim needing special treatment.

Refacing kitchen cabinets is a great cost-saving approach to kitchen remodeling. By ordering new, unfinished doors and drawer fronts and using the simple finishing techniques of whitewashing or pickling, you can bring a warm country feel to your kitchen at a fraction of the cost of new cabinets.

Whitewashing bare wood

We prefer using alkyd paint to get the effect of *whitewashing,* the washed-out, weather-beaten effect, because it's slower to dry than latex paint. On bare wood, be prepared to work quickly, which means you must plan your approach beforehand. Practice on an inconspicuous area like the bottom or back of the wood so that you can experiment with the process.

Whitewashing involves working in a small area no larger than three feet wide. Apply the paint with a wide brush and then follow up with a quick rub down using burlap rags. We find that the rough surface of burlap creates a nice effect on the bare wood. Yes — this is messy work, so wear rubber gloves.

Apply the paint following the grain of the wood and working from the top to the bottom. Then wipe away the excess paint in the same direction. As you wipe, you leave behind a lovely splash of color in the wood that gives a muted, weathered appearance.

When the paint dries, the surface is ready for a protective coat of polyurethane.

Burlap is cheaper than a paint brush. You can find it in fabric stores in 48- and 64-inch widths. Buy a half yard for a large area (like a door), and cut it into palm-size rags. Your best bet is to buy a colorless, lint-free, natural shade of burlap because if it's colored, the color may bleed into the paint.

Pickling bare wood with dye

Coloring with dye is another option for a more subtle and softer-looking finish than wood stain. Use it to glaze, or *pickle,* a base coat of flat white latex paint. Liquid dyes come in a rainbow of colors and are available at hardware stores, craft centers, and even some grocery stores.

Follow these steps to create a pickled finish on unfinished or old wood that's been stripped of its paint or varnish.

1. **Apply a coat of flat white latex paint with a 3-inch-wide foam brush.**

   To feature the wood grain, apply a thinned down paint so the grain shows through.

   Foam brushes are an inexpensive alternative to traditional brushes. They are disposable and handy for touchups.

2. **Wipe off the paint before it starts to get tacky on the surface.**

   Remove most of the paint to create a translucent white film. Let it dry overnight.

3. **Pour the liquid dye into a plastic container or Styrofoam food tray.**

4. **Use a foam brush to apply the dye following the direction of the wood grain.**

   To get dye into tight spaces, use a small, angled foam brush. Immediately wipe off the excess with a rag. Let the dye dry.

5. **Apply two coats of polyurethane as a protective topcoat.**

Stenciling everything under the sun

A stencil is a decorative design reproduced on a surface with paint. The design can be applied on walls or anywhere you can apply paint. Apply a stencil on painted surfaces to call attention to the ceiling, windows, or doorways; or stencil a wainscoting (a decorative covering or treatment on the lower portion of a wall). Choose an informal floral design rather than harder-to-position and less-forgiving geometric patterns.

Precut acetate stencils have designs drawn in a wide variety of patterns and styles, and you can find them at paint and craft stores and home centers. The stencil has registration holes that you use to align the repeating pattern as you relocate the stencil along the wall or other surface.

Thanks to the miracles of modern science, you can create a stencil of any design you like, subject to copyright limitations. Bring a design to a good copy and duplicating service, which can enlarge or reduce it to any size you want and copy it in black-and-white or in color onto clear acetate (transparency). Although waxed manila paper is the traditional stencil material, acetate and Mylar stencils are transparent so that you can see previously applied colors. This makes it easier for beginners to reposition the stencil accurately. A simple design may involve one sheet; more complicated designs may involve several overlays. Have as many copies made as colors you intend to use. Then make the cutouts with a mat knife as shown in Figure 13-5.

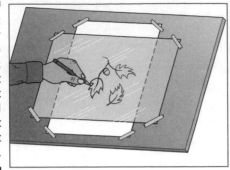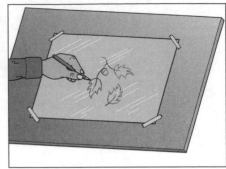

Figure 13-5:
Trace your design onto acetate; then tape it to a mat board and cut it out with a craft knife.

For your shopping cart, choose a quick-drying paint — acrylics are a good choice because they come in many colors. Buy a stencil brush, drafter's masking tape, and spray-mount adhesive.

Follow these basic steps for stenciling a room border, which you can apply to virtually any stenciling project:

1. **Beginning at a corner of a room, measure down from the ceiling to the point where you want the top or bottom of the stencil to be and pencil a tick mark at this point.**

2. **Use a 4-foot level, or a shorter one coupled with a long straightedge to draw a level guideline, as shown in Figure 13-6.**

   If you have a couple of helpers, mark tick marks at each corner; stretch a string between your marks and adjust it until it is level. Then make new marks every couple of feet and connect them with a straightedge instead of leveling each time. If your ceiling is way out of kilter, you may want to follow the ceiling by measuring down from it every 4 feet and connecting those points with a straightedge.

3. **Align the edge of the acetate with the pencil line and attach it to the wall with spray adhesive or low-tack painter's masking tape.**

   Continuous patterns will simply wrap corners all the way around the room. Start in the least noticed corner because when the design comes back to that point there will likely be a mismatch or otherwise cheated pattern. With *non-continuous* borders, treat each wall separately, centering the pattern so that the ends fall equidistant from each corner. To center a pattern, mark the center point of the wall and start your first stencil centered over that mark or with an edge aligned with the mark, whichever makes the pattern come out best at the corners.

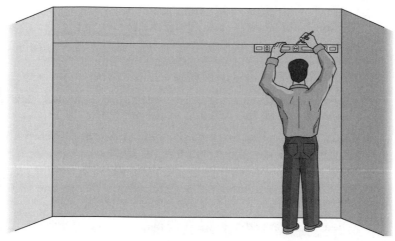

Figure 13-6:
Use a level and straight-edge to mark a lightly penciled guideline.

4. **Pencil a registration mark in one of the pair of precut registration holes and use it as an easy reference point the next time you move the stencil.**

   If your stencil does not have registration holes, cut a small V-notch about an inch in from each corner on the top or bottom edge of the stencil. Notch all stencils for other colors in the exact same locations.

   When the next stencil will wrap a corner, measure where the angle will occur and score the stencil with the dull side of a utility knife. Score the backside for inside corners and the front side for outside corners. Then the stencil will bend in place.

5. **Pour paint into a small container. Dip the brush in the paint and blot it in felt or paper toweling to remove the excess.**

   You actually use very little paint to stencil, but most patterns require more than one color. For example, a floral design may use two shades of green for the leaves and stem, and two shades of pink for the flowers. Even if you're using one stencil for several colors, it's best to do one color at a time and mask off the unused cutouts. If the stencil has images of footballs, beer kegs, and hot dogs, you may want to check with your spouse before painting.

   A dry brush gives you more control over how much paint you put on the wall. This, in turn, lets you use shading for special effects, such as making the edges of flower petals lighter than the interior parts.

6. **Dab the paint inside the cutout of the design, working your way around from its edges and filling the center of the design last.**

Hold the stencil against the wall as you paint. Don't brush in the normal fashion or you may drive paint under the stencil. The stencil brush is round and squat, kind of like a sumo brush, making it easy to dab.

7. **When you finish painting one color in all the cutouts, carefully peel the acetate from the wall and avoid smudging the fresh paint.**

8. **Clean off any paint from the back of the acetate. Then realign and mount the stencil in the adjoining location.**

9. **Repeat this process until the first color of the design is complete and use the same guideline and registration marks for any additional stencils and colors.**

When the paint is dry, erase your pencil lines and marks.

Part V
The Wonderful World
of Wallpaper

In this part . . .

Even a quick glimpse of the wallpaper hung by a previous owner can make your anxiety soar. In this part, we leave the psychological impact of irksome wallpaper to therapists and focus instead on hanging the wallcoverings you want and getting rid of those you don't. And for people who have run out of pictures to hang over all the tears and stains, we include a few quick, easy wallpaper repairs. By following the simple instructions in this part, you can make your home a more pleasant and eye-pleasing place to be.

Chapter 14

Wallpapering Basics: First Things First

. . . .

In This Chapter

▶ Deciding what wallcovering to buy

▶ Estimating needs and buying wallcoverings

▶ Gathering the right tools and supplies

. . . .

*W*allcovering adds rich texture and interest to walls and other surfaces in your home that plain paint can't. You can choose from a virtually unlimited variety of patterns and styles in fabric, foil, natural grasses, papers, wet-look vinyls, and dozens of other materials. A room papered with your favorite pattern is a welcome sight that draws you inside; just seeing it makes you smile. Wallpaper is one of those "little things" that make a big difference. In this chapter, you can explore your options.

Selecting the Perfect Wallpaper

Yes, the choice can be daunting, but allow yourself time to peruse as many wallpaper books as you can find. We admit that this undertaking can involve beaucoup time, but doing so gives you a good idea of the style and designs that you like — *really* like. And you want to really like the wallpaper you choose because you'll be looking at it for quite some time.

Locate and take full advantage of a knowledgeable wallpaper supplier. You need professional expertise to help you choose a paper that's appropriate for your skills and experience and to calculate how much paper you need. A wallpaper expert can suggest the necessary wall preparations and materials (such as primer/sealer and liner paper) and offer advice on using the right adhesive according to the type of wall surface and wallcovering. A professional also can help you plan proper seam placement, which not only improves the appearance of the finished product but can also substantially simplify the work (music to a do-it-yourselfer's ears!).

Determining how much work you can handle

Wallpapering sometimes requires the skills and experience of a lifelong professional and the eye of a true artist. Yet it also can be done perfectly by a first-time do-it-yourselfer. The degree of difficulty is determined by the chosen wallcovering, the condition of the surface, the complexity of the room, and how many thumbs you have.

To help you identify wallcoverings that are appropriate for you, ask yourself the following questions:

- **Am I choosing a wallcovering suited for my skill level?** Describe your experience and level of comfort to your wallpaper salesperson, who can suggest professional installation for wallcoverings that demand greater skill, or at least caution you about the potential difficulties or quirks of a wallcovering that you're unfamiliar with. Take a trip to the library to find out more about hanging the particular type of wallcovering that you are considering.

- **Are my walls and ceilings reasonably straight, level, and truly vertical? (If they are, alert the media.)** Even the easiest-to-hang self-adhesive wallpaper can be a bear to hang when nothing is that perfection called *true*. If you're working with less-than-perfect walls but still want to do the job yourself, look for patterns that are more forgiving (see "Selecting patterns that suit the room" later in this chapter) and try to use some of the tricks of the trade (described in Chapter 16) that disguise rather than emphasize problems.

- **Will I be hanging my wallcovering on a standard, easy-to-paper surface, such as plaster and drywall? Or will I be covering a problem surface, such as concrete block and wall paneling?** It's true that you can wallpaper just about anything (excluding your car), but only when the surface is properly prepared. Work with your salesperson to determine what work and skills are necessary, and then decide whether you have the skills and inclination to do the work yourself.

Many types of wallcovering are available. Each may require slightly different preparation, application, and finishing work according to its characteristics. We describe some of the most popular wallcoverings and some key things that you should know when you buy wallcovering in the section "Choosing a workable material." Ask your dealer whether the wallcovering material or its pattern will complicate hanging. (Hint: Don't buy any wallcovering with the kind of complex design that Martin Handford, the illustrator of the "Where's Waldo" collection, has made famous.) Also, try to find out whether the wallcovering you select has any special instructions. For example, make sure that you know how to position and match the pattern. With some papers, pattern matching can get pretty confusing! If window treatments are in your decorating plan, don't forget to ask to see sample books of wallcoverings that have coordinated fabrics.

For information on choosing, buying, and installing wallpaper borders, see Chapter 16.

Choosing a workable material

In spite of its name, wallpaper isn't always made of paper. The type of material and coatings used to make and color the wallcovering determines its appearance (natural, shiny, metallic, or wet, for example) and greatly affects how easy or difficult the covering is to hang. For example, with some coverings, you must be very careful not to get *any* paste on the decorative surface. We don't know how you work, but we couldn't even imagine doing that!

The material and coatings also determine how durable, stain-resistant, and easy-to-clean it will be. A paper may be washable or scrubbable (or neither), which is usually determined by how much cleaning the paper or color can handle. You can occasionally sponge a *washable* wallcovering with warm, soapy water. *Scrubbable* coverings are made of tougher stuff and can take more frequent washes that. Scrubbable papers are ideal for hallways, stairways, a toddler's room — where smudges (and worse) are inevitable, and kitchens where spills and greasy grime tend to build up on the walls. Choose a paper that is suitable for the planned location, considering both the type and amount of abuse you expect the wall to take. Like choosing a spouse, you may have to compromise, but you shouldn't go so far as to completely disregard either appearance or practicality. Here's how your choices stack up:

- **Standard papers** are inexpensive and generally easy to hang. Just be careful not to tug on paper too hard as you position and reposition the sheets on the wall. Standard papers tear quite easily, soil easily, and are relatively difficult to clean because they lack a protective coating. However, if money is an obstacle, you'll be thrilled to hear that these papers are relatively cheap.

- **Vinyl-coated papers** have a paper backing and a paper surface that's sealed with a liquid vinyl. This makes the wallcovering washable, meaning that you can safely sponge it off with soapy water.

- **Solid sheet vinyl wallcoverings** are made by binding vinyl to cloth or paper backing. These wallcoverings are the most rugged, stain-resistant, and scrubbable. Vinyl wallcovering is an excellent choice for kitchens.

   Vinyls are the best choice for a beginning wallpaper hanger. Not only are they the easiest type of wallcovering to hang, but they're also easy to live with — they're durable, soil-resistant, and easy to clean. They're even easy to remove.

✔ **Foils and Mylars,** which have a thin, shiny metal coating, reflect a great deal of light. This feature makes them a good choice for small rooms with little or no natural lighting, such as an interior powder room. The wall surface must be in nearly perfect condition, however, because the wallpaper's shiny surfaces accentuate any imperfections.

Even though hanging reflective wallpaper on walls with imperfections isn't a good idea, you can improve the results by first covering the walls with a heavy *liner paper,* which is designed to bridge small cracks and imperfections. Foil and Mylar papers are expensive, and liner paper installation can be a bit advanced for the everyday do-it-yourselfer, so we recommend that you call a pro for this job.

✔ **Grasscloth, hemp, and other cloths-on-paper** are richly textured, woven coverings with laminated paper backing. Although grasscloth is traditionally made of a vine, many modern synthetic versions are available. All are good choices to cover less-than-perfect walls, but they are expensive and relatively difficult to hang. If you are experienced and want to try one of these natural-looking coverings, discuss the installation requirements in detail with your dealer.

✔ **Flocked papers** have raised, velvety patterns and are good choices for covering walls that have minor surface imperfections. The washable flocks are easier to install than nonwashable ones, but both are expensive, and installation generally requires a pro. If you are experienced and want to step up to a more advanced project, discuss the installation requirements in detail with your dealer.

Knowing what's on the backside

Your primary concern is rightly focused on the front side of the wallcovering. After all, that's the side that shows. However, what's on the backside counts, too. In particular, the back may be prepasted or not, and the type of backing determines how it will eventually be removed.

Here are the two primary differences on the backside of wallcoverings and what they may mean to you:

✔ **Prepasted and unpasted:** Perhaps the most obvious difference on the backside of wallpaper is the presence or lack of paste. The vast majority of in-stock wallcoverings are prepasted. Activate this factory-applied adhesive by applying a pre-paste activator or by dipping the paper in a water tray, as we describe in Chapter 16.

✔ **Dry-strippable and peelable:** This feature will be a greater concern down the road when you, or the next occupant of your home or apartment, wants to remove the paper. *Dry-strippable* paper peels off in its entirety. *Peelable* paper peels off but leaves behind its paper backing. This backing can be papered over (assuming that it's in good shape) or removed with a wallpaper remover solution before painting. Keep in mind that strippable wallpaper or the paper backing of peelable wallpaper is easily removable only if the substrate was properly sealed before installation (see Chapter 16 for additional information on primers).

Selecting patterns that suit the room

Without a doubt, the most important factor in choosing wallpaper is choosing a pattern that you like. (Actually, that's the second most important factor. The first is choosing a pattern that your spouse likes.) You also must make sure that the pattern "works" in the particular room that you plan to paper — in other words, it should achieve your design goals. Because patterns often affect the degree of installation difficulty, you also want to choose one that is appropriate for your skills if you plan to hang it yourself.

Here are some basic aesthetic guidelines to consider when you're selecting a pattern:

- ✔ Vertical stripes or patterns make the ceiling appear higher.
- ✔ Horizontal stripes or patterns seem to widen a room and bring ceilings down.
- ✔ Large patterns generally don't look good in a small room because they tend to overpower the space and make it seem smaller. A large, open pattern looks best in a larger space.
- ✔ A mini-print or a paper with a small pattern or geometric design suits smaller dimensions.
- ✔ Dark colors make a room seem smaller.
- ✔ Wallpaper with a light background makes a room look larger.
- ✔ A pattern of ducks ice-skating makes any room look silly.

Matching repeating patterns

If you look at a roll of wallpaper, you can see that patterns repeat themselves every so many inches or feet along the length of the roll. This is called a *vertical repeat*. The pattern on one strip may align with another adjacent pattern horizontally or at an angle. How the designs on one strip are positioned in relation to the same designs on adjacent strips is called the *pattern match*.

Pattern matches come in five types: random match, random texture, straight-across, half-drop, and multiple drops. (The term *drop,* in this sense, refers to how much the pattern drops to match the adjacent strip.) Ask your dealer about the implications of the pattern for your particular project and about any special cutting and installation requirements.

The following list describes the five types of pattern matches shown in Figure 14-1.

- In a **random match,** such as a vertical stripe, you don't need to match patterns, but you do need to install each drop with the same edge always on the left.

- **Random texture** wallcoverings such as grasscloth don't have a pattern; therefore, matching is not necessary. However, the left and right sides of a roll often have often shading differences that can cause problems. Installing the paper as it comes off the roll juxtaposes a light edge with a darker one, making the shading difference more obvious. To overcome this problem, manufacturers often recommend flipping every other drop.

- **Straight-across** patterns line up and match horizontally but may also be laid diagonally on a wall. The pattern always looks the same on every drop from the ceiling or other horizontal elements, such as chair molding and the tops of windows.

- **Half-drop** patterns line up or match on a 45-degree diagonal line rather than a horizontal one. Each strip is positioned so that it is above or below the adjoining strips at a distance equal to one-half the vertical repeat. Every other drop looks the same at the ceiling.

- A **multiple drop** (called ⅓ multiple drop, ¼ multiple drop, ⅕ multiple drop, and so on) is similar to the half-drop; the difference is that the amount you offset on each strip varies. The higher the multiple (3, 4, 5, and so on), the less often a design repeats itself at the ceiling line. This pattern is great for out-of-level ceilings but can be very, very confusing.

Hanging wallpaper with a low vertical pattern repeat (a few inches versus a foot or more) is easier and wastes less paper.

Buying Wallcovering

In many cases, calculating how many rolls of wallpaper you need is very straightforward. Just figure the area you need to cover and divide that number by the area each roll covers. However, many times you're better off letting the dealer figure your needs. In either case, get out your tape measure and a pad of paper.

Sketching the layout

Make a simple sketch of each wall in the room, including any doors, windows or other openings. Get out your tape measure and grab a helper; measure the dimensions (width and height) of all the walls and openings. Then calculate the areas of each by multiplying width times height. Add up all the wall

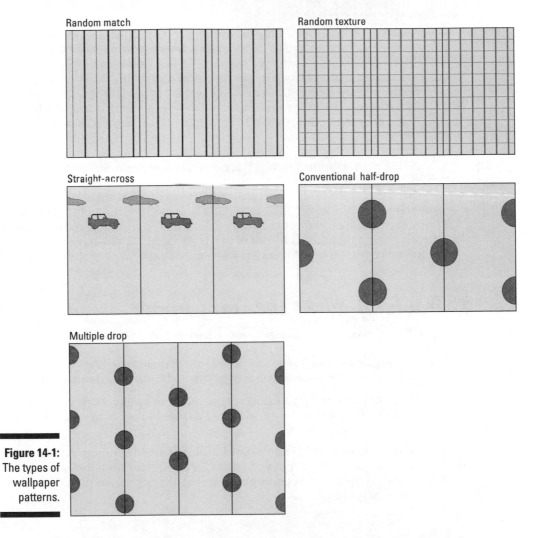

Random match

Random texture

Straight-across

Conventional half-drop

Multiple drop

Figure 14-1:
The types of
wallpaper
patterns.

areas, and then add up all the opening areas separately. For the *total area to be covered,* subtract the total area of the openings from the total area of the walls, and multiply that number by 115 percent to allow for waste.

Estimating the number of rolls to buy

For random texture, random, or straight across patterns in a typical room, you can handle the figuring. For example, for a bedroom with two doors and two windows, just divide the total square-foot area you need to cover (see "Sketching the layout") by the *total coverage* figure of the roll of wallpaper that you're buying to determine the total number of rolls that you need. Most likely, the answer isn't an even number of rolls, so round up to the next highest number to get the number of rolls that you need to buy or order.

If your project is complex — lots of cutting, irregular openings, an out-of-square room — or if your wallcovering has a tricky pattern or is otherwise a difficult type to hang, we strongly recommend that you let an experienced salesperson estimate you needs. The assistant can evaluate the pattern repeat, the pattern match, the length and width of the wallpaper, the complexity of the job, how the covering is sold (single, double, or triple rolls), the size of the rolls, and other factors to determine the amount of wallcovering that you should buy.

When you buy wallpaper off the shelf or when you receive paper that you preordered, make sure that the pattern numbers on all the rolls are the same and that the pattern is what you ordered. Also verify that the *dye lot* (or *run*) of all the rolls is the same. Each time there is a different run of the paper at the factory, changes can occur in the coloring, quality, or appearance of the coating. Keep a permanent record of this information. If you have to order additional paper, be sure to request the same pattern number and dye lot.

Tracking down the right paper

You can purchase your wallpaper from a number of sources:

- **Wallpaper outlets:** These stores offer the largest selection of carryout paper and have a library of manufacturer's books to order from.

- **Home centers and paint stores:** Most of these retailers offer a modest selection of wallpaper-to-go and keep a large library of manufacturer's books to order from.

- **Mail-order catalogs:** Some manufacturers publish catalogs with pages of actual wallcoverings that you can order by phone. Look through the advertisements in decorating magazines for information on ordering these catalogs.

Tooling Up for the Task

After you determine what you need to do to prepare the surface (see Chapter 15), it's time for a trip to the home center, paint store, and hardware store. The tools that you need for wallpapering may vary from our suggested list. For example, even if we suggest a break-away razor knife, your utility knife with a sharp blade will work just fine. Refer to Chapter 10 for information on interior-preparation tools and supplies.

This list and Figure 14-2 show you the tools, supplies, and other items that a do-it-yourself paperhanger typically needs:

- 2-foot level (or a bubble stick)

- Adhesives, activators, or water tray (as required)

- Break-away razor knife
- Bucket, sponges, and clean rags
- Canvas drop cloth
- Flat, hard, work table (half sheet of plywood on sawhorses)
- Metal straightedge (such as a 6-inch taping knife or painter's trim guard)
- Paint roller and tray (for prepasted activator or unpasted paper)
- Pencil
- Plastic drop cloth
- Plumb and chalk line
- Seam roller
- Sharp scissors
- Smoothing brush or plastic wallpaper smoother
- Spackling compound, primer/sealer, sizing, and liner paper, all as needed for preparing the walls
- Step stool or ladder
- Tape measure
- Work lights and extension cords
- Oh, and don't forget the wallpaper

Figure 14-2:
Wallpapering tools, equipment, and supplies.

Plumb and chalk line

Break-away razor knife

Seam roller

Smoothing brush

Choosing Your Wallpaper Adhesive

Wallpaper adhesive is generally available premixed in *standard* and *heavy-duty* versions. Standard is fine for most wallcoverings, but some types (heavy grasscloths, for example) require greater holding power. Tell your wallcovering dealer the type of paper and the surface it will be applied to, and he or she tells you whether a heavy duty adhesive is required. If you are applying vinyl over vinyl or intend to put a border on top of vinyl paper, you need vinyl-to-vinyl adhesives, which bond to just about any surface without priming. (See Chapter 16 for more information about borders.)

Chapter 15

Getting the Surface Ready

· ·

In This Chapter

▶ Cleaning and setting up the room

▶ Repairing and preparing wall surfaces for wallcoverings

▶ Removing wallpaper

· ·

Many of the preparations that you need to make before hanging wallpaper are the same steps that you take in preparation for interior painting. You want to set up a clear, well-lighted, and safe work area and then take the necessary steps to assure that surfaces are smooth and generally in good condition. In most cases, you need to prime and seal the existing wall surface to assure that the wallpaper adheres properly and that it can later be removed without damaging the wall. Refer to Chapter 10 for additional information.

Clearing and Cleaning the Room

To get the room ready for work, remove as much furniture as possible. Ideally, you want a completely empty room, but you can get by with a good 3 feet of work area in front of the walls. In addition, you need a work area where you can set up a table to roll out, measure, and cut wallpaper into strips.

Remove the covers on electrical receptacles and light switches and cover the face of the fixtures with masking tape. Also, remove any heating grates or wall-mounted light fixtures.

 Before you remove a light fixture, shut off the power to the room from the electrical panel. Put a piece of tape over the circuit breaker as a reminder to others to leave the power off. Then verify that the power is truly off by using a neon circuit tester. Cover any exposed wires with electrical tape. If you don't have a circuit tester, you can try another option: Plug in a radio that works and turn it on. If you hear music, the electricity is still on.

Do a quick once-over to dust and clean the walls and woodwork. Remove any fuzzy-wuzzies and cobwebs from corners and, if the woodwork is dirty or greasy, wash it in a phosphate-free household cleaner according to the directions. Avoid using cleaners containing phosphates such as TSP (trisodium phosphate). They are bad for the environment and leave a residue on the wall that prevents primer/sealers from bonding properly.

If you have any mildew, eliminate the source of the problem, such as moisture within a wall or a lack of proper ventilation. Then kill the mildew spores and remove the stain. Use a solution of 1 part household bleach and 3 parts water with a little non-phosphate cleaner or detergent. Sponge or spray-mist the stains with the solution and let it sit for at least 15 minutes. Bleach is not good for painted surfaces, so after it has done the deed on the mildew, stop the bleaching action by rinsing well with a neutralizer, such as clean water or a vinegar-and-water solution. Repeat the beaching and neutralizing processes, if necessary, until the stain is gone.

Never mix bleach with ammonia; it produces a lethal gas.

Remove other stains the best you can and seal any that remain by following the advice in the sidebar, "A primer on primers."

If you're planning to paint the woodwork in the room to match the new wall-covering or if your ceiling could stand a fresh coat of paint, paint before you hang. Then you don't have to be so concerned about protecting the walls or spend so much time carefully cutting in. In addition, getting wallpaper adhesive off a painted surface is no problem, but removing paint spatters or drips from wallpaper can be a disaster.

Preparing Wall Surfaces

You can apply wallpaper successfully to a variety of surfaces if you take the necessary steps to prepare the surface. You want smooth walls without any holes, cracks, popped nails, or other bumps that would telegraph through the paper. For information on drywall and plaster repairs, see Chapter 10 and also check out *Home Improvement For Dummies,* by Gene Hamilton and Katie Hamilton (published by IDG Books Worldwide, Inc.). In addition to following the surface preparation work described in Chapter 10, you also need to be aware of some special preparation considerations for wallpaper.

In most cases, you'll be applying wallpaper over painted drywall or plaster walls or over existing wallpaper on these same surfaces. But occasionally, you may want to apply wallpaper over problem surfaces, such as plywood, metal, prefinished paneling, concrete block, and ceramic tile. If you want to install wallpaper on such surfaces, we suggest that you get detailed instructions from your dealer. In some cases, the task calls for hanging a liner paper to level the playing field (see Chapter 14 for more information). In other cases, covering the surface with drywall may be easier.

Smoothing painted walls

To guarantee good wallpaper bond and future removability, you should coat all painted walls with an acrylic wallpaper primer/sealer (see the sidebar, "A primer on primers"). Use 80- to 100-grit sandpaper to machine-sand oil-painted and glossy surfaces before sealing them, but be careful to not sand into the drywall paper covering. If you do, it gets all fuzzy. (Refer to Chapter 8 for more on tools, abrasives, and other techniques.) If latex paint comes off when you rub it with a wet cloth, it is of poor quality, and you should use the pigmented variety. You must either machine-sand painted walls until they are smooth or have them professionally skim-coated with joint compound and then prime them.

A primer on primers

The key to good wallpaper adhesion is the proper condition of wall surfaces. If you start with a perfectly clean, painted wall, you're likely to get good results with any prepasted wallpaper. However, you're *guaranteed* to get good results if you first apply an acrylic wallpaper primer/sealer to the wall. Ironically, a primer/sealer not only promotes adhesion but also makes it easier to strip the paper off when you get tired of it or when the next owner prefers another wall finish. Primer/sealer makes it easier to position the wallpaper without stretching it, and that means fewer seams opening up when the paper dries.

If you're papering over new drywall, applying a coat of primer/sealer is a *must*. If you don't start with a primer/sealer, which soaks into and seals the paper surface of the drywall, you'll never be able to remove the wallpaper without doing serious damage to the drywall. If your walls have ink, lipstick, crayon, nicotine, or other stains, seal the stains or they will bleed through both the wallpaper primer/sealer and the paper itself. For this, you need an acrylic pigmented stain-killing primer/sealer. However, stain-killers are not wallpapering primer/sealers, so you must follow up with a primer/sealer made for wallcoverings.

Acrylic all-surface wall-covering primer/sealer goes on white but becomes clear as it dries. Pigmented acrylic all-surface wall-covering primer/sealer is more expensive than the clear stuff, but it helps to cover dark or patterned surfaces and prevent the color or pattern from showing through the paper. It's a good idea to tint a primer to the approximate color and shade of the wallpaper background so that the wall color doesn't show as much if the seams open slightly. Both primers perform equally well on porous and non-porous surfaces.

A coat of wall-covering primer/sealer takes two to four hours to dry, so paint it on the day before papering or at least a few hours before you hang the paper. Be sure to read the instructions from the wallcovering and paste manufacturer and consult your dealer regarding priming/sealing requirements for your project.

Sealing new drywall before papering

New drywall (including patched areas on existing walls) must be well sealed before you install wallpaper. First, apply a coat of oil or latex drywall primer/sealer and follow up with a pigmented wallpaper primer/sealer.

Removing Wallpaper

If you want to feel a sense of power, stand in a large room with the world's ugliest wallpaper and imagine that you can change the destiny of that room. (Dynamite is not an option.) In a perfect world, you could gently pull at a loose seam, and the old paper would miraculously peel off the wall, leaving no residue or adhesive — just a nice clean surface.

In the real world, that scenario is very unlikely, but you don't have to dread the task of removing wallpaper. Although taking down wallpaper isn't fun, it's a good example of grunt work that any do-it-yourselfer can accomplish. The downside is that it's a messy and time-consuming job; the upside is that it's a no-brainer and doesn't require expensive tools or even talent.

Knowing what you're up against

Before you can determine the best approach to use, you need to know the type of wallcovering and the type of wall surface that's under the wallpaper. In most cases, walls are either drywall (gypsum sandwiched between layers of paper) or plaster smoothed over *lath* (either strips of wood or a metal mesh). You can usually tell what you have by the feel (plaster is harder, colder, and smoother than drywall) or by tapping on it (drywall sounds hollow and plaster doesn't). If you're in doubt, remove an outlet cover to see the exposed edges. It's important to remember that drywall is more vulnerable to water damage; you must avoid over-wetting it. And use care when you're scraping, because drywall is more easily gouged than plaster.

What about the wallpaper? Be optimistic — assume that the paper is *dry-strippable*. Lift a corner of the paper from the wall with a putty knife. Grasp the paper with both hands and slowly attempt to peel it back at a very low angle. If it all peels off, you're home free.

If the wallpaper doesn't peel off or if only the decorative surface layer peels off, you must saturate the wallpaper or the remaining backing with water and wallpaper remover solvent and then scrape it off.

Some papers, such as foils or those coated with a vinyl or acrylic finish, are not porous. If you're removing such wallpapers, you must scratch, perforate, or roughen the entire surface to permit the solution to penetrate below the nonporous surface to the adhesive layer below (see "Choosing a removal technique" later in this chapter). You can test for porosity by spraying a small area with hot water and wallpaper remover. If the paper is porous, you can usually see the paper absorb the water immediately. After the paper is wetted, you can scrape it off.

Now that you know what you're dealing with, you can choose an appropriate removal technique for the entire surface. Depending on your situation, you can choose one of three wallpaper-removal approaches — dry-stripping, wallpaper remover, or steam. Read the how-to for each approach later in this chapter in the section "Choosing a removal technique."

Preparing for the mess

All wallpaper removal approaches are messy, so take the necessary precautions to protect your floors. For all removals except dry-stripping, we recommend that you lay down a 3-foot-wide waterproof barrier around the perimeter of the room. You may find the pre-taped plastic drop cloths more convenient and reliable, such as adhesive polyethylene sheeting. To prevent the watery mess from getting on your floor, tape the plastic to the top edge of the baseboard or, even better, to the wall just above the baseboard, which prevents water from seeping behind the trim. (You can remove the tape when working on the bottom inch of the wall.) Cover the outer 2 feet of plastic with canvas drop cloths or a few old absorbent towels in the area where you are working. Be very careful where you step; the plastic sheeting is very slippery.

Water will probably end up dripping down the walls and under your feet. For that reason, you need to tape over switch and receptacle covers or shut off the circuit breaker at the electric panel. Use an extension cord to bring power from another room for work lights and the steamer.

Tape down two layers of plastic on the floor. That way, you can roll up the top layer with all the paper goo, and the second layer will protect the floor while you sponge the adhesive residue off the wall.

Keep plenty of old dry towels or rags around to mop up, in case (or should we say *when*) your protective measures fail.

Gathering tools and supplies for removing wallpaper

You need only a few basic tools and supplies for wallpaper removal, but you may want to check out "Choosing a removal technique" later in this chapter for the specific tools you need. The following list describes these tools.

- **Razor scraper:** This push-type wallpaper scraping tool (about 3 to 4 inches wide) looks like a putty knife but has a slot for replaceable blades so you can always have a sharp edge.

- **Paper scraper:** This nifty gadget can scrape and perforate wallpaper applied on drywall. It has a round, knoblike handle attached to a scraping blade that cuts the paper. Solvents or steam can then penetrate to the adhesive layer but can't damage the paper facing of the drywall.

- **Wallpaper remover:** Although warm water may do the trick (and is certainly priced right), you can turn to commercial wallpaper removal solvents.

- **Garden sprayer, spray bottle, or paint roller:** Use one or more of these tools to get the water/remover solution onto the wall.

- **Wallpaper steamer:** Rent one (or buy a do-it-yourself model if you've just bought a fixer-upper!).

- **Plastic and canvas drop cloths:** You need both types to adequately protect your floors from the watery mess.

- **Wide masking tape:** Tape the plastic drop cloths to the base molding to avoid ruining your floors.

- **Water bucket, towels, rags, and wall sponges:** Wash down the walls well after removing old wallpaper.

- **Trash can and plastic liner**

- **Large can of elbow grease**

Choosing a removal technique

The technique you use for removing the old wallpaper depends upon what kind of paper you're taking down and what kind of surface is underneath (see "Knowing what you're up against," earlier in this chapter). The following sections outline the steps to the different approaches.

Dry-stripping

If a wallpaper is dry-strippable, you just need to loosen each strip at the corners with a putty knife and *slowly* peel it back at a very low angle (10 to 15 degrees), as shown in Figure 15-1.

Figure 15-1:
Starting from a corner, pull off strippable and peelable papers at a very low angle.

Don't pull wallpaper straight out or you may cause damage to the underlying surface, especially if it's drywall.

After you remove all the paper, follow the adhesive removal procedures described in the next section. If only the top, decorative layer peels off, leaving a paper backing behind, that's a *peelable* paper. Dry-strip the entire top layer and then follow the procedures described in the following section to take off the backing and adhesive.

If you plan on repapering and the old backing is secure and in good condition, you may be able to hang right on top of it. Discuss this option with your wallpaper dealer.

Soaking and scraping it off

To remove nonstrippable paper or any paper backing that remains after dry-stripping a peelable paper's decorative layer — now there's a mouthful! — turn first to warm water and wallpaper removal solvent. Soak the surface with a wallpaper remover solution. Although a spray bottle works, the most effective way to get the water on the wall and not all over the floor is with a paint roller or a garden sprayer. Then scrape the sodden paper off with a wide taping knife or a wallpaper scraper.

Don't wet a larger area than you can scrape off within about 15 minutes. You shouldn't let water soak into drywall for longer than that, or it may cause unnecessary damage. Usually you can wet about a 3-foot-wide, floor-to-ceiling section at a time.

Scrape off the wet wallpaper and let it fall to the floor. The cloth drop cloth or towels that you put down (see the "Preparing for a mess" section earlier in the chapter) absorbs most of the dripping solution and keeps your shoe soles a little cleaner.

If the wallpaper is non-porous, you must roughen or perforate the surface so that the remover solution can penetrate and dissolve the adhesive. To roughen the surface, you can use coarse sandpaper on either a pad sander or a hand-sanding block. You also can use a neat gizmo called a Paper Tiger or another perforating tool devised for use on wallpaper applied over drywall. Rounded edges on these tools help ensure that you don't cause damage that may require subsequent repairs. Don't use the scraper after the wallpaper is wet; you may damage the drywall.

If you are successful using the soak-and-scrape approach, skip to the "Winding up" section later in this chapter. If not, it's time to pull out the big guns — a wallpaper steamer.

Giving it a steam bath

You're talking major work if you must remove more than one layer of wallpaper or remove wallpaper that has been painted. And if the wallpaper was not applied to a properly sealed surface, removing it without damaging the wall can be next to impossible. For these tough jobs, you may have to rent a wallpaper steamer (about $15 for a half-day) or buy a do-it-yourself model (about $50). A wallpaper steamer is a hotplate attached to a hose extending from a hot water reservoir that heats the water and directs steam to the hotplate, as shown in Figure 15-2.

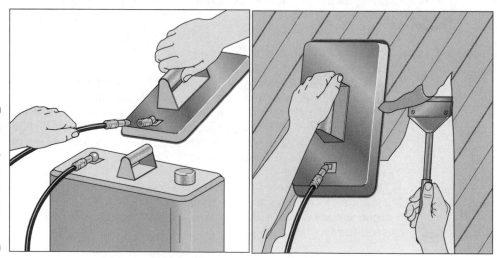

Figure 15-2:
Use a wallpaper steamer to steam and scrape away old paper.

Although you can use a steamer and wallpaper scraper with relative confidence on plaster walls, use caution on drywall, which is much more vulnerable to water damage and is more easily gouged.

Before you start steaming, prepare the room (as described in "Preparing for the mess" earlier in this chapter) to protect the floor. Fill the steamer with water and let it heat up.

Keep a baking pan handy to put the hotplate in when you're not using it.

Starting at the top of the wall, hold the hotplate against the wall in one area until the wallpaper is softened. Move the hotplate to an adjacent area as you scrape the softened wallpaper with a wallpaper razor-scraper (refer to Figure 15-2) and let it fall onto the plastic as described in the earlier "Soaking and scraping it off" section. When you're through scraping one area, the steamer usually has softened the next area, depending on the porosity of the paper.

Remember that both steam and the water that condenses from it can drip off the hotplate and burn you. To prevent hot water from dripping down your arm, stand on a step stool when you're working above chest height. Wear rubber gloves and a long-sleeve shirt, too.

Winding up

After you remove all the wallpaper and any backing, the walls are usually still quite a mess, with bits of backing and adhesive residue still clinging to them. Wash off any remaining adhesive residue with remover solution or with a non-phosphate cleaner in water, using a large sponge or sponge mop. You can use an abrasive pad or steel wool on plaster, but use caution on drywall. Avoid overwetting or abrading the paper facing.

Rinse your sponge often in a separate bucket of water, squeeze it out, and re-wet it in the removal or cleaning solution. Continue washing this way until the walls are clean.

When the walls are completely dry, make any necessary repairs (see Chapter 10) and do surface preparation work as described earlier in this chapter in "Preparing Wall Surfaces" and in the sidebar "A primer on primers."

Chapter 16

Hanging Wallpaper

. . . .

In This Chapter

▶ Planning seam location

▶ Hanging wallpaper, step-by-step

▶ Administering wallpaper first aid

▶ Adding wallpaper borders

. . . .

Hanging wallpaper — the stuff of this chapter — usually is a relatively simple process. Just follow the steps — measure, cut, apply paste (or activate pre-pasted wallcoverings) and smooth it on the surface. It is also a Dummies-approved project for first-timers, provided you start with relatively simple projects and standard papers. (For more on choosing wallcoverings and factors that may complicate wallpapering see Chapters 14 and 15.) So if you're hanging wallpaper for the first time, start in a bedroom and tackle a kitchen or bath when you have more experience. Oh, do you say that a kitchen or a bathroom is the only room that you want to paper? Then by all means start there, but be prepared for a challenging job.

We've interviewed a lot of do-it-yourselfers and one thing is pretty consistent. Most of them are like us — they don't wallpaper with loved ones. Call it stressful, call it time-consuming; we call it a solo sport.

Plan Before You Hang

A famous baseball player once claimed that "Ninety percent of this game is half-mental." Well, we're not sure about his math skills, but we are sure that two of the most important parts of wallpapering are half-mental — visualizing exactly where you want your seams to fall and then determining where to hang the first strip (called a *drop*).

Locating seams

To avoid unpleasant surprises that result from poor seam placement or having patterns cut off in awkward places, plan before you start hanging wallpaper. Take a few minutes to evaluate the room to determine where you want each seam to fall and where the patterns will begin relative to the ceiling or the corners of a room. Ask yourself:

- **Which is the most dominant wall?** That wall will be your showpiece, and the one that your guests will look at most closely. Plan to lay seams where they will be least noticeable. Although seam planning should start on the dominant wall, it's not the place you want to start papering.

- **How are windows, doors, or focal points (such as a fireplace) spaced on the wall?** Try to minimize the impact any one special feature has on the wallpaper layout. For example, if the wall has two windows, a symmetrical approach works best. Simply start by centering a seam or a strip on the wall between the two windows and work your way out to the corners.

- **Where do you want the kill point?** The *kill point* is where the final seam is located. Because you will be working around to the kill point from two directions, one or both of the last two strips will need to be cut to fit the remaining unpapered space. This means that the pattern probably won't match at the final seam. A good inconspicuous place for the kill point is usually anywhere over an entry door. Your eye is not usually drawn there, and the vertical mismatch will be limited to about a foot.

- **Are the ceilings and walls reasonably level and plumb?** Ceilings that aren't *level* and walls that aren't *plumb* present a problem when you're wallpapering. Because the patterns on the paper are truly horizontal and vertical, they make out-of-whack walls and ceilings even more noticeable.

- **Does the wallpaper pattern create any special need?** With a very large pattern, cutting the paper vertically at a corner of a room may cause a noticeable break in the pattern. To overcome that problem, start working from the center of the wall or from another spot.

In cases where precise placement of seams is important, you must know the *expanded width* of the paper. Most papers expand a percent or two — as much as an inch — after the paste is wetted or applied, while some papers don't expand at all. Paste and book a foot-long, full-width cutoff for the specified time. (To learn how to do this, you'll have to read ahead in this chapter to "At Last You're Ready to Paper," even though you're not.) Then measure the width and use that figure, not the dry width, for laying out your seams.

Working around unleveled ceilings and plumb walls

If you have ceilings that are badly out-of-level, avoid a straight-across pattern (one in which the pattern placement is the same distance from the ceiling for every strip). A horizontal pattern would emphasize the out-of-level ceiling. Consider instead a vertical pattern, such as stripes, or *drop-match* pattern (one where every other strip starts with the same pattern). The larger the drop, the less evident any horizontal pattern elements. Similarly, if you have out-of-plumb walls, avoid vertical patterns because a vertical pattern may start on one wall and cross over to the other at inside and outside corners.

You may be able to further minimize such problems, at least on the most noticeable wall, by adjusting the position of the paper to avoid having pattern elements very close to the edges of ceilings or outside corners. The more space you have between your design elements, such as sheep, the easier it will be to adjust the position so that the sheep don't lose their heads.

No hard and fast rule exists about pattern placement. Do whatever you think will look best in the most noticeable areas. Follow a truly plumb guideline or one that is not plumb but is perpendicular to the ceiling, described in the following section "Finding a starting point." You can even compromise between the two guidelines.

Sometimes evaluating a situation and imagining the results are very difficult. Undoubtedly, pattern placement is one area where experience pays and when a professional installer earns his money.

Finding a starting point

If you've planned seam placement, you can start wallpapering wherever you want, with one exception — avoid starting with either of the two strips that will lie on either side of the final seam (kill point). You want these two drops to be the last ones you do because both drops may have to be cut simultaneously, and that requires that they both be wet enough to peel back and reposition.

Keep in mind, however, that it's usually easier for a right-handed individual to work counterclockwise around the room, and a left-handed person to work clockwise.

Wherever you start, don't rely on a corner of the wall or the edge of a door and window trim to guide the first piece. Instead, use a plumb and chalk line (or a carpenter's level and pencil) to create a straight, vertical (plumb) guideline, as shown in Figure 16-1. Position the plumb or level at the desired location. Install the first drop about $1/8$ inch from the guideline.

If an out-of-level ceiling calls for it, then here's how to establish an out-of-plumb vertical guideline:

1. **Measure about 4 feet down from the ceiling at each corner and snap a chalk line between the two points, as shown in Figure 16-1.**

2. **Use a framing square (or any object that you know has a square corner, such as a plywood scrap) to draw a line perpendicular to the chalk line.**

3. **Extend the out-of-plumb line using a pencil and a straightedge until the line runs from the floor to the ceiling.**

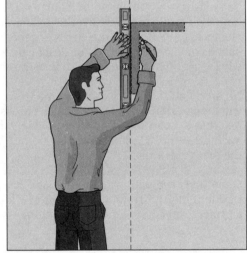

Figure 16-1: Making a guideline.

If ceilings are fairly level, use a plumb and a chalk line to establish a plumb line.

When following an out-of-level ceiling is better than hanging paper plumb, make a guideline that is perpendicular to the ceiling.

At Last You're Ready to Paper

With all the planning complete and your first guideline established, it's finally time to hang the paper. Well, it's almost time. First, make sure that your spouse is out of the house and that your tools, work area, and hands are all clean as a whistle. Then reverse-roll every roll of wallcovering.

To *reverse-roll,* place a roll in an empty water box or cardboard box positioned on the floor at the end of your cutting table. Draw one end up onto and down the length of the table, pattern side up. (You may have to flip the roll end for end in the tray to make this possible). Then reroll the paper so that the pattern faces in. After it is fully rolled, roll the entire roll back and forth under the pressure of outstretched hands. Then unroll the entire roll in back-and-forth folds at the base of the table so that the top end of the pattern is on the top of the pile. Now you're ready for cutting.

Reverse-rolling allows you to inspect every roll for obvious imperfections and lessens the paper's tendency to curl or roll up during the soaking or pasting process. If you find flaws, you have two options: You can return the roll immediately (you can't return a cut roll), or you can keep it if you determine that you have enough paper to cut out the defect.

Cutting strips of wallpaper

Cutting wallpaper involves two steps: First, you rough cut the wallpaper; then you trim the wallpaper in place for a precise fit.

When you rough cut, first draw the paper, design side up, onto your table. Then cut a strip to size with a pair of large scissors or shears. Always pull the top of the strip up to the same end of the table for cutting, and plan to leave a 2- to 3-inch allowance at the top and bottom of each strip. Keep these other points in mind:

- ✔ **For papers without any vertical pattern repeat, such as woven coverings and those with vertical stripes, or for papers with a vertical repeat of less than 3 inches,** just measure the height of the wall and add about 5 inches (total) for top and bottom allowances. For example, cut 101-inch strips for a 96-inch wall.

   When installing every other strip upside down is called for (such as for grasscloths and other woven wallcoverings), clip the upper-right corner of every top as you cut it so that you know which way is up (or down) when you hang it.

- ✔ **For papers with a vertical pattern repeat that's more than 3 inches,** place the paper on the floor at the base of the wall and, while holding the paper against the wall, carefully pull up enough paper to reach the ceiling. Move the paper up and down to adjust the position of the most dominant pattern, such as the largest flowers in a floral pattern, for best looks. Then mark the paper at the intersection of the ceiling. Take it down for cutting. First, cut the top 2 to 3 inches above your mark. Then measure and cut the bottom so that the full strip is 5 to 6 inches longer than the height of the wall.

   If the vertical pattern repeat is more than 3 inches, always use the pattern as your guide instead of just cutting a measured amount from the end of the roll. You'll be less likely to make errors or generate unnecessary waste.

✔ **For a straight-across pattern** (one in which the pattern placement is the same distance from the ceiling for every strip), cut all full-length strips so that they are identical to the first — that is, the same length and always starting at the same point on the pattern.

✔ **For paper with a half-drop pattern** (see Chapter 14 for a description of this pattern), only every other strip (number strips 1, 3, 5, and so on) will be cut at one point on the pattern. To determine where to cut the alternating strips (number strips 2, 4, 6, and so on), roll out the paper side-by-side with the first strip and align the patterns correctly, making sure that the top of the uncut paper extends above the top of the odd strip. Then mark and cut the top and bottom of the even strip in line with the odd strip. Measure and cut all future even-numbered strips from this point above the dominant pattern.

When you are cutting alternating strips at different points on the pattern, as you do for drop patterns, keep the different strips that have been cut in separate piles, all oriented the same way.

When Henry Ford wallpapered his house, you can bet that to maximize efficiency, he cut nearly all the full-length strips that he needed in advance. To minimize waste, he would then have used any shorter cutoffs above and below windows or above doors. But if *you* take this approach and cut the first one or two *drops* (or strips) wrong, then you've cut them all wrong. To avoid a scenario where you are wondering whether perhaps it would be cheaper to lower the ceiling than to buy new paper, we suggest a more cautious approach. Cut only the first two strips; use them to mark the next two as a pattern for future strips, but don't do any more cutting until you've successfully hung the first two strips. Even then, don't cut all the strips. Instead, do enough for one wall at a time. Now you know why Ford went into the automobile industry and not wallpaper hanging.

Pasting the wallpaper and relaxing with a good book

After you cut the first drop, it's time to either activate the paste on a pre-pasted wallcovering or apply paste to an unpasted wallcovering. The procedures are generally quite straight forward, but be sure to follow the manufacturer's instructions for the particular wallcovering that you're hanging. For example, instructions may say to fold the paper and let it relax for a time before you hang it — a process called *booking*.

During the time that the wallpaper relaxes, it may expand as much as ½ inch or more. After the paper is hung and it dries on the wall, it tends to pull itself nice and tight on the wall, but the adhesive causes it to hold its expanded size. Booking the paper keeps the paper moist during this relaxing time.

The success of your project depends on proper application of the right adhesive. For example, if you apply too much adhesive on grasscloth or fabric coverings, the paste will seep through the backing and onto the decorative surface. Too much adhesive can also cause excessive shrinking or slow drying, which can create mildew problems. Too thin and — you guessed it — it won't stick on, or the edges will curl. The backing of the wallcovering and the type of wall surface determine the type of adhesive you should use, how thick it needs to be mixed, and how much you should apply, but you need to consider other factors, too.

Activating prepasted wallcoverings

The dry paste on the back of prepasted wallcoverings must be *activated* (liquified), either by soaking the wallcovering in water or by brushing on a pre-paste activator, which is like a thinned wallpaper paste. If you're using a pre-paste activator, follow the same procedure as described for applying paste (see "Doing it the old-fashioned way") but use an activator.

If you are using the water-soak method, follow the manufacturer's guidelines:.

✔ **If instructions say to go directly from the bath to the wall**, place the water box in position at the base of the wall. Submerge the loosely rolled strip in the water bath for the specified time and then hang it as described in "Hanging your first strip," later in this chapter.

✔ **If instructions say to book the wallcovering,** loosely fold the backsides of the strip together so that the pasted sides are over each other as follows:

1. Fold the bottom end up to about one-half or two-thirds of the way up the paper.

2. Fold the top down to just meet that point. Be careful not to crease the paper at the folds.

3. With the pasted sides together, fold the strip in half or roll it up loosely and set it aside to relax for 5 to 10 minutes, as suggested by the wallcovering maker.

The following tips help you lessen the chances of making an error when you hang the booked strip on the wall.

✔ Follow the same sequence and procedure every time you book and fold or roll a strip.

✔ When you book, fold, or roll a pasted strip, make sure that the end that will hang up to the ceiling is on the top of a fold or the outside of the roll.

✔ Lay a booked strip down to relax facing the same direction every time.

Doing it the old-fashioned way

If you're using unpasted wallcoverings, use a *standard* premixed wallpaper paste unless the manufacturer (or dealer) recommends a *heavy duty* paste for the particular wallcovering that you have chosen. Then follow these steps:

1. **Lay one or more cut strips on your pasting table.** Make sure that all the strips are oriented in the same direction and that the pattern-side is facing down.

2. **Position the top of the first strip at one end of the table and apply the paste to at least the top half of the paper.** Use a short-nap paint roller or a pasting brush to spread the adhesive as uniformly and smoothly as possible.

3. **Book the top half of the strip by folding the pasted surfaces together.**

4. **Slide the booked end down the table so that you can paste and book the rest of the strip.**

5. **Loosely fold or roll the booked strip if the manufacturer recommends a resting time before hanging it.**

Don't paste more than one strip at a time, or one may dry prematurely while you're hanging another.

Hanging the wallcovering

To hang the drop, follow these steps:

1. **Grasp the top edge, and peel open the fold, which you made when booking the paper.**

   Leave the other half booked for the time being.

2. **With one hand on each edge a few inches down from the top, hold the drop up in place on the wall.**

   Align the edge about ⅛ inch away from the vertical guideline; and locate the top with the dominant pattern at the planned distance from the ceiling. This procedure automatically leaves the proper 2- to 3-inch allowance at the top and the bottom.

You don't want the edge right on the guideline because the chalk or pencil line may show through the seam. If the edge is not a uniform ⅛ inch from the guideline, peel the paper back as needed to reposition it; do the same to remove any large folds or air bubbles. Do not force badly misaligned paper into position by pushing it. Such an action stretches and may tear the paper and may also result in an open seam when the paper dries. If the paper needs only slight adjustment, push carefully with two outstretched hands, or three if you've got them.

3. Smooth this upper half of the strip, as shown in Figure 16-2.

Make your first strokes vertical ones, up and down, along the guideline. Then brush horizontally from the guideline toward the opposite side and finish with diagonal strokes.

4. Grasp the bottom end and peel it apart until it hangs straight.

Smooth it as shown in Figure 16-2. (On subsequent strips, you will work from the seam, as you now work from the guideline.)

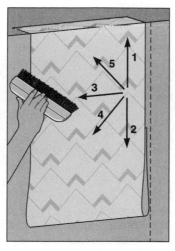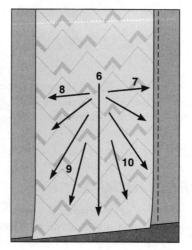

Figure 16-2:
Use a smoothing brush or plastic smoother to smooth the wallcovering onto the wall.

Continue with the remaining drops — paste-book-hang, paste-book-hang — one next to the other. As you get the "hang" of it (sorry), a helper can paste, book, and then relax while you hang.

Trimming the paper

Trim the allowance at the ceiling and baseboard (see Figure 16-3) by using a breakaway razor knife guided by a metal straightedge, such as a taping knife or a painter's trim guide. Change blades very often to assure that you are using only the very sharpest blade, or you may tear the paper. Alternatively, you can crease the paper at the ceiling-wall corner, peel it back to cut along the crease with shears, and then smooth it back onto the wall.

If your walls are drywall, paper reinforcing tape and joint compound cover this ceiling-wall joint. Use just enough pressure to cut the wallcovering in a single pass, but not enough to cut into the drywall or the paper tape. Oddly enough, the sharper your knife is, the easier this will be to do.

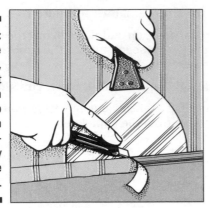

Figure 16-3:
Trim the allowance, using just enough pressure to cut through the wallpaper cleanly in a single stroke.

Before you move on to the next drop, use a damp sponge to remove any adhesive from the face of the wallcovering. Wiping up wet paste is easier than trying to get it off after it dries. Also, wipe adhesive off the ceiling, baseboard, and other trim.

Smoothing seams

For a perfect seam, start with proper wall preparation (priming/sealing), proper choice and application of the adhesive, adequate booking/relaxing time, and proper hanging techniques. The seaming method you choose depends in part on the location — mid-wall or at the corners.

By far the most common type of mid-wall seam is the *butt seam*, where the two edges touch but do not overlap. As you hang each drop, position it right next to the preceding one so that the edges just touch. If you don't get it quite right, just peel it back as needed to reposition it. If the paper still needs very slight adjustment, push carefully with two outstretched hands. Do not force badly misaligned paper into position by pushing it. Overworking the paper will stretch it, and when the paper returns to its normal expanded size, the seam will open. This is the numero uno cause of open seams. You may also tear the wallcovering.

Use a seam roller to seal the seam. Be firm, but don't press so hard that you roll out all the adhesive. As you complete hanging each drop, always make a point to check the previous seam. If the edge has lifted, lightly reroll it. If it has pulled apart slightly, smooth the paper toward the seam or give it a little tap toward the seam with the smoothing brush.

At inside corners (and sometimes at badly out-of-plumb outside corners), use a *wrap-and-overlap seam*, in which one drop wraps the corner about ½ inch and the other drop overlaps the first drop and ends right in the corner. For details on how to make this seam, see the sections "Papering inside corners" and "Papering outside corners," later in this chapter.

Getting some relief

Anytime you turn a corner or paper around an obstacle, such as a window, you need to make what is called a *relief cut* in the paper. Only one cut is required at right angles. When papering around rectangular obstructions, such as electrical outlets, however, you need to make four cuts; one cut must originate from each corner, and the cuts should connect to form an *X*. You need to make many closely spaced relief cuts around a curve, such as an archway or the base of a round light fixture.

To make a relief cut, smooth the paper as closely to the obstacle as possible. Then either make the cut in place with a razor knife or crease the paper at the edge of the obstacle and peel it back to make the cut. The following situations call for relief cuts:

- **Inside and outside wall corners:** Smooth the wallcovering up to the corner. Make a relief cut out from the corner. Start the cut precisely at the ceiling-wall-corner intersection and extend it to the edge of the paper. Then you can wrap the corner.

- **Electrical switch and receptacle boxes:** Paper over the outlet. Starting at each corner, make a diagonal cut so that all cuts connect to form an *X*. Then trim the flaps by making cuts from corner to corner around the perimeter.

 In the preparation stages for wallpapering (see Chapter 15), you should have shut the power off, removed cover plates, and taped over the face of the receptacles or switches. These steps are necessary to eliminate any electrical hazard associated with wet adhesive, cutting, and damp sponging around all electrical outlets. These precautions also keep the devices adhesive-free. Otherwise, the next time you plug in a lamp, you won't be able to unplug it.

- **Window and door trim:** Cut the paper, leaving a 2-inch allowance at the trim. Smooth the paper up to the side of the trim and crease it into the corner formed by the trim and wall. Make a diagonal relief cut starting precisely at the 90-degree corner of the trim and extending out to the edge of the paper. You can then smooth the paper over the window and door. After the paper is smoothed and the seam is rolled, trim the flaps with a razor knife and straightedge as described in the "Trimming the paper" section earlier in this chapter (see Figure 16-4).

- **Round or curved obstacles:** Smooth the paper up to the closest edge of the obstacle and make a relief cut up to that edge. Smooth a little more and make one relief cut on each side of the first cut. Continue smoothing and cutting.

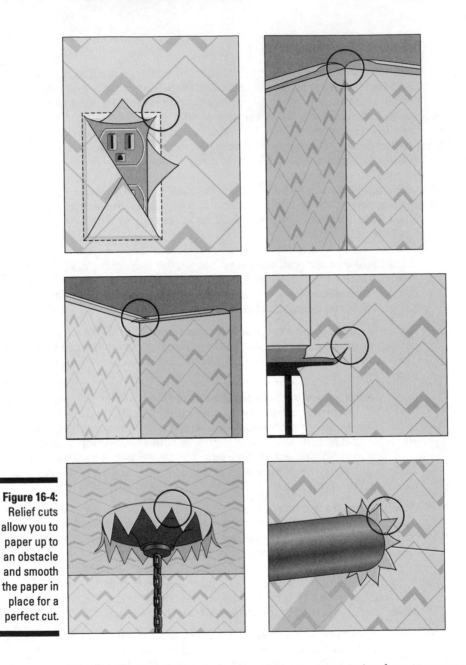

Figure 16-4:
Relief cuts
allow you to
paper up to
an obstacle
and smooth
the paper in
place for a
perfect cut.

✔ **Handrail or pipe:** Assuming that you cannot simply remove an obstacle that you cannot go around, such as a handrail or a pipe penetrating a wall, you must make a single cut from the obstacle to the nearest edge of the paper. Then you can proceed with the multiple relief cuts as described for round or curved obstacles. As you complete the circle, smooth and seam the long cut as you would any butt seam (see the section on "Smoothing seams," earlier in this chapter).

Sometimes the pattern itself suggests where a cut can be least conspicuously located — along the stem of a flower or the edge of a line in a geometric pattern, for example.

Papering inside corners

Never wrap wallpaper more than ½ inch around an inside corner with a drop. Even if the walls are perfectly plumb, the paper will pull away from the corner as it dries, making it vulnerable to tearing and/or wrinkling. Instead, make a wrap-and-overlap seam as shown. Use the wrap-and-overlap seam for out-of-plumb outside corners, too, as shown in Figure 16-5 and the following steps:

Figure 16-5: Use a wrap-and-overlap at inside and out-of-plumb outside corners.

1. As you reach the last strip before a corner, measure and cut the strip lengthwise so that it will wrap the corner about ¹/₂ inch.

2. Hang the strip but peel it back from the corner a few inches.

3. Using a vertical guideline that's about ⅛ inch farther from the corner than the narrowest width of the cutoff, apply the next drop on the adjacent wall, allowing it to wrap the corner.

4. After you have smoothed the second drop in place, trim it at the corner using a breakaway razor knife guided by a metal straightedge.

5. Toss the trimmed paper and peel the paper back from the corner enough to allow you to reposition the first drop.

6. With the first drop wrapping the corner and smoothed in place, smooth the second drop over the first.

Smooth the paper with a side-arm seam roller, which has no frame on one side of the roller so that you can get into corners with it.

Papering outside corners

Outside corners present two problems. First, because they physically stand out, people often brush against or bang into them. And second, because outside corners also stand out in the sense that they are eye-catching, and you want things in such a position to look as nice as possible. For these reasons, avoid placing a seam right at the corner where it may be brushed apart or be more noticeable.

If the corner is perfectly plumb, you can just round it. However, if it is out-of-plumb, you can use the wrap-and-overlap technique as described in the previous section, but with two differences. First, instead of wrapping the first drop about ½ inch (Step 1), wrap the corner at least 3 inches to assure that it will stay put; second, instead of having the second drop end right at the corner (Step 4), measure, cut, and position it so that it stops about ¼-inch shy of the corner (see Figure 16-5). Both cuts are located by measurement and made on the cutting table, not in place.

Making cuts along the length of wallpaper is usually done with a special (read: expensive) 6-foot-long magnesium-alloy straightedge. As a substitute, you can use about a 4-inch-wide strip of ¼ inch plywood. If you don't own a table saw, ask your lumber store to cut the plywood for you.

Cutting wallcovering dulls blades very quickly. Snap off dull blades on a breakaway razor knife or change blades often on another type of cutter.

Applying the final strip

As you close in on the kill point — the location that you planned for the final seam (see the "Locating seams" section at the beginning of this chapter) — stop when you have done all but the drop on each side of the last seam. At that point, the unpapered gap on the wall will measure something under the width of two rolls. When applied, therefore, one drop will overlap the other, and you must double-cut to make the final seam. Plan this cut at a location where the pattern mismatch will be least noticeable. For example, if there is open background on both drops at any point where they overlap, then make the cut there, as shown in Figure 16-6.

Planning this double-cut is easier when the paper is dry. Place two strips on your worktable so that, together, the width is equal to the width of the unpapered wall area. Tape them in position with a low-tack (easy-to-remove) tape, such as painter's masking tape. Then lift and reposition the top layer so that you can locate the best place for a seam. Mark or measure the location and make the cut after you have hung both strips.

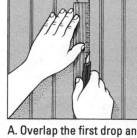  

Figure 16-6:
Use the double-cut method to make the final seam.

A. Overlap the first drop and cut through both pieces using a knife guided by a metal straightedge or level.

B. Peel off the cut-away pieces of both drops.

C. Gently but firmly seal the seam with a seam roller.

Quick Fixes for Wallpaper

Two of the most typical repairs for wallpaper are fixing seams that lift off the wall and pull away or patching torn or stained areas. The fixes are surprisingly easy — after you know how. Read on.

Loosey goosey seams

To reglue the edges of wallpaper that have pulled away from the wall, use wall-covering *seam sealer*. It comes in a small, squeezable tube with an applicator at the tip so it's easy to apply. The best part is that the sealer dries clear, leaving no telltales of the repair work.

Here are the simple steps to bond those loose edges of wallpaper:

1. **Gently peel back the loose wallpaper without stretching or tearing it.**

2. **Use a clean wet rag or sponge to soften the old glue.**

   Wipe away as much of the old paste that you can reach on the back of the paper and the wall.

3. **Carefully put the nozzle of the opened tube of seam sealer behind the paper, and squeeze the seam sealer onto the wall.**

4. **Gently smooth the edge of the wallpaper against the wall removing any excess sealer with a damp rag or sponge.**

   Hold the paper carefully and firmly in place for several seconds.

5. **To seal the edges, use a seam roller to *lightly* apply pressure.**

   If more sealer oozes out of the seam, wipe it with a damp rag or sponge.

Repairing a tear or stained area

Don't worry, things may look bad, but you can easily patch a torn or stained area in wallpaper. Easily that is, if you have extra wallpaper to cut a patch the size of the damaged area. For a problem area — larger than about a foot square — you're better off replacing the whole strip (which we talk about in Chapter 15 in the section about how to remove wallpaper).

But for small patches or stains, here's how to correct the damage. Begin by assessing the pattern and how it relates to the damaged area so that you can cut a patch piece that will blend in. Follow these steps, which are illustrated in Figure 16-7, to correct the damage:

1. **To make a patch piece, unroll a piece of matching wallpaper on a flat surface and find an area large enough to cover the damage.**

2. **Hold the patch piece over the damaged area and secure it with masking tape or drafting tape, which doesn't stick as tightly as other tapes.**

   Carefully align the pattern on the patch with the damaged area.

3. **Use a razor knife to cut through both the scrap piece and the paper underneath.**

   It's important to cut through both layers in a single pass for a clean cut with sharp edges.

4. **Untape the scrap from the patch, remove the damaged wallpaper, and clean the wall area so that it's free of any old wallpaper paste.**

   Check out Chapter 15 for tips on doing this.

5. **Coat the back of the patch with wallcovering adhesive (or seam sealer for a small patch) and position it carefully.**

6. **Hold the patch in place until it feels secure, and use a damp sponge to smooth the paper and wipe away any excess adhesive from the face of the paper.**

7. **Use a wallpaper seam roller to seal the edges of the patch.**

   Roll it gently so that you don't squeeze out the adhesive or seam sealer. When the patch dries you won't be able to find the patch.

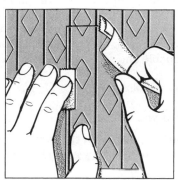

A. Cover the damaged area with a large scrap of wallpaper, lining up the patterns, and affix it with drafter's tape. (Steps 1 and 2)

B. Cut around the damage with a razor cutter, pressing through both sheets. (Step 3)

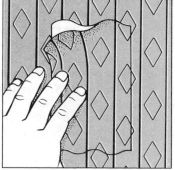

Figure 16-7: Patching damaged wallpaper.

C. Remove the damaged piece, and replace it with the new cutout. (Steps 4 to 9)

Border Incidents

We don't know of a faster way to change the look of a room than adding a wallpaper border. You can use border in all kinds of places and ways. Apply a border at the ceiling, as a chair-rail, or maybe as a detail around windows or doors. Wherever you hang a border, it's sure to enhance the room. And talk about easy.

Sizewise, borders can be a few inches or a foot wide, and the patterns and styles are almost as bountiful as wallcoverings. You'll find them coordinated with wallcoverings and fabrics, but you can also get your hands on a huge variety of patterns just waiting to bring a splash of color and pizzaz to ordinary plain walls. Most are prepasted and strippable and sold in rolls of 5 or 7 yards long.

Here's how to determine how many spools you need:

1. **Measure the length of the area you intend to border.**

2. **Divide that figure by the length of the spool that you are buying to determine the number of spools without a waste factor.**

3. **Add about ½ yard extra for every spool to allow for matching, and add an additional ½ yard for every corner or miter, such as when you are bordering windows.**

You can apply a border to any painted wall or on top of wallpaper that has been up for at least two days. Generally, borders look best on neutral backgrounds, but many patterned papers have borders with coordinating colors or patterns. Borders can also be stenciled using a decorative painting technique described in Chapter 13.

In a small room, a border at the ceiling level will make the space look larger. But don't assume a border has to go at the ceiling-to-wall joint, which can sometimes be rough. For a different look, you can also place a border a couple inches below the ceiling. Placed at a chair rail height (24 to 36 inches from the ground) a border tends to make the room look smaller because it divides the walls.

Straight-as-an-arrow borders

Even some newly built homes won't have walls and ceilings where everything is true (level, plumb, and square), but you can establish a horizontal guideline with a carpenter's level and measuring tape to act as a guide for hanging a wallpaper border.

To establish a level line below the ceiling, use a measuring tape and a carpenter's level to establish guidelines on the walls around the room as follows:

1. **Use masking tape as an experiment to help decide where you want to position the border.**

   Attach the masking tape lightly at different heights to see different effects the border will have on the room.

2. **When you decide where you want to install the border, mark the location on one wall at a corner.**

   Measure down from the ceiling or up from the floor, depending on which distance is shorter.

3. **Hold the level flat against the wall at the point you marked and adjust the level it until the bubble is centered.**

4. **Draw a light penciled line on the wall at that mark.**

5. **Work your way around the room using the level in the same manner to create a line on all the walls of the room.**

Border work

You're ready to hang the border, but first make sure the walls are clean (no dust bunnies in the corner) and remove electrical outlet covers if the border will be installed over them. Plan the job to begin and end in the least conspicuous point of the room so the joint of the two end pieces will be less noticeable, which in many rooms is a corner behind the door.

To hang a border, follow these steps:

1. **Get the adhesive working by activating it.**

   Read the directions for prepasted borders, which usually involve soaking them in water.

2. **To hang a border that's not prepasted on painted walls, use any premixed wallpaper adhesive.**

   For hanging either a prepasted or non-prepasted border on top of a wallcovering, use a vinyl-to-vinyl adhesive for better adhesion. Apply with a wallpaper brush, paint roller, or a clean paintbrush (foam or man-made bristle) spreading the adhesive on the back of the border. Make sure to coat it evenly, especially on the edges.

3. **Fold the wet pasted sides together, accordion-style to keep the adhesive most. (This is called *booking*.)**

4. **Carefully align the top or bottom edge of the border just on top of the guideline to conceal it, unfolding the booked strip as you work along the wall.**

5. **Gently but firmly, smooth the border on the wall with a smoothing brush or a large, damp sponge.**

6. **As you continue to hang the rolls of the border, butt the joints together so they're smooth and evenly aligned.**

   If the pattern does not match exactly, overlap the new roll over the previous one until the pattern aligns. Then cut through both layers with a sharp razor knife, guided by a ruler or other metal straightedge. This process, called *double cutting,* assures a perfect match every time. (Refer to Figure 16-6.) Then peel back the border to remove the cutoffs, and press the ends of the border back into place.

7. **When you get back to the point where you started, overlap the end of the border onto the beginning for cutting.**

   Peel it back and overlap it again as needed to see the least conspicuous location to double-cut the border. Usually, but not always, cut at a point where there is either no pattern or very little pattern.

8. **Lightly roll any seams with a seam roller.**

Using corner miter cuts on borders

Use a *miter cut* (cutting two pieces at a 45-degree angle so when joined they meet at 90 degrees at right angles) where a horizontal border joins a vertical one. A miter cut is a *double cut* because you cut two overlapping pieces at once. An outside-corner miter cut is when a border outlines a door or window, and an inside-corner miter cut is when a border turns and runs up the side of a window or doorway. Here are the steps to follow, as shown in Figure 16-8.

1. **Cut the the horizontal border to extend at least a couple of inches beyond the corner of the window or door casing.**

   Don't press border down firmly because it will be trimmed and peeled back.

2. **Cut the vertical border and hold it so that it overlaps and covers the horizontal border forming a small cross.**

   Cut both strips long so that you can match up the pattern by moving the vertical strip up and down, or the horizontal strip back and forth. Although you can certainly get a perfect match on one side of a door, you just as certainly will not get a perfect match on the other side. This means that, as you are moving the one horizontal and two vertical pieces, you strike a compromise that looks best at both corners. Although borders are often placed up against the casing, no hard, fast rule says that you must position them this way. You can also space the borders an equal distance from all sides of the casing.

3. **Use a taping knife or ruler to lay a straightedge, on a diagonal line from the corner at the trim to the opposite corner.**

4. **With the straightedge to guide you, carefully cut through both layers of the border with a sharp razor knife.**

5. **Remove the bottom horizontal cut-away piece by first lifting up the vertical border and then carefully removing it.**

6. **Reapply the vertical border so that it forms a perfect 90-degree mitered joint with the horizontal border.**

A. Apply a horizontal border and lay a vertical border over it. (Steps 1 and 2)

B. Align a straight edge diagonally across the intersection (Step 3)

C. Cut through both layers with a razor knife. (Step 4)

Figure 16-8:
Use a double-cut miter cut for a border that outlines a window or the top of a doorway.

D. Remove the cut-away pieces and apply the vertical border. (Steps 5 and 6)

E. Seal the edges with a seam roller. (Step 7)

7. **Carefully press the two joining edges together and seal them with a seam roller.**

    The seam roller presses the edges tight against the wall. For details about this tool, refer to Chapter 15.

8. **Let the joint dry and then ue a damp sponge to lightly remove any adhesive that may have oozed out from the seam.**

Part VI
The Part of Tens

The 5th Wave   By Rich Tennant

"Frank and I decided to go for a sort of speckled finish."

In this part . . .

Welcome to The Part of Tens, a ...*For Dummies* tradition. We're sure glad (and we're sure you will be, too) to have this special place for handy tips to make your life a little easier. In this part, we offer decorative painting tips and a chapter offering ten great painting and wallpapering Web sites.

Chapter 17

Ten (Or So) Decorative Painting Tips

A s you gain experience using decorative painting techniques, you soon discover that behind the few basic principals of creative painting, such as broken color, subtractive and additive approaches, and a few standard glazes and tools, lies thousands of little tips, custom tools, and techniques. You find many tricks of the trade in books and magazine articles while exploring the possibilities in painting, and undoubtedly, come up with a host of your own resourceful techniques as you do the work. The following are a few of our favorites.

Mind Your P's: Preparation and Planning

As always, it pays to plan ahead if you're embarking on a decorative painting project. Work goes more smoothly and you get better results.

Spatter-proofing the work area

Protect areas that you don't want painted or spattered. Mask trim, glass, mirrors, and other fixed obstacles. Remove electrical outlet plates, door hardware, and other easily removed obstacles. Washes and glazes are usually thinner than paints, so cover floors with dropcloths or the like.

Protecting your hands

Many techniques, such as sponging and ragging, are quite literally hands-on jobs, so you need gloves to protect your hands. Rather than use household latex or rubber gloves, try surgical gloves. You can hardly tell that you have them on. Surgical gloves allow much greater dexterity than household gloves, which can feel like more like boxing gloves after awhile. You can buy surgical gloves at most drug stores.

Testing before you paint

Room-size projects call for large-scale testing of your techniques and color choices. For just a few dollars, you can buy a full 4 x 8 sheet of drywall and experiment until your heart's content. Bring along a drywall knife to your supplier so that you can cut the drywall into three or four manageable-size pieces.

When you complete a project, why not experiment with other decorative painting techniques that intrigue you by trying different applicators or techniques using the leftover paint. You can paint plain brown kraft paper or tissue paper for custom gift-wrapping or card stock for one-of-a-kind note or gift cards.

Calling it quits for the day

Techniques can vary from day to day and person to person. If you cannot complete an entire project at one time, work to a natural stopping point, such as the corner of a wall or end of a group of cabinets. Stopping and starting up the next day will often result is noticeable variations *(signatures)*. By the same token, when you are working with a partner, resist the natural temptation to share the more creative decorative work and the routine base-coating work. Let one person handle each job in its entirety.

Techniques to Try

Although we encourage you to experiment and come up with you own techniques, you don't always have to reinvent the wheel. The following are some tried and tested techniques that decorative painters have been using for years that novices should keep in mind.

Enhancing wood grain

If you are whitewashing or liming a wood surface, try brushing the surface with a wire brush in the direction of the grain. This creates tiny crevices or scratches that will hold paint after wiping the surface with a cloth.

Creating visual effects by fading colors

Fading one color into another can produce very interesting results. For example, fading from dark to light as you move up a wall can visually lift a ceiling. Fading can also act as a transition between a wall and ceiling color, thereby eliminating a distinct line between the two. For example, when painting clouds on a ceiling, reinforce the effect by smoothing the transition between the "earth" (floor and lower walls) and the "sky" (upper walls and ceiling).

Fooling the eye with patterns

By applying paint in patterns, you can change the apparent proportions of a room. The following two techniques use vertical patterns to make a room seem taller. Rag rolling — rolling a painty rag over a wall where paint has dried, or rolling a solvent-soaked rag over a just painted wall before it dries — is typically done in vertical strips.

Another technique, which creates the same illusion, uses a satin or semigloss clear finish to create a stripe pattern. This technique can be done on a plain painted wall or on a wall that has been painted by another decorative technique, such as ragging. Just follow these simple steps:

1. **Using a long straightedge and a level to guide you, mask vertical strips from the ceiling to the floor, by using painter's masking tape.**

   The stripes can be the same size and evenly spaced or vary in width and spacing, but try to maintain a repeating pattern — for example, wide-narrow-narrow-wide, wide-narrow-narrow-wide, and so on.

2. **Apply a clear finish to the entire wall.**

3. **Remove the tape.**

   The shiny, clear-coated surface contrasts with the flat (dull) uncoated areas to produce a subtle vertical pattern.

Avoiding trouble in corners

Inside corners present a problem because the tendency is to double-coat them accidentally — first, when you apply paint to one wall and then again when you apply paint to the adjacent wall. Whenever possible, adapt your applicator specifically for corners. When sponging, for example, carefully slice one side of a sea sponge with a serrated kitchen knife (or a fine-tooth hacksaw blade) so that the edge is straight and angled back slightly. When the sponge is pressed against one wall, the sponge won't contact the adjacent wall. Use small pieces of sponge, artist's brushes, or similar tools to touch up or maintain better control in inside corners.

Hazing to tone down bold colors and patterns

If your color choices seem too bold after a project is complete, a good way to tone the colors down is to apply a thin white glaze. Apply the glaze using the same applicator that you used to create the effect, such as a sponge, stippling brush, or rag. This technique can also soften some patterns that you may wish were less pronounced.

Protecting your creations

While most painting jobs are certainly satisfying, the creative elements in decorative painting make it particularly rewarding. To make sure your creations last for a long time, use the best quality paints and glazes available. For additional protection, apply a clear polyurethane coating (see Chapter 4) to the outer surface to protect against abuse, wear, or heavy cleaning.

Working as a team

Work with a partner whenever you're using a *subtractive* process — that is when you're applying a glaze and then removing part of it to expose the color below. While one member of the team applies the glaze, draws guidelines, masks off, and/or prepares the cloths, sponges, brushes, or other tools, the other concentrates on working the glaze with a solvent rag, comb, or other tool according to the technique being used.

Chapter 18

Ten Great Painting and Wallpapering Web Sites

Despite our best efforts in the preceding pages, and all the other books and magazine articles that you may have browsed in your search for information to help you with your painting or wallpapering project, inevitably you will have questions or need information not found in general literature.

We've done a fair share of surfing the Net, both as professional writers and in search of resources to help us with our own home improvement projects. We've gathered some Web sites — ten to be exact — that we find most helpful with painting, finishing, or wallpapering projects. Some of these are manufacturers' sites, which include interactive store locators, calculators, color selectors, detailed product information, instructions, and links to other great sites, including both e-mail and toll-free links to technical and customer support departments where you can get quick responses to specific questions.

Even if you can get all the help you need in a paint store, who wants to stand in a paint aisle reading fine print or try to get the attention of a salesperson when people are impatiently "tsk-tsking" in line behind you?

Tooting Our Own Horn

You won't be surprised to hear us suggesting that our site www.housenet.com does a pretty good job featuring how-to information about painting and wallpapering. The site has also has calculators to help you figure a job and has contractors who monitor the message boards to answer your specific questions.

Starting on the Right Foot

Often the most challenging part of a painting project is preparing the walls and surfaces, especially if you have stains or mildew to deal with. Zinsser, a longtime a manufacturer of surface application products, features "Applications and Solutions" on their site, www.zinsser.com, which is a helpful guide for anyone faced with not-so-perfect walls or surfaces to paint or wallpaper.

Taking the Mystery out of the Creative Touch

The Benjamin Moore site features some good step-by-step instructions about decorative painting at their site www.benjaminmoore.com with color descriptions about how to do sponging, ragging, rag-rolling, dragging, color washing, and smooshing — well, maybe not smooshing, but they'd be happy to hear from you when you invent the technique! Handy exterior and interior paint calculators make quick work of figuring how much paint you need to buy.

Finding a Photo Finish

Another paint manufacturer's site is www.ppgaf.com by Pittsburgh Paints, where all their paint companies are featured. Wondering about what kind of finish to use on a weathered deck or any kind of house siding? You find application notes and coverage for all their products and an online paint school covering such topics as types of paint, surface preparation, adhesion and applications problems, and a glossary of paint terms.

Also, Minwax, a maker of stains and finishes does a nice job of helping consumers choose the right shade of stain or finish with their "Wood Finishing Sourcebook" at www.minwax.com. The site features extensive information, ideas, and tips for transforming unfinished and old woodwork and restoring damaged finishes.

Putting Retailers to Work for You

A trade organization, the Paint & Decorating Retailers Association offers consumers some good advice at their site www.pdra.org with everything from solutions to problems and answers about painting, wallcoverings, floorcoverings, and exterior stains. And if you can't find a solution to your problem — click, click — and your question is e-mailed to an expert who will try to help.

The home improvement retailer, Lowes, features painting information in a big way at their site www.lowes.com. You find extensive how-to illustrated information with an emphasis on solving paint problems inside and outside the house. Browse by category or type in a search word or two to find useful, specific articles.

If you're looking for ideas to wallpaper a room, check out www.wallpaperstogo.com, a retailer's site where you can take a Model Room Tour for ideas about decorating the kitchen, bath, living and dining rooms, bedrooms, and hallways. Explore the effects of texture and color before you make a commitment. You find tricks of the trade, a calculator, and message boards at this site.

Another wallpaper site to visit is www.decoratewaverly.com, a manufacturer's site that does a nice job of featuring ideas to decorate a room with wallpaper and matching fabric. For example, you can read an article "Use Wallpaper to Create the Look of Tile," and then click to get a better look at swatches of the wallpaper and fabric used. Sure beats lugging that heavy wallpaper book around!

Imperial Wallcoverings features the artists who design their wallcoverings with some background about their designs and the artists themselves. At www.imp-wall.com, you find how-to information and a designer showroom tour where you can click to enlarge the patterns for a better view.

Index

Discover Dummies™ Online!

The *Dummies* Web Site is your fun and friendly online resource for the latest information about *...For Dummies*® books on all your favorite topics. From cars to computers, wine to Windows, and investing to the Internet, we've got a shelf full of *...For Dummies* books waiting for you!

Ten Fun and Useful Things You Can Do at www.dummies.com

1. Register this book and win!
2. Find and buy the *...For Dummies* books you want online.
3. Get ten great *Dummies Tips*™ every week.
4. Chat with your favorite *...For Dummies* authors.
5. Subscribe free to *The Dummies Dispatch*™ newsletter.
6. Enter our sweepstakes and win cool stuff.
7. Send a free cartoon postcard to a friend.
8. Download free software.
9. Sample a book before you buy.
10. Talk to us. Make comments, ask questions, and get answers!

Jump online to these ten fun and useful things at
http://www.dummies.com/10useful

For other technology titles from IDG Books Worldwide, go to
www.idgbooks.com

Not online yet? It's easy to get started with *The Internet For Dummies*, 5th Edition, or *Dummies 101*®: *The Internet For Windows*® 98, available at local retailers everywhere.

Find other *...For Dummies* books on these topics:

Business • Careers • Databases • Food & Beverages • Games • Gardening • Graphics • Hardware
Health & Fitness • Internet and the World Wide Web • Networking • Office Suites
Operating Systems • Personal Finance • Pets • Programming • Recreation • Sports
Spreadsheets • Teacher Resources • Test Prep • Word Processing

IDG BOOKS WORLDWIDE BOOK REGISTRATION

Register This Book and Win!

We want to hear from you!

Visit **http://my2cents.dummies.com** to register this book and tell us how you liked it!

- ✔ Get entered in our monthly prize giveaway.

- ✔ Give us feedback about this book — tell us what you like best, what you like least, or maybe what you'd like to ask the author and us to change!

- ✔ Let us know any other ...*For Dummies*® topics that interest you.

Your feedback helps us determine what books to publish, tells us what coverage to add as we revise our books, and lets us know whether we're meeting your needs as a ...*For Dummies* reader. You're our most valuable resource, and what you have to say is important to us!

Not on the Web yet? It's easy to get started with *Dummies 101*®: *The Internet For Windows*® *98* or *The Internet For Dummies*®, 5th Edition, at local retailers everywhere.

Or let us know what you think by sending us a letter at the following address:

...*For Dummies* Book Registration
Dummies Press
7260 Shadeland Station, Suite 100
Indianapolis, IN 46256-3917
Fax 317-596-5498

BESTSELLING BOOK SERIES